This book is dedicated to (in alphabetical order):

Warren Beatty
Glenn Beck
Arthur Asa Berger
Tim Blair
Susan Castillo
Noam Chomsky
Jason Clarke
Stephen Colbert
Alan Colmes
Richard Condon
Ann Coulter
Larissa MacFarquhar
Morris Dickstein
Andrew Ferguson
Dan Flynn
Al Franken
H. Bruce Franklin
Roger Friedman
Ben Fritz
Nibir Ghosh
Bernard Goldberg
Thomas Grant
Robert Greenwald
Sean Hannity

David T. Hardy
Christopher Hitchens
James Earl Jones
Anthony Jay
Naomi Klein
Dave Kopel
Jesse Larner
Rush Limbaugh
Jonathan Lynn
Jamie Malanowski
Robert W. McChesney
Michael Moore
Rupert Murdoch
Jeffrey Ogbar
Bill O'Reilly
David Rampton
T.V. Reed
P.J. O'Rourke
Larry J. Sabato
Eric Schlosser
Tobin Siebers
Aaron Sorkin
Irving Wallace
Howard Zinn

Ars Americana, Ars Politica

ARS AMERICANA, ARS POLITICA

Partisan Expression in Contemporary American Literature and Culture

Peter Swirski

July 2010

To David,

As Always,

Pete

McGill-Queen's University Press

Montreal & Kingston · London · Ithaca

© McGill-Queen's University Press 2010

ISBN 978-0-7735-3765-1 (cloth)
ISBN 978-0-7735-3766-8 (paper)

Legal deposit third quarter 2010
Bibliothèque nationale du Québec

Printed in Canada on acid-free paper that is 100% ancient forest free
(100% post-consumer recycled), processed chlorine free.

This book has been published with the help of a grant from the Canadian Federation
for the Humanities and Social Sciences, through the Aid to Scholarly Publications
Programme, using funds provided by the Social Sciences and Humanities Research
Council of Canada.

McGill-Queen's University Press acknowledges the support of the Canada Council for
the Arts for our publishing program. We also acknowledge the financial support of the
Government of Canada through the Book Fund for our publishing activities.

Library and Archives Canada Cataloguing in Publication

Swirski, Peter, 1963–
Ars Americana, ars politica : partisan expression in American
nobrow culture / Peter Swirski.

Includes bibliographical references and index.
ISBN 978-0-7735-3765-1 (bound) ISBN 978-0-7735-3766-8 (pbk)

1. American literature—20th century—History and criticism.
2. Politics and literature—United States—History—20th century.
3. Authors, American—20th century—Political and social views.
4. American literature—Political aspects. 5. Politics in literature.
I. Title.

PS228.P6S95 2010   810.9'35873   C2010-901808-7

This book was designed and typeset by studio oneonone in Sabon 10/13

Contents

Ars Americana, Ars Politica

All I desire is that humane values be maintained in our institutions, codes of conduct and systems of thought. It is probably nothing more than old-fashioned liberalism. (1986)

• John le Carré, *Conversations with John le Carré*

Introduction

American Art, Political Art

Life and Times of Frederick Douglass, The Gilded Age, The Iron Heel, Boston, It Can't Happen Here. On a classic Carson show, this list would be an invitation to look for a common denominator – which in this case would not be difficult to find. Thematically and stylistically dissimilar as these five books are, all are classics of American literature. More to the point, all are classics of American *political* literature. Fictional or factual, journalistic or speculative, published in the nineteenth century or the twentieth, all have greatly enriched our understanding of the United States and of the sociopolitical forces that on occasion threatened to tear it asunder.

But while much remains to be learned from the old masters, many of us are less inclined to take seriously the modern crop of writers with a cause. This is to some extent understandable, insofar as much of contemporary political art is hard to assimilate in terms of the inherited interpretive canons. In content, modern-day artists with a political axe to grind steer clear of the formulas of Marxist vintage. In style, they work outside the tired highbrow vs. lowbrow dialectic. Freely mixing commitment and entertainment, ideological partisanship and slick consumer appeal, they forge a different kind of art than what we've grown used to heaping plaudits upon.

Hence *Ars Americana, Ars Politica*. In the first study of its kind, I look at a group of modern American political works that, while immensely popular, have as yet failed to attract the imprimatur of the canon. Looking at their mix of soap-box and box-office appeal, I examine not only the partisan credentials of this new brand of art *engagé* but also the nobrow style in which it conducts its political business. Partisan and nobrow, the five works at the heart of my study amount to nothing less than a novel sociocultural formation. Acknowledging this, I analyze their politically combative nature and crossover artistry in order to set the record straight on both counts.[1]

To claim that the works I discuss – *The Man* (1964), *Death of a Politician* (1978), *Parliament of Whores* (1991), *Bulworth* (1998), and *Stupid White Men* (2002) – are modern classics is arguably to overstate the case.[2] To maintain that they have received their deserved share of critical notice – or, indeed, acclaim – is equally open to argument. Either way, the matter can be settled only by inspecting their politics and aesthetics in detail. W.H. Auden protested famously that in "our age the mere making of a work of art is a political act." But even his polemical tone fails to do justice to the works at the heart of my study. This is because partisanship is not merely a part of their artistic agenda – it is their *raison d'être*.

As such, the main thrust of my analyses is historical and reconstitutive. Neither exclusively literary-critical nor entirely sociopolitical, *Ars Americana* brings the last five decades into focus in order to recast them in a critical light. "Critical" means here as much "metaliterary" as "sceptical," in the sense of a skeptical inquiry into the myths prevailing in modern political discourse. Driven by the political art under the microscope, chapter by chapter I revisit the familiar and the less familiar episodes from the 1960s to the present day to see if the popular memory of them holds up under critical scrutiny.

Between Irving Wallace's political and riotous bestseller *The Man* and Michael Moore's political and riotous bestseller *Stupid White Men*, lies most of contemporary American politics and history. Sandwiched between them are Richard Condon's irreverent *Death of a Politician*, P.J. O'Rourke's impudent *Parliament of Whores,* and Warren Beatty's iconoclastic *Bulworth*. Fictional or journalistic, historical or satirical, conservative or liberal, all five have one thing in common: they are not merely political, but political with a vengeance.

Even a thumbnail sketch drives home the point that this kind of art should come equipped with shock-absorbers.

In 1964, with LBJ hustling to clinch the vote on Civil Rights, *The Man* puts a Black man in the White House and chronicles the hell that breaks loose. In the post-Watergate 1970s, *Death of a Politician* vivisects the career of a Nixon look-alike who sells his soul to the weak-eyed devil of rapacious folly. In a revisionist retrospective on the 1980s, *Parliament of Whores* takes the whole American government to the cleaners, before hanging them out to dry. In 1998 *Bulworth* turns the sign of the times, a Demublican Senator, into a gangbanger rapper and a devil-may-care Socialist. And in the first decade of our millennium *Stupid White Men* goes bare-knuckled after the forty-third Executor-in-Chief of the American Dream.

Not surprisingly, to balance their political superstructure, all five writers search for a balance between *engagé* and commercial. Political discourse laced with socioeconomic history is, after all, hardly a surefire recipe for box-office success. Realizing this, in quintessential nobrow fashion, all five authors court both the discerning intellectual and the mass consumer with oodles of political lore, fortified by fast and furious rhetoric. Entertaining, ambitious and political to the core, *The Man*, *Death of a Politician*, *Parliament of Whores*, *Bulworth* and *Stupid White Men* transcend the highbrow/lowbrow dialectic, proving that in some cases there is little virtue in separating culture into art and bestsellers.

Bristling with political polemics, historical analyses and even economic statistics, they challenge the stereotype of popular blockbusters. Fusing brainy content and journalistic élan, they exemplify the demotic power of political art that resonates with mass audiences. My interest in them is, in fact, in direct proportion to their fusion of partisan politics and popular appeal – in short, to their nobrow quotient. Today, when politics-as-usual has alienated so much of the American electorate, it is frequently popular artists (not to say polemicists) who stoke the public's interest in matters of government.

Touching on controversy that is not only political but politically, well, touchy, our nobrow quintet exemplifies what the uproar is about. Uproar may be, in fact, a euphemism in a time when partisan rough-and-tumble dismays even the seen-it-all Washington pundits. Sniping from the gutter is a time-honoured tactics, concedes

Popular art meets politics.
In 1964, in bed at St. Joseph's Infirmary in Atlanta: Martin Luther
King reads Irving Wallace.
By permission of David Wallechinsky and Amy Wallace

John Geer in *In Defense of Negativity*. But even he might flinch from
the lowlights of the congressional and presidential campaigns of the
last decade. Not that there is anything new about hitting opponents
below the belt. Nineteenth-century American politics brimmed with
accusations that might make even today's tabloids blanch, from matri-
cide and cannibalism to venereal disease and bestiality.

It is only recently, however, that negative politics have gone first
mainstream and then primetime. Most historians point to Richard
Nixon's butchery of Democrat Jerry Voorhis as the watershed,
recording how the future president's 1946 campaign, full of half
truths, full lies, and innuendoes, opened the can of worms of
modern electoral sleaze.[3] Lee Atwater's campaign on behalf of
Bush the Father – notorious for the so-called Willy Horton ads
that hung a black parolee's murders on Michael Dukakis – was only
a logical step forward. By now, everybody is in the game. The pub-
lic may not condone negativity but, as focus-group research
shows, it continues to fall under its spell.

Despite protestations of civility, the partisan arena is a blood sport, more suited to pay-per-view than C-SPAN. The same goes for the popular culture that feeds off it. It is true that one should not judge a book by its cover, but what if the cover says it all? From Al Franken's *Rush Limbaugh Is a Big Fat Idiot and Other Observations*, to David Hardy and Jason Clarke's *Michael Moore Is a Big Fat Stupid White Man*, political writing today is a take-no-prisoners free-for-all. But when *Bowling for Columbine* gets banned even in Massachusetts and the *American Spectator* crucifies Barack Obama in an online post as "Il Duce, Redux?," it is time to peel truth out of the political candy wrapper.[4]

> Sociological novels such as Sinclair's *The Jungle*
> (1906) and proletarian novels such as Steinbeck's
> *The Grapes of Wrath* (1939), for example, are
> excluded.
> • Joseph Blotner, *The Modern American Political Novel*

In "Why I Write," George Orwell staked out his position with habitual clarity: "No book is genuinely free of political bias. The opinion that art should have nothing to do with politics is itself a political attitude."[5] While his point is well made and well taken, in this day and age any cultural expression can be – and has been – argued to be political. Stories and novels written without politics in mind are frequently pressed into service of political and, even more frequently, politically correct agendas.

Art, after all, does not fight back even when it is arbitrarily plucked out of its sociohistorical context. Much of the time, however, such cultural *Anschluss* makes little sense. There is little, for instance, to deter deconstructions of *The Adventures of Huckleberry Finn* as a homoerotic idyll, but doing so hardly proves that Twain was into queer politics. Logically speaking, if everything under the sun is political, then nothing is.

As if to corroborate this point, many critical studies extend the mantle of political art provocatively far afield. Nibir K. Ghosh's *Calculus of Power: Modern American Political Novel* (1997), for instance, maintains that novels such as *The Awakening*, *Fear of Flying* and *Slaughterhouse-Five* are political, putting his endeavour in peril of equivocating politics with practically any type of social concern.

Praiseworthy intentions aside, however, there is little that is political – and, even less, partisan – in Kurt Vonnegut's realistic fantasy about Billy Pilgrim unstuck in time, stumbling to the fire-bombing of Dresden.

Aware of such perils, other critics justify their definition of political art somewhat more carefully. Yet the very proliferation of such definitions means that the prospect of a consensus on what is – and isn't – political art remains dim.[6] Unable to lean on an accepted definition, let me begin with a few examples, instead. First, cultural expression doesn't have to deal upfront with politics to have a political dimension. In dissecting sundry elements of America's socioeconomic system, Mike Davies's *City of Quartz* or Eric Schlosser's *Fast Food Nation* spare only a passing glance to the branch of the spin industry known as politics. The touchstone is their attitude: muckraking, reformist, topical.

Conversely, a story set in the White House is not yet *per se* political, for the same reason that a doctor-nurse romance is not a medical book. Starring a lone legislator, and unfolding at the backdrop of the Capitol Hill, an espionage thriller may display all the requisite props. But a typical thriller, even when draped in red, white, and blue, has nothing political about it. What is missing? For one, the touchstone attitude. This is why *The West Wing*, set in the White House and pushing the liberal Democratic agenda, is unequivocally political. This is why *Murder at 1600*, set in the White House and pushing a Wesley Snipes crime mystery, isn't.

Spurred by similar considerations, some scholars raise their criteria of political art considerably higher, even at the risk of letting a few classics fall by the wayside. Thus when Joseph Blotner, in the epigraph preceding this section, excludes *The Jungle*, it is because Sinclair's masterpiece does not meet his criteria of political art. This is not to take anything away from Sinclair's stature as one of America's foremost writers in the first half of the twentieth century – not, to be sure, because he left an aesthetically superlative body of work, but because he revolutionized the manner in which many Americans approached their lives and their expectations of these lives.

When Sinclair was starting out, there was no minimum wage, no right to bargain collectively, no employer liability for work accidents, no maximum working hours, no unemployment compensation, no voting rights for women, no health insurance, no laws against price-fixing, and little if any supervision of banks, stock exchanges, or insurance companies. These are only some of the domains in which his writing and tireless public campaigning brought about reform. And yet, the point stands. Activist and muckraking to the core, *The Jungle* is not primarily concerned with politics, and even less so in the self-censored version canonized in eight hundred editions worldwide.[7]

To recap, a political work should, at the very least, be political in setting and attitude. Necessity does not, of course, entail sufficiency and, as I show in this book, the most politically engaged writing of recent times stands apart in another crucial respect. All the same, a work held to be political in any comprehensive sense will at the minimum display a political tenor and a political vehicle. Novel or reportage, minimalist realism or hyperbolic satire – no matter. Make appointees, electees, activists, lobbyists, ideologues or other political operators jockey for power and you have the makings of a political work.

This is where many critics pack their analytic tool-kits up – if, indeed, they venture this far. After all, as prominent a theorist as Irving Howe is content with a disjunction of political action and political setting, rather than their conjunction. A political novel, he argues, is one "in which political ideas play a dominant role *or* in which a political milieu is the dominant setting."[8] These days, this implicit dilution of political purpose in political art has gone even further. Fuelled by postmodern scepticism, cultural criticism has become heavily politicized – and largely apolitical. As Tobin Siebers shows in *Cold War Criticism and the Politics of Skepticism*, the Foucauldian premise that everything is political all too often signals a flight from organized politics.

In itself avoiding partisanship is nothing new. It is for the same political-yet-apolitical reasons that heart-warming blandishments such as *Mr. Smith Goes to Washington* got their Oscars and a place in the sun. But all you need to do is put Capra's and Beatty's scripts side by side to calibrate the distance between what goes by "political" in Tinseltown – and what is. This is also where *Ars Americana* departs from its predecessors. Unlike Howe, I take political setting *and* activist attitude to be necessary ingredients of political art. But taking my cue from modern political culture and political art in the United States, I also take "political" to rhyme with "partisan."

This is a radical move, to the extent that partisanship is what typically gets defined *out* of aesthetically-driven criticism. In my view,

Pressing panic buttons at Fox.
Warren Beatty's *Bulworth*: two thumbs way up.

this is an error. If our critical efforts are to be of more than academic interest, partisan involvement must not be used to justify the exclusion of any form of cultural expression. Can one really come to terms with the '60s without coming to terms with the Black Panther Party and its community-program socialism? Or with the '70s without Nixon and his paranoid presidency? Where would the '80s be without Reaganomics or the '90s without Clinton's Demublican centrism? Or the 2000s without the neocon revolt under George W.

– or, for that matter, without the rabble-rousing libertarianism of Michael Moore?

Circulating among tens of millions of readers and viewers, the works at the heart of my study are in the mass-culture frontlines of America today. Given this, considerations of partisanship cannot but be central to *Ars Americana, Ars Politica*. An ideological and rhetorical "arms-race" is now part and parcel of the political mainstream, and any cultural critique that keeps partisan expression at arm's length is going to fall short when it confronts art that prides itself on taking political sides. It may be, in fact, that only by shrugging off the aesthetized canons of response can we mete out interpretive justice to such programmatically partisan and no-brow art.

On the other hand, even as one may debate the meaning of partisanship in the context of cultural criticism, there is little doubt what partisanship means in the electoral trenches. It means Katherine Harris, co-chair of W.'s 2000 election campaign (in 2006 thwarted in her bid for a Senate seat), turning away thousands of Florida voters on suspicion they would cast their ballots for Gore. It means the Democratic presidential hopefuls campaigning in 2008 without an ideological position on key issues such as energy, trade, tax cuts, and even Iraq – content to identify themselves as non-Republicans, instead. It means, in short, that political parties exist primarily to win elections, not to govern.[9]

> I stress this empirical approach - this commitment to practical criticism - because it has been my experience that a certain kind of mind, called, perhaps a little too easily, the academic mind, insists upon exhaustive rites of classification.
> • Irving Howe, *Politics and the Novel*

In conjunction with political setting and political attitude, my third criterion – clear and present partisanship – sets the bar much higher than most scholarship of political art does. The difference is evident in comparison with Gordon Milne's classic *American Political Novel*. Dwelling on muckraking exposés of economic avarice and corruption, this meticulous study never remarks on the fact that the political art it talks about has precious little to say about politics.

THE MAN

DAY	PAGES WRITTEN
October 31, 1963	7
November 1	3
2	0
3	0 ·
4	12
5	8
6	12
7	3
8	7
9	3
11	21
12	10
13	23
14	17
15	9
16	0
17	0
18	21
19	7
20	16
21	8
22	4
23	2
24	4
25	0
26	6
27	8
28	0
29	21
30	0
December 1	0
2	16
3	18
4	3
5	8
6	14
7	0

DAY	PAGES WRITTEN
December 8	0
9	0
10	1
11	18
12	19
13	9
14	0
15	0
16	18
17	22
18	1
19	4
20	1
21	0
22	0
23	11
24	0
25	0
26	14
27	9
28	0
29	0
30	12
31	0
1964 — January 1	0
2	17
3	15
4	2
5	0
6	19
7	9
8	16
9	17
10	4
11	0
12	0
13	18

LIFE MAG interview

JFK funeral

Irwing Wallace's handwritten worksheets for *The Man*.
Note the time of completion: the 1999 edition states that the
novel was written nine weeks before JFK was assassinated on 22
November 1963. Not so. Wallace began work on *The Man* nine
weeks before the assassination but, as his scrupulous notes
record, did not complete it until 8 March 1964.
By permission of David Wallechinsky and Amy Wallace

1964

THE MAN

DAY		PAGES WRITTEN		DAY		
JANUARY	14	17		FEBRUARY	20	23
	15	15			21	14
	16	10			22	0	Rewriting
	17	9			23	0	"
	18	0			24	13
	19	0			25	11
	20	20			26	20
	21	13			27	14
	22	4			28	20
	23	17			29	14
	24	5		MARCH	1	0
	25	0			2	24
	26	0			3	23
	27	10			4	17
	28	14			5	15
	29	12			6	21
	30	0			7	28	5:55 afternoon
	31	0			8	12	5:14 afternoon
FEBRUARY	1	2				
	2	0				
	3	20				
	4	18				
	5	16				
	6	16				
	7	7				
	8	0				
	9	1				
	10	20				
	11	4				
	12	17				
	13	18				
	14	19				
	15	0				
	16	0				
	17	16				
	18	12				
	19	17				

Finished book on page 1166 at 5:16 in afternoon, Sunday, March 8, 1964.

This is emphatically not the case with *The Man*, *Death of a Politician*, *Parliament of Whores*, *Bulworth* and *Stupid White Men*. In their partisan involvement, they redefine the meaning of art *engagé*.

American Political Novel supplies another instructive foil for the book in your hands. Even as Milne aims for a comprehensive survey of the genre, Irving Wallace's political romance about a Black President does not even rate a mention. Neither does *The Man* make the seemingly all-inclusive study by Ghosh – nor indeed any other critical study of political art to date. No doubt, everyone is entitled to his own, no matter how idiosyncratic, selection of political art. But, surely, there is something amiss if a comprehensive, no-book-left-behind survey of the political novel fails to even mention a 750-pager that defined "political" in its time.

All this begs a number of questions about *The Man* and, by extension, about the five works at the centre of my study. Is Wallace's epic not political enough? Hardly, given that its fierce activism actually led to death threats against the author. Is it not representative enough? Hardly, given that the privations of African Americans have always twined with the political and moral course of the country. Is it too obscure? Hardly, given Wallace's sales of two hundred million and readership in excess of a billion, to which *The Man* contributed a lion's share. Or is it, as Norman Mailer put it, that a bestseller is by definition not art and can be safely relegated to the cultural dumpster?[10]

Here, at last, we come face to face with the type of cultural prejudice latent in critical investigations of political art. Do commercial bestsellers like Wallace, Condon and Beatty, who sold their talents to the movie factories of Hollywood, deserve to rest spine to spine with Douglass, Twain, and Lewis? Do, for that matter, pop journalists such as O'Rourke and Moore? The full answer to this question would take a book in itself (fortunately, such a book already exists).[11] But any version of the answer must begin with the recognition that many of America's greatest artists fused their intellectual ambitions with popular forms. It was in this very spirit that Mark Twain bragged that he wrote for the millions, while Henry James only for the elite few.

The same attitudes permeated the writings of Douglass, London, Sinclair and Lewis. Even as they pursued aesthetic goals, they pursued mass audiences no less, recognizing that the latter were crucial to the dissemination of their views. *Ars longa, vita brevis* indeed, for while reformers pass out of sight, the words of the reformers – to rephrase Auden – are modified in the guts of the living. Well aware that, to be effective, a preacher needs a congregation, few American political writers turned up their noses at mass appeal. Looking askance at contemporary art of a similarly nobrow character only perpetuates our residual elitism.[12]

Popular art has a way of changing the way we see the world, if not the world itself. If one is to believe Abraham Lincoln's alleged greeting to Harriet Beecher-Stowe, *Uncle Tom's Cabin* started the biggest war between Waterloo and the First World War. With the backing of another president, *The Jungle* helped bring about the Pure Food and Drug Act and Meat Inspection Act of 1906 – even as Sinclair rued that he had aimed for the country's heart, not its stomach. *1984* armed successive generations with a lexicon with which to take government to task: Big Brother, newspeak, thought police. *Catch 22* changed attitudes to war and bureaucracy for the flower-power decade and beyond.[13]

Seen in this light, the bias behind the collection *Understanding American Politics Through Fiction* is nothing short of procrustean. Even though its editors concede the utility of political art, they approach it primarily as a narrative vehicle for "the less familiar factual and theoretical material written by political scientists."[14] In other words, because political art is engaging and political science is a bore, the former is employed as a ramp by which readers can safely climb to the latter. Far from a political medium in its own "write," literature is relegated to the role of a handmaiden to the social sciences.

In contrast, I want to argue that when it comes to political art, there is every reason to look for the Horatian ideal of enlightenment via entertainment. "Education sugarcoated," is how Irving Wallace expressed his responsibility vis-à-vis the reading public. "ENTERTAINMENT FOR THE SAKE OF LITERATURE," echoed Richard Condon. "Although I'm trying to say things I want to say politically," argued Michael Moore about *Capitalism: A Love Story*, "I primarily want to make an entertaining movie."[15] No need, in other words, to evoke Mao Tun or *Mao II* to appreciate that popular art is more than a vessel for social-scientific theories.

Political "artertainment" can, in other words, not only inform but inspire political action. Sometimes, as in the case of Marvin Gaye's *What's Going On,* popular art goes platinum not despite

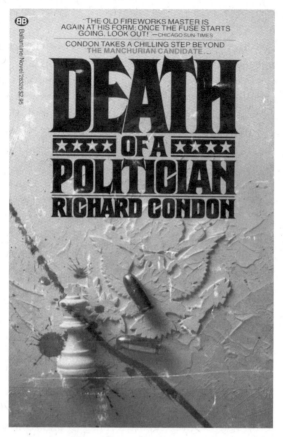

Lone king, bullets, blood spatter, Great Seal of the
United States.
High-octane revisionist history: cover of the paperback
version of Richard Condon's *Death of a Politician*.

but *because* it is political. This is precisely the case with Wallace,
Condon, O'Rourke, Beatty, and Moore. With full deliberation, their
political thrusts and rhetorical feints are crafted to encourage sober
thought as much as stir up raw emotion. With sophisticated argu-
ment rubbing shoulders with argumentative sophistry, they turn
partisan art into a visceral experience.

Ranging from the Black Panthers and the Socialist left, through
the Democratic centre-right and the Republican right-of-centre, to
loose-cannon independence, they cover among them the entire
American political spectrum. Enjoyed by tens of millions of potential
voters, they exemplify the populist grassroots of American arter-
tainment and of the American democracy. They focus on how

political hierarchies operate, and on how to disempower the powerful. But instead of theorizing or speechifying on behalf of this or that ideology, they dramatize politics by showing how power relations gone awry affect Mr and Mrs Doe.

The jury is out on whether our modern quintet are fit successors to the Twain-Douglass-London-Sinclair-Lewis axis. *Ars Americana* is but one exhibit in the case. What is clear, however, is that an artistic fusion of partisan content and bestselling entertainment demands analysis in terms of its effect on American political art. Popular culture has always been identified with the lowest common denominator. Little regard has been given to the possibility that popular forms may appeal to wide audiences because of their ability to identify and satisfy a taste shared among a large number of people. The largest cultural denominator, however, need not be the lowest.

> Likewise, if the literary critic may object
> that the book contains too much talk of politics,
> the political scientist may feel that it contains
> too little.
> • Walter Rideout, *The Radical Novel in the*
> *United States, 1900-1954*

To be effective, art has to be original. It has to be capable of doing things that seem never to have been done before. Noble in its social and political aspirations, American *littérature engagé* has not, however, been the paragon of artistic innovation. The genius of Dos Passos and Warren notwithstanding, far more typical is the classic proletarian novel: all agitprop with a consolation romance thrown in like an extra olive in a weak martini. Conformist in style – realistic at best, plodding at worst – in form it rarely departs from a rise-and-fall *Bildungsroman*, more often than not tempered with an almost Sophoclean doom.

Hemmed in by the zero-sum dialectic of class struggle, political nuance or even basic economic logic often go the way of the dodo. To propose that indiscriminate strike action can force a company's closure and thus permanent unemployment, that worker-run enterprises are as prone to feuding and fraud, that union bureaucracies can be as rigid as federal departments, is simply an ideological misstep. Moreover, as critics from Daniel Aaron to Walter Rideout laboured to point out, cardboard characters rarely foster aesthetic or emotional engagement. Far from the psychological subtlety of Paul Auster's *Leviathan*, the generic cast is limited to the oppressed labourer, the tyrannical foreman, the greedy capitalist, the despicable scab, the indomitable organizer, the love *immaculata*. Little more than authorial mouthpieces, they make you ache for their plight – not for them.[16]

Such are the conclusions of scholarship ranging from Morris Speare's pioneering *Political Novel* to Michael Wilding's *Political Fictions*.[17] Indeed, disappointed with what they find on the domestic front, scholars frequently turn to Europe in search of political art worthy of the name. Undoubtedly, political literature on the other side of the Atlantic can be as blistering as anything published in the USA today. For proof, look no further than John Le Carré's *Absolute Friends* or Alistair Beaton's *A Planet for the President*. All the same, it is hard to avoid the impression that some home-grown critics remain deeply ambivalent about political art.

Beguiled by this or that version of formalist aesthetics, itself rooted in German romanticism and its myths of pure art, they look askance on partisan literature that rolls up its sleeves and gets its hands dirty. Because it is seen as extrinsic to art, political commitment is frequently applauded – but from a safe distance. This ambivalence is exacerbated vis-à-vis partisan art, and even more so in a nobrow incarnation. Indeed, if one were to summarize the attitudes prevalent in critical circles, the relation between politics and art is seen not so much as the creative tension of a jazz duet but as the stultifying combativeness of a marriage on the rocks.

Arthur Koestler penned some of the most famous political works of the twentieth century, including *Darkness at Noon* and *The God That Failed*. Yet even he bemoaned: "I have spoiled most of my novels out of a sense of duty to some 'cause'. I knew that the artist should not exhort or preach, and I kept exhorting and preaching."[18] The words may have changed during the decades that separate Koestler from Phillip Roth, but not the sentiment. In the latter's *I Married a Communist*, a leftist of the old school declares: "Politics is the great generalizer, and literature the great particularizer, and not only are they in an inverse relationship to each other – they are in an *antagonistic* relationship."

The problem with such a polarization is that by stigmatizing politics as a trespasser it denies the very *raison d'être* of political art –

and leaves critics very little to talk about. Recognizing this awkward fact, some scholars openly militate against studies that "'say' politics while merely doing literature."[19] As if in response, the raft of revisionist studies in the 1990s marked a departure from the generation of formalist criticism ill at ease with partisan causes. And rightly so. Segregating art from politics makes little sense, for it is this extra-literary dimension that permits artists to bring the visible world to justice.

It is for this reason that, instead of taking Wallace, Condon, O'Rourke, Beatty, and Moore at their word, I scrutinize their partisan politics *critically*. It would be disingenuous to deny that it takes consummate skill, not to say artistry, to entice mass audiences away from Jerry Springer to a close encounter with history, statistics and ideology. All too often, protest art groans under the weight of *gravitas*, preaching to the choir while the congregation wanders off in search of lite entertainment. Our modern quintet mines a radically different formula, seasoning politics with partisan irony, riotous humour and rhetorical sophistry.

For a title, *All the Trouble in the World* may not sound overly risqué, but whoever heard of *The Lighter Side of Overpopulation, Famine, Ecological Disaster, Ethnic Hatred, Plague, and Poverty?* It turns out that millions of Americans did, turning P.J. O'Rourke and his unrepentant brand of hit-'em-where-it-hurts Republicanism into a goldmine. Generally speaking, if the public can be taken to vote with their wallets, American consumers of political art seem perfectly willing to put entertainment ahead of party lines. This buyer's market means, in turn, that no matter what Wallace's, Condon's, O'Rourke's, Beatty's, and Moore's leanings, their priority is to optimize the ratio of politics to fun.

It is in this light that we must evaluate their efforts to overcome mass complaisance, if not downright ignorance, about the ways of the government, while diverting audiences with every partisan joke, hyperbole, and occasional expletive at their disposal. It is with this partisan and nobrow aesthetics in mind that I revisit the core issues that defined their respective decades: the transnational legacy of the Black Panthers and the Black Power movement – the mythology of the presidency and the reality of Nixon's terms in office – the price tag of Reaganomics and bipartisan realpolitik – the political legacy of Socialism and the role of the mass media – and the political spin-sanity in the USA today.

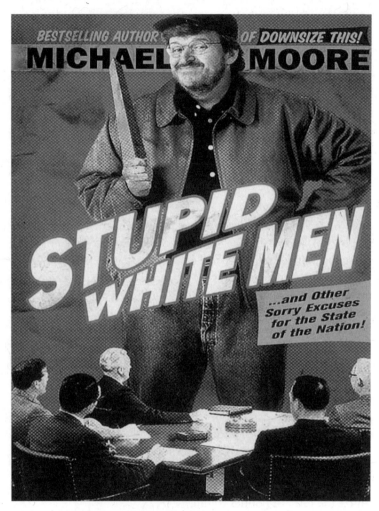

Spinsanity and American civics.
In-your-face: Michael Moore teaches a lesson in *Stupid White Men... and Other Sorry Excuses for the State of the Nation!* Cover of the first edition.

Although all these issues have received their share of analysis and diatribe, rarely has the work of political scientists and historians been correlated with that of popular artists. Rarely has political and socio-economic data been fed into the same cultural equation that includes rhetorical variables such as irony, litotes, rapping idiom, or satiric *bon mot.* There remains, in short, a chasm between what cultural critics talk about and what Washington pundits hang their professional hats on. A new cultural formation, intent on engaging the public with a nobrow *mèlange* of political savvy and revisionist history, is an obvious starting point for bridging it.

That the chasm remains as wide as ever is borne out by a recent collection of essays by political scientists engaged in teaching political literature. Noting the "dearth of general discussions"[20] of literature and politics, the editor of *Reading Political Stories* bewails the dearth of studies that successfully combine the science of politics and the art of storytelling. Indeed, as he points out, the only professional journal ever to provide a forum for cultural criticism and political science folded after only one issue. Seen in this light, crossover collections, such as Patrick Deneen and Joseph Romance's *Reading America* (2005), are winter swallows rather than harbingers of spring.

Examining the modern mix of blockbuster entertainment and political analysis, *Ars Americana* aims to bridge this chasm. As with all cross-disciplinary ventures, there are inherent risks. Upon finishing this book, readers versed in literature and other forms of artistic expression may feel that there is more politics and history here than they care to know. Conversely, readers at home with politics, economics, social studies and related disciplines may conclude that literary-narrative and art-cultural matters receive undue attention. In either case, I hope it means that both sides discovered here things they did not know but hopefully found worth knowing.

> "America" is a laboratory for examining the shifting connections between politics (in the broadest sense) and cultural expression.
> • Sacvan Bercovitch, *Ideology and Classic American Literature*

In *The Art of Protest*, T.V. Reed describes his study in the following terms.

This book hopes to prove useful to three main types of readers. For students and general readers new to the subject, it presents an introduction to social movements through the rich, kaleidoscopic lens of artistic and cultural expression. For scholars of social movements, it offers intriguing observations on particular movements and useful insights into various ways to think about the relations between culture and social change.[21]

His words are doubly apt for, by dint of substituting "political" for "social," they sum up the intentions behind *Ars Americana* as well. All too many critical studies discuss political art while abstaining from investigating the political structures these works evoke. In contrast, my approach hinges on integrating the narrative and sociopolitical perspectives across various art forms – from prose fiction to essayistic nonfiction to film script.

To be sure, even as our interdisciplinary methods converge, there are differences. A prominent scholar and activist, Reed declares himself to be "interested in social movements as sites for the production and reception of cultural texts," another way of saying that the cultural texts he is interested in are the social movements themselves.[22] True to his word, *The Art of Protest* tries to include in this pantextual category such forms of direct action as sit-ins, strikes, boycotts, and other forms of civil disobedience. In contrast, I limit myself to the more intuitive and, frankly, more plausible expressions of art, even as I spare no effort to flesh out its political context.

There is also the awkward fact that political art selected for academic criticism is almost invariably left-wing, proletarian, or liberal. To an outsider it might appear that the American right has never put pen to paper in defense of their conservative, republican, or libertarian beliefs. However, unless we wish to risk of becoming culturally irrelevant, we can ill afford to imitate Horatio Nelson and feign to be blind in one eye (always the right, it would seem). Moved by these considerations, where *The Art of Protest* openly restricts itself to the left side of the political spectrum, I take under the microscope the best-selling book of essays from the self-styled Republican Party Reptile.[23]

Even as Bill O'Rilley, Ann Coulter or Sean Hannity – bestselling partisan Republicans all – attract their share of cultural and political commentary, Patrick Jake O'Rourke remains a less known quantity. And not only in academic circles. Al Franken's recent partisan best-

#1 NATIONAL BESTSELLER

P.J. O'ROURKE

"Outrageous . . ., it is insulting, inflammatory, profane, and absolutely great reading."
—*The Washington Post Book World*

Parliament ★
of Whores

A Lone Humorist Attempts to Explain the
Entire U.S. Government

WITH A NEW FOREWORD BY ANDREW FERGUSON

Lone pen-slinger rides into town.
Cleaning up the cesspool on the Potomac: P.J. O'Rourke's
Parliament of Whores.

seller, *Lies, and the Lying Liars Who Tell Them* goes full throttle
after the Coulter-Riley-Hannity axis but omits to give the time of
day to *Parliament of Whores* and its author. Redressing this omis-
sion, I test the integrity of O'Rourke's Republican tenets while cheer-
ing for one of the funniest primers on the ways of the government
from either side of the political aisle.

As exemplified by the 2008 presidential race, not to mention the
perpetual Congressional equilibrium, the choices for the electorate
are limited in practice to the Democratic centre-right (Obama/
Clinton) and the Republican right-of-centre (Romney/McCain). This
pragmatic construction of partisanship fails, however, to reflect

the party politics favoured by the writers – novelists, journalists, scriptwriters – I study. As such, reflecting their commitments, *Ars Americana* looks at partisanship inside and outside the electoral mainstream, placing Black Panthers, socialists and independents alongside that premium instrument of American government, the Democrats and the Republicans.[24]

Having said that, I do not aim for a comprehensive coverage of today's political parties or even of political art. Even in the case of the political novel, hardly an over-analyzed genre at that, the task would be insuperable for any one monograph. Staying in the realm of the possible, I instead use the selected quintet as a lens to focus light on the partisan and cultural questions they so sharply illuminate. Along the way, I analyze their rhetorical stratagems, if only to clear the smokescreens dispensed by the writers themselves and their critics. Much like Morris Dickstein's recent *A Mirror in the Roadway*, my approach is thus historicist and experiential, even as it is political.

All studies of mass culture necessarily assume that the political messages expressed therein have the power to affect the attitudes of readers and viewers. Do political leanings in blockbuster entertainment really translate into changes in political opinion? Are the changes detectable in editorials, legislative agendas, or even voting patterns? Even the most tentative of such correlations would make understanding popular art vital to the appreciation of the factors that shape the political awareness of the American public – or lack thereof. Selling in the millions, bestsellers that steep themselves in politics should have a measurable impact on public opinion in the country. Given this, the nature, efficacy and, not least, accuracy of such mass political education is surely of profound interest and importance.

Inevitably, having been created with the aim of reshaping the political culture of our time, our five works become political instruments in their own right. Given that they openly identify with political parties or with identifiable political agendas, it is important to investigate how they further such political programs. Understanding to what degree these bestselling opinion-makers succeed in this task is crucial. All this is to say that, by focusing on the issues that drive these authors and their firebrand art, I reject the postmodern denials of authorship and intentionality – and thus the denials of the very conditions of political engagement in our culture.[25]

At the outset of the *Annals*, the Roman historian Tacitus swore (tongue in cheek) that he would conduct his audit of emperors from Augustus to Nero *sine ira et studio* – without anger and partisanship. While it may be arguable whether such Olympian detachment is at all possible, critical objectivity is a goal worth aspiring to, especially when it comes to politics and government. Should *Ars Americana* be judged to fail in this respect, let me assure you that it is not for the lack of effort in reconciling the analytical and the polemical but because of the urgency of concerns that, while rooted in history, continue to play havoc with our present.

Americans also believe that the man who has succeeded, by definition, will become a good man. It's part of the presidential image. (1977)

• John le Carré, *Conversations with John le Carré*

Chapter One   1960s

The Return of the Black Panther: Irving Wallace's *The Man*

Few postwar American writers could rival the popularity of Robert Ludlum. But only a few of the millions of loyal readers who followed his heroes through labyrinthine webs of deception, corruption, and intrigue expected more than a cursory treatment of political issues. After all, the author himself boasted on more than one occasion that he did not spend much time on things that don't move the story. To many it comes as a surprise, then, that an informed view of politics and political machinations forms the background of many of Ludlum's plots. In the case of slightly more ambitious – if always action-driven – thrillers like *Trevayne*, it even surges into the foreground.

Published in 1973, just as the full range of Nixon and Liddy's crimes was being hauled into the open, *Trevayne* plumbs the murky corridors of party and military politicking. In the manner of Richard Condon, it depicts a corrupt government within a government, where Congress and the presidency can be bought and sold in the name of political expediency. It would have been hard for readers to miss the correlations with contemporary politics. By 1976, of course, when Robert Redford and Dustin Hoffman portrayed Bob Woodward and Carl Bernstein in *All the President's Men*, it was all over. The footage of Nixon on the White House lawn, boarding the chopper that would whisk him into forced retirement, had long since become part of national history and conscience.

In 1976 another political thriller climbed the bestseller lists. Irving Wallace's *The R Document* also depicted a government conspiracy that turned the presidency into a puppet show. There was no mistaking the scorn both writers heaped on the Republican cabals. Echoing Wallace in the introduction to a post-Irangate edition of *Trevayne*, Ludlum glowered:

> one of the truly great achievements of man is open, representative democracy ... But wait. Someone is always trying to louse it up. That's why I wrote *Trevayne* nearly two decades ago. It was the time of Watergate, and my pencil flew across the pages in outrage. Younger – not youthful – intemperance made my head explode with such words and phrases as *Mendacity! Abuse of Power! Corruption! Police State!*"[1]

Much has been made of Ludlum's persistent suspicion of the existence of high-level government cabals. Accused of conspiracy mania or even paranoia, he has always countered with the same argument: in less than twenty five years the White House was infiltrated not once, but twice by the Watergate and Iran-gate cliques, who deemed themselves above all scrutiny. This is no longer the age of Aquarius, he insisted – it is the age of conspiracy. Defending himself from similar charges, Wallace scoffed at those who scoffed at his depiction of an FBI cabal plotting to take over the government. After Watergate and all the shenanigans in the Executive Branch "all the dirty stuff in real life will give absolute credence to my fiction."[2]

The similarities between Wallace and Ludlum are not confined to political conspiracies, a theme to which they returned on numerous occasions. Both were popular, not to say populist, bestsellers who gauged their success by how much sleep readers were prepared to forego in order to reach the last page. In the context, the joyous confession of a *Washington Post* reviewer of *The Bourne Identity* also sums up *The R Document*: "It's a lousy book. So I stayed up till 3 a.m. to finish it."[3] And if their mind-boggling sales – in each case approaching a quarter *billion* copies – are anything to go by, both have consistently proven equal to the task of keeping readers awake.

Inflicting insomnia with edge-of-the-seat suspense does not, of course, favour intense character study, and, in this respect, what is true for Ludlum is again true for Wallace. Many of their dramatis personae are evoked with such monochromatic strokes of the pen that they are only fuel for the narrative engine which races from one hairpin turn to the next. Contrived and melodramatic, the plots crescendo to an obligatory confrontation between good and evil which, however complicated on the surface, is always clear-cut. Both authors luxuriate in stylistic overkill in which three adjectives are always better than one. The results? Tomes whose page length exceeds that of many dictionaries.

The juxtaposition with Ludlum does not, however, do Wallace many favours. By and large, for example, it obscures not only the commitment with which he approached his *metier* but also the finer aspects of his prose. In *The Man*, for example, in the scene when a black writer, Leroy Poole, briefly recollects his youth, Wallace's impressionistic staccato prose suggests that his normally plodding narration may have been a matter of choice rather than lack of skill. As for commitment, here is Wallace on Wallace:

> when you write a book that also affects the reader for better, improves him, gives him more love and understanding of his fellows, then you feel a deeper satisfaction for having produced your novel. This, apparently, is the extra dividend factor that makes *The Man* so important to me.[4]

Two decades after his death, the author and the novel that was so important to him have by and large faded from the public eye. But not so long ago Wallace's popular outreach made him what only a handful of writers ever dream of being: a public educator. "The world is crowding us too much, flowing vats of information and experience into us at great speed," he stressed. "Unadulterated fiction can no longer compete with actuality. So fiction must absorb actuality and then it must make an effort to exceed it."[5] Hence the reportorial style that, for many, defined the Wallace experience.

This commitment to fact-in-fiction is nowhere more apparent than in *The Man*. Among Wallace's historical fictions, this one may have been the hardest to swallow for a nation torn asunder by civil rights riots, punctuated by the slayings of JFK, Malcolm X, MLK, and RFK. As if to prove the point, even as the novel got legs in bookstores, the author received death threats for daring to write about

He's here! He's here!
Future history: poster for the British edition of *The Man*.
By permission of David Wallechinsky and Amy Wallace

a Negro in the Oval Office.[6] In this context it matters little that, as biographer John Leverence points out, under actual federal law Wallace's hero would have been swiftly removed from the job. By putting a Black president in the White House, the writer forced a generation of middle-class whites to face what most would rather not: Black Power.

```
Shall I say the man? If there is a man on earth,
he is a man.
```
• Frederick Douglass, *My Bondage and My Freedom*

Wallace made a name in Hollywood writing for James Cagney, Doris Day, Peter Lorre, Natalie Wood, Karl Malden, and Rock Hudson, to mention only a few. Yet, no matter how successful he was as a script-writer, he always saw himself as a novelist first. In his prolific publishing career he contributed to a thousand and one magazines, at one point or another ghost-writing for Boris Karloff, Gracie Allen, W.C. Fields, Red Skelton, Bob Hope, and even the president of Mexico. In addition, he published sixteen books of nonfiction, not to mention a bevy of articles in the *Britannica, American Oxford Encyclopedia*, and *Collier's Encyclopedia.*

All this pales, however, next to his chief source of fame: an almost uninterrupted procession of bestselling novels, eleven of which – including *The Man* – were sold to the movies. Prodigious quantity is, of course, one thing and quality another. Reviewing Wallace's 1962 sensation *The Prize*, the *New York Times* may have compared its author to France's great realist Honoré de Balzac, but Richard Lingeman's appraisal of the 1972 blockbuster *The Word*, was far more typical. Opening with a cheerful reference to the "Kick Irving Wallace Day," it summed up the view of the East Coast establishment in a list that opened with "contrived" and finished with "lousy."[7]

Unfazed, Wallace continued to release a string of chart-toppers while, as always, educating his readers by peppering fiction with historical fact. He also continued to defend this documentary aesthetic with which, like Sinclair Lewis's before him, his name would become synonymous. Like Lewis, he employed fulltime researchers to scour for historical details to use in their fictions. Like Lewis, on more than one occasion he reiterated his position: "I'm interested in the novel of ideas."[8]

The joints creak occasionally where story and history – the latter often ill-camouflaged as outright lectures – meet. One reviewer even wondered if the whole point of this research was to demonstrate that Wallace was a serious author.[9] Yet, for all his faults, Wallace never lost the knack of keeping even the most critical of his critics turning the pages. Echoing the 3 a.m. reviewer who could not put Ludlum down, even Richard "Kick Irving Wallace" Lingeman

The Man made its mark politically and on the bookstands.
Supernova: Irving Wallace receiving the *Bestsellers Magazine*
award for the paperback of 1965 from Robert Kirsch, book
critic of the L.A. *Times*.
By permission of David Wallechinsky and Amy Wallace

likened the experience to watching a late-night movie, "and find-
ing oneself unable to turn it off until the last plot has flipped its last
flop ... and it is 3 o'clock in the morning."[10]

Although he wasn't, Lingeman could have been describing *The
Man*. One part mawkish melodrama, one part edge-of-the-seat
thriller, Wallace's epic mines a theme that, as the current presidency
shows, is never far from America's headlines: the state of the union

as reflected by the state of its black minority. Activist to the core, it typifies its author's determination to bridge fact and fiction – so much so that it even reproduces a fictional *New York Times* op-ed which liberally educates Americans on the history of their country's racial rights and wrongs. At other times it reads like a tourist brochure with page after page of a set-piece tour of the White House.

Aside from anything else, however, *The Man* is eerily prescient. In one of the most dramatic coincidences in literary history, Wallace wrote about the death of his fictive president only days before Kennedy left for Dallas to be assassinated military-style. As if that were not enough, *The Man* sets its fictional presidential impeachment proceedings in the mid-seventies, again uncannily predicting the future. And even though Wallace had Malcolm X as a model for the charismatic leader of his fictive Turnerites, he invented this armed, black-clad, direct-action Black Power group a full two years before Huey P. Newton and Bobby Seale founded the Black Panther Party for Self-Defense.

The Man wasn't Wallace's first stab at dealing with racism and the plight of blacks. In the 1950s he developed two storylines about these essentially American themes. The first had a family move into a new neighbourhood – a commonplace experience unless you're black and it's white. The second was about a black student who gets turned down by an Ivy League university. Sidestepping formula, Wallace had a white lawyer take up the case, only to realize that the student didn't deserve to be admitted. In the end, however, Wallace decided for a time that he had nothing to say that hadn't been said better by black writers themselves.

Then one night in 1964, at the Cannes Carleton, he revealed that he had written a novel about a black in the White House. "The hell you have," growled James Baldwin. "What credentials do you have to do that?"[11] None, replied Wallace, except for the same poetic licence that lets you write about whites. More to the point, he continued, written by a *white*, this Trojan horse would be read by people who would never deign to buy Ellison or Wright. And his was right. Many readers of *The Man* wrote in to confess to past bigotry and a profound change in attitude. That alone made it all worthwhile, confessed the author, the fact that "what I've written has not only entertained people, but has actually changed them, educated them, made them better human beings."

Going to meet The Man.
A stranger in a strange land: Irving Wallace researching
The Man at the White House, 1963.
By permission of David Wallechinsky and Amy Wallace

The genesis of this most political of Wallace's novels is scrupu-
lously recorded in his notebooks. In mid-September 1963, he got
permission to visit the White House on the condition that he would
not disclose the president's consent. During the four days he spent
there, he enjoyed a personal tour with Kennedy's press secretary,
Pierre Salinger, interviewed the president's private secretary, sat in
the chair in *the* office, roamed the private quarters in the West Wing,
soaked in the nitty-gritty of the daily grind of the wheels of gov-
ernment – and left to start the book. In a mere four months and a
week, the manuscript was finished, 1,166 handwritten pages in all.

The publication of *The Man* in 1964 coincided with the first pro-
duction of Amiri Baraka's *The Dutchman*, commonly regarded as
the birth of Black Power theatre. Unlike *The Dutchman*, however,
The Man became the fifth highest seller of 1964, trailing only *The*

Political political.
In 1964, at the John Washington Carver Institute: Irving Wallace receives the Supreme Award of Merit for *The Man*.
By permission of David Wallechinsky and Amy Wallace

Spy Who Came In From the Cold, Candy, Herzog, and *Armageddon.* With a combined seventy-one weeks on the *New York Times* and *Time* bestseller charts, it went gold in hardcover, platinum in paper, and multi-platinum in the Reader's Digest Book Club, not counting seventeen foreign editions and the 1965 *Bestseller Magazine* Award for the paperback of the year.

Most of all, however, it hit the mark politically. Within six weeks of its publication, Wallace was awarded the Supreme Award of Merit and Honorary Membership from the George Washington Carver Memorial Institute. Underscoring this contribution to breaking down race barriers, the award was presented to him by Mallie Robinson, mother of the first big-league black baseball player, Jackie Robinson. The dedication explicitly honoured the author of *The Man* for his "Outstanding contribution to the betterment of race relations and human welfare."[12]

> One flash from the heart-supplied intellect of
> Harriet Beecher Stowe could light a million camp
> fires in front of the imbattled host of slavery,
> which not all the waters of the Mississippi, min-
> gled as they are with blood,could extinguish.
> • Frederick Douglass, *My Bondage and My Freedom*

From clues strewn over the first three chapters, the internal chronology in *The Man* can be reconstructed as follows. Contrary to real life, Lyndon Johnson serves only a year and three months, i.e. the remainder of Kennedy's term. He is succeeded for one term by the president known only as the Judge (modelled after Harry Truman, after he had retired in the Midwest). The Judge is followed by another nameless chief executive known only as TC – short for The Chief. When the novel begins TC's secretary has been with him for six years, but it is unclear whether this includes his time as a senator. Assuming it does not, TC has served all but a year and five months of his second term when fate strikes.

Matching this chronology to actual events, LBJ's first term would have run the remainder of JFK's, i.e. until January 1965. The Judge would have then been succeeded by TC in January 1969. Add his two terms – less a year and five months – and The Man succeeds The Chief in 1975. Together with Wallace's 1964 letter to his publisher, which situates the book's action ten years in the future, it is clear that this is future history. Despite this, there is a feeling of anachronism when events and attitudes that clearly belong to the 1960s are said to occur a decade later. This temporal dislocation persists even in the film version, despite Rod Steiger's desultory update of the plot (which whitewashed America's racial wars by setting them in South Africa).[13]

The story revolves around Douglass Dilman, an inconsequential black senator who happens to be the president pro tempore of the Senate and thus fourth in line of succession. With the vice-president's seat temporarily vacant, TC and the House speaker (third in

succession) leave on a state visit to West Germany to haggle with
the Russians over respective spheres of influence in Africa. Then the
unthinkable happens. While the American delegation is together for
a conference call, the ceiling caves in and kills them all. Dilman is
sworn in as president among racial tension and intrigue, and takes
the line of least resistance until the time when he's ready to prove
that he is, indeed, The Man.

That time comes when, abetted by his cabinet, Congress slaps
him with impeachment charges for incompetence, gross dereliction
of duty, attempted rape of his Southern-belle social secretary, and
even spying for the Soviets. Long before that, however, Dilman has
been humiliated everywhere he turns – even when he has nowhere
left to turn. Refusing to sign a Minorities Rehabilitation Act that
would mostly line the pockets of big business, he is vilified even by
America's blacks, who need the crumbs from this bipartisan loaf.
Adding injury to insult, he barely escapes assassination by a rene-
gade member of the Turnerites, an organization of black militants
whom he had crushed when they put "Freedom by all means nec-
essary" into action.

Recognizing the president's integrity, a few individuals stand by
him during impeachment hearings orchestrated by redneck Con-
gressman Miller and patrician Secretary of State Eaton. In the end,
it comes down to a climactic showdown in the Senate, symbolized
by a vote to determine if Dilman is to be removed in ignominy or
allowed to get on with the job. Like Restoration president, Andrew
Johnson, Wallace's CEO squeaks by with a margin of one. Hard-
ened by the ordeal into the man we always knew he was, on the last
page, "feeling assured and purposeful, feeling good, he entered his
Oval Office to begin a day's work" (740).

Wallace makes it easy to lambaste his design: a protagonist equiv-
alent of a lump of coal who, under political heat and pressure, hard-
ens into a diamond in the rough. Unfortunately, Dilman is no Jed
Bartlett (even less Winston Churchill who, on one account, would
stroll around the White House at night clad only in a maduro cigar).
The Man is a saccharine cartoon, with no sexual drive, no hobbies,
and no distinguishing characteristics except his racial cross. Like
Jesus, jeered and taunted when stumping across the country, only
to be betrayed and tried in ignominy, he bears the crown of thorns
with the fortitude of a martyr. And the thorns keep coming: enough
crises to fill the first four seasons of *The West Wing*.

But we move from character to politics and *The Man* turns into a different sort of beast altogether. The name Douglass Dilman alludes to Frederick Douglass, a slave jailed for stealing his master's property (himself), who rose to be not only a national statesman but a 1872 vice-presidential candidate. It was the closest America would come to a black president until more than a century later, when Jesse Jackson won eleven primaries, briefly becoming the Democratic frontrunner before losing to Michael Dukakis. Bobby Kennedy's prophecy as Attorney General that in thirty or forty years America would have a Negro president has still not come to pass. Although, technically, forty years from RFK's assassination expired only in 2008, Barack Obama is half-white.

It is true that Dilman doesn't get elected fair and square (but then again neither did George W. Bush in 2000). Wallace's artifice is really a sign of the times when only blind chance – colour-blind, that is – could put a Negro in the country's driver seat. Like TC, Dilman is really a victim of circumstance. He is put on trial even before the Senate hearings through racial scorn, bigotry, and flaming hatred. In a mocking bow to Richard Wright, overnight this self-effacing individual becomes America's most Visible Man. And, like Beatty's Senator Bulworth, resigned to electoral failure, the black president commits political suicide by speaking the truth about big business and race relations.

To Wallace's credit, from time to time he shades his mostly black-and white characters in a more lifelike grey. Congressman Zeke Miller is not a mere caricature of a Dixie plutocrat but a real-life composite of the racist platform espoused by the Orval Faubuses and Strom Thurmonds of the era. Leroy Poole is both a living indictment of homegrown apartheid and, in Dilman's words, a reverse race chauvinist. The most enigmatic portrayal, however, is reserved for the lightning rod of the novel: the Turnerites. On the one hand, their name links them to the 1848 slave revolt led by the American Spartacus, Nat Turner. On the other hand, during Dilman's Cabinet meeting, the attorney general implicitly compares them to the KKK.

In the incident that triggers Dilman's crackdown, the group picket a department store owned by the local Grand Dragon who blinds one protester with acid. In retaliation the picketers assault him and vandalize storefronts. Armed police and dogs rush to the scene, sending two Turnerites to the county hospital – one blinded, one crippled for life – and the other ten to jail. In the end, no charges are brought

In a composite nation like ours, made up of almost every variety of the human family, there should be, as before the law, no rich, no poor, no high, no low, no Black, no white, but one country, one citizenship, equal rights and a common destiny for all.

A government that cannot or does not protect the humblest citizen in his right to life, Liberty and the pursuit of happiness, should be reformed or overthrown, without delay.

Fredk Douglass

Washington D.C. Oct 20. 1883.

Black vice-presidential candidate in 1872.
Source of the epigraph to *The Man*: Frederick Douglass's manuscript in Irving Wallace's personal collection.
By permission of David Wallechinsky and Amy Wallace

against the Klansman. A kangaroo trial of the blacks, presided by a local judge known for letting off lynchers, ends in the harshest verdict possible: ten years each, including the blinded victim.

Incredibly, the president shrugs off the verdict: the blacks "got the raw end of the stick" (220) but "that's not unusual, wrong though it is" (221). And while the whole incident is over as far as he is concerned, the violence escalates. The remaining Turnerites kidnap the racist judge who, days later, dies of gunfire in circumstances that make it difficult to determine whether it was murder or self-defense. Dilman mobilizes the FBI, outlaws and hounds the Turnerites, and eventually refuses to commute the death sentence of their captured leader. In the end, only Leroy Poole, a writer, is left to guard the group's memory.

> In the national District of Columbia, over which the star-spangled emblem is constantly waving, where orators are ever holding forth on the subject of American liberty, American democracy, American republicanism …
>
> • Frederick Douglass, *My Bondage and My Freedom*

Having worked in McCarthy's Hollywood, Wallace had plenty of experience with political censorship. Which is not to say that he was a stranger to the other kind. The first Italian edition of his Kinsey-type novel, *The Chapman Report* was to be published during the 1960 Christmas season but had to be delayed after an intervention from the Vatican. "Postpone it at least until Lent," came the directive from the Holy See, tactfully skipping "or else."[14] Equally offended by the book's sexual frankness, the German Home Office also tried (unsuccessfully) to ban it.

Wallace despised censorship in any guise. "Some things we know are obscene," he wrote,

> like injustice and crime promoted by the White House, like mass murder on the ground in Vietnam and from the air in Cambodia, like ignoring the impoverished and the minorities and the elderly while playing footsy with the wealthy multi-national corporations.[15]

The diversity of love and lovemaking, on the other hand, he sneered, is legislated obscene. Only,

> neurotic weirdos like Richard Nixon, Ronald Reagan, Strom Thurmond feel that prosecuting a book or a film is more important than cleaning up a ghetto or fighting social injustice or stopping killing abroad.

Wallace's political involvement went far beyond taking a stand against censorship. A lifelong liberal, in 1968 he fiercely supported Eugene McCarthy although, characteristically, when the latter lost the party nomination, Wallace refused to vote at all. Like Norman Mailer and Hunter J. Thompson, though without their unquenchable thirst for self-promotion, he reported on the 1972 conventions for the *Chicago Sun-Times/Daily News*. Like Warren Beatty, he was active on behalf of George McGovern, writing numerous articles for the senator's campaign sheet, notable for their early record of Watergate.

His nose for politics and injustice was so acute, in fact, that right in the middle of a lucrative career he put novel writing aside in order to research a muckraking article, "How Young Lawyer Nixon Bungled His First Case." Nixon's debut at the bar, he uncovered, had been so awful that he ended up being sued by his client's family. The presiding judge actually concluded that Nixon might lack the ethical qualifications to practice law and threatened to get the Bar Association involved. A bungling two-timer shrouded in self-denial and injured innocence, Wallace's Nixon has all essential qualities of the man recreated by Richard Condon.[16]

For a political novelist, there is arguably no grander theme than the presidency. This is because, as exemplified by the White House and amplified by the media, America's view of *the* office is seldom far from mythopoeic. Be that as it may, *The Man* was not Wallace's first treatment of the presidency. In 1941 he wrote a film story whose title explains, perhaps, why it was never optioned by Hollywood. Political and historical, *Madame President* was based on the life of Victoria C. Woodhull, Equal Rights Party suffragette who – with Frederick Douglass on her ticket – ran for president against Ulysses Grant in 1872.

Tailored and manicured, the country's chief executive is part of the national iconography, together with the flag, the combat fatigues, and the apple pie. The president, as one pundit puts it, "embodies America's projected national hopes and beliefs and serves as the maker and manipulator – as well as the inheritor and servant – of the icons of the myth of America."[17] Even as other analysts warn that "Americans have an over-developed tendency to president-worship," this fixation, counters James Oliver Robertson in *American Myth, American Reality*, "is part of our nationalism, our search for national unity and wholeness in a single person."

MADAME PRESIDENT

by

Irving Wallace

It is a summer's evening in the year 1870, and Delmonico's famous restaurant is crowded with the cream of Manhattan society. There is gayety, noise, as couples joke and laugh and converse -- when, suddenly, a hush sweeps over the restaurant, then a silence. All eyes stare in one direction.

For, during the excitement, two women have entered, and taken a table near the doorway. Two women, unescorted, in a public place after six o'clock in 1870! Unheard of! Scandalous!

The two women -- Victoria Woodhull, and her sister, Tennessee Woodhull, are once again shocking staid New York. Everyone has heard of the Woodhull sisters -- those daring Ohio suffragists battling for the equality of women.

Charlie Delmonico, genial restaurant owner, hurriedly approaches them. He is tactful.

"There's only one way to save you," he whispers. "I will pretend you just dropped in to speak to me, and then, as we chat, I will escort you to the door."

The Woman?
Breaking another political taboo: page 1 of Irving Wallace's typescript of *Madame President*.
By permission of David Wallechinsky and Amy Wallace

Presidential Messianism may be par for the course for the Washington spin machine, but the reality is as always more prosaic. First, the Office is too big for any person. As Wallace recounts it in *The Man*, the president is:

the chief Executor, overseeing the execution of our laws, exercising important powers of appointment and removal. He is chief of state, national host to an endless stream of native and foreign visitors. He is Commander in Chief of the Army and Navy and Marines and Air Force, with the Pentagon dangling from his civilian lapel. He is arbiter of both Houses on the Capitol Hill, able to influence Congressional activity, able to nullify its accomplishments by veto. He is Ambassador to the world, making deals with international leaders, ironing out treaties, selecting foreign diplomat puppets ... he runs his political party, he molds public opinion, he sees that his voice is heard in the United Nations, he acts as a superpoliceman in areas ranging from strikes to race riots to big-business monopoly (69–70).

The ascension of Theodore Roosevelt, who consistently polls as one of America's greatest presidents, provides another reality check for White House mythology. Roosevelt was bumped to vice-president from governor of New York because the party kingmaker, Senator Tim Platt, wanted to bury the "damn cowboy" out of the way of the state political machine. The rest of the plot could have come straight from Wallace, insofar as the untimely death of William McKinley plucked the progressivist VP from obscurity and put him in the Oval Office. Roosevelt's double term is another exhibit in the case of presidential myth vs. reality. For all the rhetoric about reform – Teddy was sometimes called a steam engine in trousers – the record shows that his administration acted less than Taft's.[18]

Since then, the gap between presidential myth and truth has grown into a chasm. In the few decades between *The Man* and *Stupid White Men*, there was Johnson's deceit about ground-level genocide in Vietnam and Nixon's deceit about genocide from the air. There were ignominious removals of Agnew and Nixon from office. There was Reagan and – as Condon reels it off in *The Emperor of America* – "the Grenada mockery; the Lebanese disasters; the Iran-Contra scandals; the Persian Gulf debacles; the Libya fixation; the Supreme Court appointment messes; Congressional committee exposures; the charges, arraignments, and indictments of high Federal officials beyond any count of corruption in White House history."[19]

After Reagan there was Clinton and the "bimbo eruptions" (so dubbed by his own campaign team). Although, as the bumper stickers pointed out, when Clinton lied, nobody died, things changed under

George W. Bush's deadly farce of the Iraqi weapons of mass distraction which, among others, drove the country's CEO to veto legislation outlawing torture. In *The Man*, Wallace's fictional president slams the Russian empire for destabilizing world peace by invading rundown mineral-rich countries and installing puppet regimes. What would he say about the American war on a rundown oil-rich country master-minded by a president whom world-wide polls named as the greatest danger to peace on earth?[20]

> At the same time that they excluded a free
> colored man from their cars, the same company
> allowed slaves, in company with their masters
> and mistresses, to ride unmolested.
>
> • Frederick Douglass, *My Bondage and My Freedom*

In the 1896 case of *Plesy vs Ferguson*, the Supreme Court upheld an 1890 Louisiana law that mandated segregation on state rail cars. Homer Plesy, an octoroon and, like Rosa Parks six decades later, a conscientious objector, was arrested for boarding a car reserved for whites. Although white-looking, he was found legally black when it was shown that his great-grandmother was black and was declared guilty. In a pattern that would continue for decades, abroad the US armed and incited people under colonial regimes to fight for their inalienable rights, while at home it turned a blind eye to racial repression governed by a constitution that enshrined the inalienable rights of whites.

This landmark case set the law for the half century that followed. The 1948 desegregation of the armed forces, ordered by Truman, was the only example of lasting racial reform. Elsewhere, America remained a bastion of institutionalized apartheid while bearing the torch for the so-called free world. Worse, as the expediently stoked fear of postwar communism sidelined social reform, civil liberties already in place were scaled down or even rolled back. Allies of the nascent civil rights movement, such as Eleanor Roosevelt, and institutions such as the Civil Rights Congress or the Southern Conference for Human Welfare were red-baited to the point of irrelevance.

The Cold War reduced racial equality to a pawn on the chessboard of international public relations. From tax rebates to superhighway construction, the government spearheaded programs that benefited the segment of society equivalent to the voting majority: the white middle class. Meanwhile millions of blacks, including the demobilized members of the armed forces, were left at the mercy of America's volatile markets. In a display of economic hypocrisy that has not changed an iota today, Big Business demanded socialist-style bailouts and subsidies while shedding workers by the thousand in the name of free-market competition.[21]

As Michael Levine documents in *African Americans and Civil Rights*, the decade between *Brown* and the Civil Rights Act came close to engulfing the country in protests, riots, marches, boycotts and other signs of a nation in turmoil. World opinion, especially Soviet newsmakers, made much of the apartheid permeating the life of the self-proclaimed leader of the liberal world order. Smarting at the loss of prestige on the international arena, Eisenhower admitted as much on national television. "We are portrayed as the violator of those standards of conduct which the people of the world united to proclaim in the Charter of the United Nations." Ordering troops to Little Rock, he said, would restore "the image of America ... with liberty and justice for all."[22]

Political rhetoric aside, *Brown vs Board of Education* did not change matters just because it became law. Dixie states and local authorities, dead-set on keeping Jim Crow intact, resorted to closing public schools and other highjinks to avoid compliance with what they regarded as interference with the South's internal affairs. *Brown II* – which in 1955 called for desegregation with all deliberate speed – was declared null and void by six Southern states, which then went so far as to establish penalties for obeying the ruling.[23] In this climate one can only celebrate Wallace's courage in creating his political epic, all the more so in that his fiction is truer to history than most readers would suspect.

Black Man in the White House sounds like the working title of *The Man*. Instead, it is a true account published in 1963 by the first black to serve as a presidential aide. Until then, in a rarely aired chapter of America's apartheid, black White House employees had always been servicemen. E. Frederic Morrow, with a career in public relations, was ostensibly hired by the Eisenhower team to help with policy. In reality, hiring him was a crass tactics to court black support in northern swing states. As Morrow reveals, his elation at this high-profile racial watershed was soon replaced by disgust. Not only did white secretaries refuse to work with him, but he was banned from being alone with any female employee, lest he sexually molest her.

Is it really a surprise that Wallace's black president insists on keeping doors open when conferring with his white secretary?

Even as he signed the Civil Rights Act and the Voting Rights Act into law, Lyndon Johnson's feelings were captured by the remark commonly attributed to him: "I'm signing away the Southern vote for twenty years." Be that as it may, what was revolutionary for the federal government was too little too late for the black minority. As lax enforcement of the acts became the norm, less appeasement-directed factions clamoured for faster reforms. Many – much like Wallace's fictive Turnerites – espoused the confrontational posture of Malcolm X, overlooking the fact that, for all his violent rhetoric, Malcolm carefully stayed within the law (the essence of his tactical success).

Of all Black Nationalist groups in the United States, the Black Panthers became the most visible and the most feared by the authorities and their main constituents: middle-class whites. Arch-symbols of social activism and activist socialism, the Panthers were recast in the media as revolutionary exponents of military self-rule. In reality, while equating non-violence with acquiescence to white ideology, they only denounced separatist leanings among African Americans, advocating integration into the mainstream. The real difference lay in their tactics. Sociopolitical goals were to be attained by virtue of community work and radical cultural nationalism in the name of Black Pride and Power.[24]

The stage for the rise of the Black Panther Party for Self-Defense was set by the feet-dragging progress of the Civil Rights Movement and the failure to make a dent in the soft apartheid now permeating the country. The colour-coded choice of a black panther as the party icon was in defiance of the half-donkey-half-elephant ruling America. In the words of Mumia Abu-Jamal: "it is not a panther's nature to attack anyone at first, but when he is attacked and backed into a corner, he will respond viciously and wipe out the aggressor."[25] Convinced that blacks had been oppressed throughout the nation's history, like Wallace's Turnerites the Panthers set out to convince their followers to stop turning the other cheek.

The presence of this party is felt everywhere in
the republic … That party, sir, has determined
upon a fixed, definite, and comprehensive policy
toward the whole colored population of the
United States.

• Frederick Douglass, *My Bondage and My Freedom*

The party was founded in 1966 by Bobby G. Seale, its eventual chairman, and Huey P. Newton, minister of defense. Both were community college students critical of other campus groups for failing to directly serve community needs. They urged blacks to exercise their constitutional right to bear arms to protect themselves from violence, especially from the police. Predating the candid-camera days of the Rodney King beating and Michael Moore's *TV Nation*, the Panthers, "equipped with cameras, tape recorders, and a copy of the state penal code," shadowed the police, looking to catch them in the act of violating people's rights.[26]

Within two years of beginning with a handful of core members, the party roster expanded to five thousand, growing in step with their campaign against police brutality.[27] Two subsequent events raised their profile even higher. In February 1967, when Betty Shabazz, widow of the assassinated Malcolm X, flew to San Francisco for a public lecture, the party provided her security. Cued to the value of style in defining form, Newton exploited the appeal of Panther devil-may-care defiance for young black males. The instant the plane touched down, Shabazz was surrounded by a disciplined contingent of young men clad in distinctive black leather jackets and black berets, with guns, bandoliers and sunglasses completing the outfit.

A second media circus erupted three months later. While Governor Reagan fled the scene, a group of armed Panthers marched onto the floor of California legislature in advance of a vote on a bill prohibiting individuals from carrying guns in residential and incorporated areas. As Jeffrey Ogbar observes in *Black Power*, the bill would effectively "prohibit the armed Panther patrols of the police."[28] On this occasion, their flagrant demonstration of firearms and a paramilitary dress code did not have a happy ending. Bobby Seale and several other protesters were imprisoned for half a year. But coverage of the stunt swelled the party membership, so that by the summer there were party chapters in most major US cities.

The Panther iconography moved onto the international stage in 1968, when two sprinters, Tommie Smith and John Carlos, raised black-gloved fists in a Black Power "unity" salute after taking gold and bronze at the Mexico Olympics. Interpreting the clenched fists as the endorsement of the Panthers, reprisal from authorities was swift. Sent home and banned from the games, the two runners were hounded by death threats and shunned by employers, even as the party ranks swelled. The same year saw the founding of the Black Panther Movement in England, followed by Black Panther Parties in Israel and Australia in the early 1970s. As late as 1987 the Panthers even served as a model for the Dalit Panthers political party of India.[29]

Despite Mario Van Peebles's film eulogy *Panther* (1995), followed by the brilliant but marginal *A Huey P. Newton Story* (2001; directed by Spike Lee), what is remembered today is the militant arm of the Party. Nary a word about social programs. You don't read about that, sneers Roger Guenveur Smith in his virtuoso *A Huey P. Newton Story* rap,

Why? 'Cos there's no guns there, no sensationalism there, no dramatic value – doesn't sell newspapers, doesn't boost television ratings.

The programs to help blacks build and control their own communal structures and institutions were, however, not only more successful than their military posturing but more threatening to the American political status quo. No wonder that, spearheaded by a fight for redistribution of wealth and resources, their demotic challenge brought the Black Panther Party on a collision course with the powers that be.

Nothing else explains why a local ragtag group of black youths was swiftly upgraded by the FBI to the status of a national security threat and public enemy number one. The influence of the holy trinities of Marx, Engels, Lenin, and Ho Chi Minh, Fanon, and Mao, which entered the party philosophy through Newton and Seale, was of course profound.[30] Yet, the party's radical approach to social organization was overshadowed by Malcolm's battle cry of "by any means necessary" and by the public spectacles of the Panthers striding about in tight military formations and policing the police.

The pen and Underwood typewriter mightier than the sword.
In 1964, surrounded by materials for *The Man*: Irving Wallace
in his study.
By permission of David Wallechinsky and Amy Wallace

Similarly, Wallace plays up the direction-action image of the
Turnerites at the expense of their politics.

Focusing on the Panthers' paramilitary exploits – including street
gunfights with the police – to the exclusion of the grassroots
program of social welfare is a historical error that no amount of
political expediency and myopia can excuse. For, even as the Black
Panther Party has been consigned to the dustbin of American his-
tory, their strategy is being re-enacted today in the Middle East by
another sociopolitical and paramilitary faction: the Hamas (to say
nothing of Hesbollah). This time around, however, the efficacy of
demotic socialism and its perceived threat to the architects of global
world order are more difficult to conceal from public view.

As early as 1999, Kirsten Schulze traced the double-edged
nature of Hamas's liberation program in *The Arab-Israeli Conflict*.
In a script that could have been devised by Huey P. Newton, ele-
ments from Fatah, the PFLP, the DFLP, and the Palestine Communist
Party organized committees and other focus groups. These,

> were not only responsible for the *intifada* but also for social
> services ranging from supplying villages under curfew with

food and establishing education programmes to arranging
for the care of wounded Palestinians. Islamist parties such
as Islamic Jihad and Hamas, which were only starting to
become political players, became progressively involved.[31]

Indeed, virtually all commentators, no matter how virulently
opposed to the group, concede that the military wing is not their
primary theatre of operations. Reuven Paz is a Haifa University
expert in Middle Eastern history who has testified against Hamas
in several high profile court cases. Yet, in a 2001 analysis for the
Institute for Counter-terrorism, even he admits that the over-
whelming majority of Hamas's efforts go to social programs. "90
percent of its work," he acknowledges, "is in social, welfare, cul-
tural and educational activities. These are important elements of
Hamas's popularity that keep it closely tied to the public."[32]

In the *Asian Wall Street Journal* Karby Leggett reiterates that,
armed ops notwithstanding, "Hamas runs a sophisticated social-
welfare network – including subsidized food, medicine and education
– that provides relief to a population in great need."[33] Indeed, adds
Daniel Byman, the focus on public welfare is why many "states in
the Middle East – including almost every US ally – laud the Pales-
tinian terrorist group HAMAS, seeing it as a legitimate resistance
movement." Even David D. Aufhauser, who blasts this idea for the
benefit of the House of Representatives, admits: "The rest of the
world, particularly Europe (until recently) and countries in the Per-
sian Gulf, view the political/charitable wing of HAMAS differently
from its so-called military wing."

> There is not a nation on the earth guilty of
> practices more shocking and bloody, than are the
> people of these United States, at this very hour.
> • Frederick Douglass, *My Bondage and My Freedom*

Although the view is rarely voiced in public, the current overreac-
tion to the Hamas has little to do with its relatively puny military
capability and everything to do with its social welfare and social-
ist populism. The concerted effort to undermine their grassroots base
by propaganda and financial strangulation helps explain the tra-
jectory of the less prepared, more proximate, and consequently more

vulnerable Black Panthers. Together with other political movements, the party fell victim to COINTELPRO, one of Hoover's pet counter-intelligence programs formed in 1967 to – as per the Bureau's internal memo – "expose, disrupt, and otherwise neutralize the New Left."[34]

The historical record makes it clear that the FBI acted in utter disregard for human rights, America's legal codes, and even its own charter. Instructed by the director himself, agents were to prevent "black nationalist groups from 'gaining respectability' by discrediting them with unfavourable publicity, ridicule and whatever other 'imaginative' means agents could think up."[35] Commenting on such state terrorism, Noam Chomsky does not mince words:

> COINTELPRO directed against blacks was murder. Against whites it was disruption, defamation, circulating stories about sexual conduct, things like that. That was a big difference, and the difference had to do with who is privileged and who is not privileged.

The rise and fall of the Black Panther Party is the subject of a dispute that, after decades of back and forth allegations, shows no sign of going away. What was the degree of the party's control over the nationalist and socialist movement it inspired in so many of America's ghettos? The rapidity and the different conditions under which party chapters sprang up nationwide suggest, for example, a loosely run outfit. Testimonials from former members paint a picture of a movement not fully prepared for their success, lacking a coherent infrastructure or means of enforcing one.

As Charles E. Jones documents in an interview with Panther Jimmy Slater, what went on in local party chapters may have had nothing to do with the headquarters.[36] There are accounts of a prevalent lack of discipline, not to mention flouting of the prohibition against drug peddling and consumption, although claims have also been made that those may have had the party's tacit approval. Such problems were exacerbated by recruitment of members with a history of violence and, in some cases, criminal records. The prominent Los Angeles Panther leader Bunchy Carter, a former member of the Slauson gang, recruited other gang members for protection.

Given this background, it is little wonder that the FBI had an easy time going after the party, agitating the populace at large with accusations that the Panthers intended no less than to "overthrow the US government."[37] For their part, the Panthers' executive provided the authorities with just the ammunition they were after. In October 1967 Huey Newton got into a gunfight with the Oakland police which claimed the life of an officer. The shakiness of the prosecutor's case – which, nonetheless, carried the sentence of manslaughter – sparked the "Free Huey" campaign by the original Rainbow Coalition ranging from Yellow Peril, an Asian-American nationalist group, to President Sekou Toure of Guinea.

The rest of the story parallels that of other left-wing dissident groups. Harassment, suppression, disinformation, infiltration, and provocation became the party's daily bread. COINTELPRO and local police intelligence divisions delegated snitches and agent-provocateurs to enlist and work from within the party. They blackmailed other members and recruited the disenchanted ones. The disinformation unit worked overtime planting phoney documents (some, printed on the FBI stationery!) to cast suspicion on selected victims.[38] Reports compiled by the Bureau itself show that by 1969 it was targeting all forty-two party chapters for evidence of possible violations of Federal and local laws.

All in all, the threat of socialism was taken very seriously, indeed. Of all actions undertaken by the FBI against all left-wing groups between 1968 and 1971, almost eighty percent were against the Panthers. Actual crimes, like those of then vice-president Agnew, were left for law students to investigate. In the end, the toll was predictably bloody and heavy. By 1971, when the BPP effectively ceased to exist, more than two dozen core members were dead, scores of others languished in jail on various charges and dubious convictions, and hundreds more were reeling from physical and psychological damage.[39]

In the media, the Black Panthers were cast as the devils of America, a motley crew of unstable, paranoid delinquents. Public attention was riveted by their clashes with the police, so much so that "felonious" became the Panthers' second name. Almost no one outside the ghettos was willing to remember, far less give them credit for, serving the community. And yet the political efficacy of the BPP, like that of the Hamas today, owed less to their military wing than to their public pledge of working to bring "land, bread, housing, education, clothing, justice and peace."[40]

Typical chapter initiatives included practical neighbourhood "survival" programs, such as free health clinics, clothing/food drives,

community daycare that enabled single mothers to seek employ-
ment, and teaching about welfare and tenant rights. Sponsored
in part by donations from local businessmen, the Free Breakfast
for Children program proved so successful that celebrities from
Richard Pryor and Donald Sutherland to Jane Fonda and Marlon
Brando gave financial and vocal support to the party. Difficult as
it is to believe, at its peak in 1969 the party was feeding twenty
thousand children weekly.[41]

The Black Panther Party ran summer-school type programs in
the Bay Area, providing free lunches and field trips for poor chil-
dren. The Panthers also opened medical clinics that provided greatly
needed health services to the community, such as free tests for sickle-
cell anaemia, a painful genetic-mutation disease with a high oc-
currence among African Americans. They not only ran fundraisers
to build the clinics, but recruited doctors to train party members
as health workers.[42] Other grassroots programs included pest con-
trol, clothing banks, and transportation for families to visit relatives
in prison.

Not content with educating by example, the Panthers spared no
efforts to publicize their ten-point political platform. The Libera-
tion Schools were to teach the community "the beauty of socialism"
and reinforce the message that "we're not fighting a race struggle,
but in fact, a class struggle."[43] Taking their cause not just to black
communities but to other working-class communities, they published
independent newspapers, including the weekly voice of the Party,
The Black Panther: Intercommunal News Service. In 1977 their
Intercommunal Youth Institute – later renamed the Oakland Com-
munity School – was rewarded by the California legislature for
having the highest standard for elementary education in the state.

Although, like the Socialist Party more than a half-century ear-
lier, the Black Panther Party did not win, it led the political revival
in the 1960s. So much so, in fact, that several of its programs were
later adopted by various levels of California bureaucracy. This in-
cluded Free Breakfast for Children, previously banned in several
states after Hoover and local police accused the BPP of polluting
giveaways with indoctrination. COINTELPRO stopped at nothing,
in fact, to disrupt the breakfasts, from inciting rumours that the food
was infected with venereal disease to storming premises with armed
agents. Even the head agent of COINTELPRO's San Francisco office,

Charles Bates, found Hoover's campaign morally odious. Soon he himself was under attack.[44]

> America is false to the past, false to the present, and solemnly binds herself to be false to the future.
>
> • Frederick Douglass, *My Bondage and My Freedom*

Even though the man behind *The Man* passed away in 1990, in 1999 the novel was back in stores across the United States in the American Voyages edition. In a series dedicated to the reissue of historically significant popular novels of our time, the new imprint celebrated the book's timelessness or – what comes up to the same thing – its timeliness. The back-cover squib, however, included a couple of red herrings. It stated, first of all, that the novel was written nine weeks before President John F. Kennedy was assassinated on 22 November, 1963. Not so. Wallace *began* work on *The Man* nine weeks before the assassination but, as his scrupulous notes record, did not complete it until 8 March, 1964.

Likewise, the publisher's endorsement of its historical significance is something of a misnomer. *The Man* is not just historically but contemporarily significant. Why else release it thirty-five years after its original success, if not to cap the decade that gave us the 1992 Los Angeles riots and *Bulworth*? To read this massive opus exclusively as an epitaph to America's Civil Rights past is not only to dilute its purpose but to be false to our troubled present. From Africa to America, the problems diagnosed in *The Man* are back today – which is another way of saying they have never left.

The prominence of Africa in Wallace's White House reflects the *annus mirabilis* of 1960 during which no less than fifteen black nations gained post-colonial independence. They would quickly discover that statehood counts for little in the global marketplace, which wrecks people and economies as surely as guns, germs and steel. Indeed, half a century on, the continent remains dirt-poor and exploited, making headlines only in terms of human catastrophe, health epidemics, and the AIDS disaster. No wonder that, while the Bush II administration set new records for reneging on state visits, Africa has turned to China to jumpstart its own economic miracle.

None of this means, of course, that Wallace should be shelved next to Nostradamus. Inventing a black president, he certainly did not anticipate the spectacular career of Barack Obama. Inventing a black direct-action group, he certainly did not predict the Black Panther Party. Of course, the flare-up of violence, the dogged persecution, and the tragic end of Wallace's Turnerites mirror in disturbing ways the flameout of socialism in America's ghettos of the '60s. But the enduring power of Wallace's faction goes beyond glimpsing something of the country's future history. In the end, it has as much to do with harnessing literature's genius for weaving fictional scenarios and letting readers calibrate their real-life beliefs.

Even though Wallace placed his Black Power militants ten years in the future, inevitably he brought them into the living rooms of the America of the sixties. Pointedly, he did not stop with a drama of racial discrimination but went on to depict a militant black liberation movement determined to meet the government's propaganda, fire power, and intimidation in kind. Indeed, if something of this dark period in racial history is known today outside the community of race historians, it is arguably in part because of its mainstream penetration by writers like Irving Wallace.

The Black Pride seventies look good in the part-comic, part-nostalgic film tributes like *The Undercover Brother*. In the preface to Wallace' novel, James Earl Jones – who portrayed president Dilman in the 1972 film version – puts a different spin on things.

> In those volatile days of the seventies, there was a general public insistence that a black man be militant. This seemed to be expected of black men by other black men, by white men, by liberals, and even by conservatives. There was the attitude, often liberal, that said, "If I were a black man, I would sure as hell be screaming or angry." At the other end of the spectrum, there were those people, often conservative, who seemed to prefer stereotypes, saying, "Give me a black man who is yelling and screaming and I'll know what to do with *him*." (vii–viii)

Made for television, the film version of *The Man* was instead released in theatres. In the wake of the surprise success of Redford's *The Candidate*, the producers decided to roll with the political punches, perhaps aware that some Southern states refused to air TV

Moving pictures.
The principal actors, movers and shakers behind the film
The Man: James Earl Jones, Barbara Rush, Irving Wallace,
Rod Serling, Joe Sargent, and below Burgess Meredith,
Irving Wallace and James Earl Jones.
By permission of David Wallechinsky and Amy Wallace

dramas that upped the ante on racial themes.[45] Alas, where Wallace
takes the beast by the horns, the filmmakers took the path of least
resistance. Safely political, rather than *political* political, the movie
sank out of sight amid patriotic bathos and melodrama. It would

be another quarter century before Beatty's *Bulworth* would attempt to set Hollywood aflame.

American presidents have always starred in all kinds of fiction, from Tom Clancy's double-deckers celebrating America's rightwing ideology to the liberal *West Wing*, winner of a staggering twenty-six Emmys. Unlike Clancy, however, instead of reducing his president to a Captain America cliché, Wallace makes an effort to plumb the psychological depths of a man almost crushed by the weight of the Office. His narrative mix of Whitman-style panorama and Dickinson-like obsession with political detail may be a true measure of his design.

At its blockbuster best, *The Man* weaves political fiction and historical fact tighter than the woof and warp on a Pilates leotards. The Congressional newspaper, *The Roll Call*, praised it for its realism in portraying the work of the government, from its complexity to its pettiness and shortcomings. The horse trader on the Hill, the handler, the spin-master, the pollster, and the mud slinger, all star in Wallace's drama about Black Power politics. And where, in defense of artistic integrity, Faulkner contended that for the "Ode on a Grecian Urn" he would sacrifice his own mother, Wallace simply reiterated his stance from *The Man*: "I'm for commitment."[46]

Farce, chaos, the goldmakers, the charlatans,
the fantasists. We had a whole parade of them
at Watergate. (1977)

• John le Carré, *Conversations with John le Carré*

Chapter Two   1970s

The Life and Death of Walter Bodmor Nixon:
Richard Condon's *Death of a Politician*

Like Raymond Chandler and Walker Percy, Richard Condon became
a writer of fiction only in the fifth decade of his life. Author of over
twenty novels – in addition to nonfiction, plays, screenplays, and
sundry essays on food and travel – he passed away in 1996, the year
Beatty's Senator Bulworth embarked on his quixotic re-election cam-
paign. A self-confessed man of the marketplace, Condon was equally
an ambitious and complex novelist. "A writer may call himself an
artist," he said in his autobiography,

> just as an ambulance chaser may call himself a lawyer, but
> what is art is not likely to be decided for decades or longer
> after the work has been produced – and then is often rede-
> cided – so we must not feel bad if we think of literature
> as entertainment rather than as enlightenment.[1]

Yet even as he entertained Condon kept one eye on enlighten-
ment, fully aware that few things in life are as devastating as truth
– including truth in fiction whose threads weave in and out of real
life. The historical roots of such "faction" reach from Petronius's
Satyricon and its whimsical allusions to ancient mores to John

Barclay's first *roman à clef*. The French term encodes the legacy of the seventeenth-century court of Louis XIV, during whose reign the Versailles coteries developed a penchant for alluding to real-life people behind the façade of fiction. That the device quickly spread into the rest of Europe was the result, in large measure, of the titillation attendant on decoding the "key" to the hidden truth.

The inclusion of topical and often inflammatory allusions for those in the know proved irresistible to generations of readers. It also led on occasion to interpretive pathologies, whereby innocent narratives would be scoured for encrypted meanings. No matter if the author denied the presence of any political subtexts, not least for fear of getting in trouble with the censors. The crypto-readers knew better, and their suspicions were proven right every time artists protested too much, only to reveal later that there *was* a hidden message after all. As in *Foucault's Pendulum*, no matter whether the subtext was really out there, it was sometimes better to believe it was.

The enduring success of the *roman à clef* owes much to the ghost of the real world lurking, like a palimpsest, behind the story. Smuggling in references to contemporary events, more often than not of political bent, writers used a variety of techniques, from allegorical parable to homiletic beast fable. Some even went as far as to print appendices that informed the more politically challenged readers who on the page was who in the news. The telltale indexing soon went out of style – as soon, that is, as the finger-pointed VIPs started to sue for libel and defamation – but not the roasting of public figures over the bonfires of current vanities.

Famous for blurring the line between fiction and life, Condon was equally famous for painstaking research. On occasion, he would even include bibliographies of his sources, provoking Mordecai Richler to grouse that his novels were "not so much to be reviewed as counter-researched."[2] Other times he merely prefaced the story with a cast of historical characters, as if to make sure their super-villainy would not be shrugged off as mere fiction. Not that it is hard to figure out who is who in Condon's gallery of political rogues. Much of the time his characters are only thinly disguised variations on easily recognizable public figures – as they are in *Death of a Politician*.

Barring a few counterfactual twists, the novel follows the career of a Nixonesque politician through the war-scam forties, the red-scare fifties, and the freewheeling-dealing sixties. Square the nov-

Through the glasses, darkly.
Richard Condon, nobrow artist extraordinaire: author of,
among others, *The Manchurian Candidate* and *Death
of a Politician*.
Freebase.

elistic licence with the *roman à clef*'s premise of historical veracity,
and you may wonder where sober fact ends and fiction begins. How
much of the historical Richard Milhous Nixon is in the fictional
Walter Bodmor Slurrie? How much of Nixon's banker and confi-
dant "Bebe" Rebozo is in Slurrie's banker and confidant "Kiddo"
Cardozo? How much of the Miami mobster Mayer Lansky is in
Cardozo's boss, Miami mobster Abner Danzig? How much of their

venality and political power is the figment of Condon's imagination? Better still, how much is true?

Published in 1978, *Death of a Politician* trailed in the footsteps of Bernstein and Woodward's *All the President's Men* – as well as those of the film, which only a year earlier had won a bevy of Oscars for the depiction of *l'affaire* Nixon. With a Tricky Dicky look-alike in the starring role, the novel follows this political Elmer Gantry up the greasy pole of House, Senate, and White House politics. Alternating burlesque with history, it comes with a political key to unlock the secrets of the man who defined the politics of the decade. Never shy to shoot from the hip, the author documents Nixon's high-office sellout, recreating the trading history of his soul on the buyer's market while fortifying it with reams of incendiary history and speculation.

Death of a Politician was bound to set conspiracy theorists agog. Jim Garrison, Carl Oglesby, and Oliver Stone had stoked everyone's worst fears about the Kennedy assassination, tracing it to the president's intention to sideswipe the armaments industry by pulling out of Vietnam. On Condon's menu it is but an hors d'oeuvre. To pave the way for his own ascension in 1968, his Walter Slurrie joins the coverup of the assassination of the man who beat him to the presidency in 1960. True or false? You decide. In June 1968, RFK was shot dead right after clinching the California presidential primaries. In November 1968 Nixon cruised into the White House. In May 1972 George Wallace was shot during a rally in Maryland. In November Nixon cruised to a landslide.

Perhaps to sweeten the bitter political pill, Condon grafts it onto a first-class investigative procedural. Opening with a facsimile of a scene-of-a-crime form, page by page *Death of a Politician* masterminds the moves and counter-moves of a crime thriller. The pace is relentless, in the best tradition of Chandler's precept that the mystery should resolve itself in a flash of action. Condon was, of course, a self-proclaimed public entertainer whose talents had been bought earlier in his life by Disney, Fox, Paramount, and United Artists. But he can easily be mistaken for an artist, looking for suspense as much in police procedurals as in cutthroat politics, and for epiphany as much in forensics as in ethics.

Political, satirical, historical, comical, and a nobrow mystery to boot – *Death of a Politician* had the makings of a bestseller. Yet, much as *Bulworth* twenty years later, it fizzled rather than sizzled on the charts before going out of print. Never reissued, today only second-hand – and tagged as rare – copies are carried by select book traders. Not even literary encyclopaedias give it the time of day. The supposedly definitive entry in Gale's *Contemporary Authors Online* spares Condon's masterpiece not one line of analysis. *St. James Guide to Crime & Mystery Writers* fails to mention this quintessential crime mystery at all.

All this pales, however, next to the biographical chapter in Beacham's sixteen-volume *Encyclopedia of Popular Fiction*. Methodically, it enumerates every single one of Condon's major, minor, and obscure writings – even his Mexican cookbook – but not *Death of a Politician*. Why?

> A first-class red scare meant millions in increased sales, but how could the most ingenious editors and reporters keep the excitement alive without a few facts?
> • Upton Sinclair, *Boston*

No one sheds a tear when some two-bit potboiler fails with both readers and critics. But is that the case with Condon? In the early 1960s *Time* hailed him as one of the ten best novelists in America.[3] In the *New York Times*, his "cynical, hip political thrillers" were extolled by the same Richard Lingeman who never missed Kick Irving Wallace Day. The *New York Times Book Review* counted him, together with Heller, Mailer, Berger, Burroughs, Kesey, and Pynchon, as among the most distinguished postwar writers. Condon, one critic enthused, stands among the American popular novelists of his generation like a borzoi among retrievers. "Nabokov without tears," seconded another.

Condon's political dramas sold by the million in more than twenty languages worldwide, not counting braille. The author of *Death of a Politician* was, after all, the author of *The Manchurian Candidate*, the publishing phenomenon of the era. Having gone nova on bookstands, *The Manchurian Candidate* was released by United Artists as a five star film with Laurence Harvey, Frank Sinatra, Janet Leigh, and Angela Lansbury (directed by John Frankenheimer). In 2004

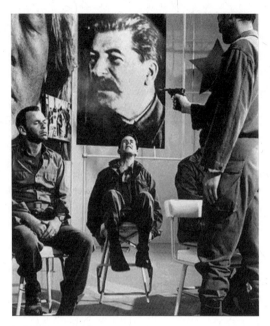

Political artertainment.
Joseph Stalin as Satan: *The Manchurian Candidate*
tapped the stoked paranoia of the Cold War.
M.C. Productions.

– by then a 100-Best-Ever Hollywood classic – the film reprised
its conspiratorial thrills under the Paramount banner, with Denzel
Washington and Meryl Streep on the marquee.

In the 1980s, changing his emphasis from politics and the Mafia
to the Mafia and politics, Condon scored a new rash of bestsellers
with the Prizzi saga (capped in 1994 by *Prizzi's Money*). The 1982
opener, *Prizzi's Honor* – chronologically the second part of the
tetralogy – was turned by John Huston in 1985 into an Oscar-
winner with Jack Nicholson and Angelica Houston. Condon's
screenplay adaptation of his own bestseller cemented his success
by winning the coveted Writers Guild of America award and a
nomination for the Best Writing Oscar and the Golden Globe.

But if Condon was far from your average writer, *Death of a
Politician* is far from an average thriller. Replete with Rabelaisian
pith and wit, it is literate and experimental, changing narrative
styles and points of view as often as Imelda Marcos changed shoes.
Set ostensibly in 1964, it defies the unity of action, dishing out a

mosaic of testimonials, profiles, and reports narrated by an ensemble of brilliantly unreliable characters. While the murder investigation races forward, the main storyline is projected in flashbacks of reconstructions. Defying linearity and chronology, it raises more questions than it answers, deconstructing the life of Citizen Slurrie with the assurance of Faulkner's *As I Lay Dying*.

As a whodunit, *Death of a Politician* is masterpiece artertainment, mixing the intellectual rigours of biography with the pacing of crime fiction. As a political *Who's Who*, it is a masterpiece satyricon with a cast straight out of Machiavelli's *Prince*. White House office-holders, godzillionaire financiers, mob bigwigs, and the ubiquitous Secret Police all came with enough "key" to identify their real-life prototypes. As a surgeon on the body politic, Condon delights in swinging a machete where other artists might have resorted to a scalpel. Putting the tri-coloured getup of Uncle Sam on the same weak-eyed devil that ran the show in *The Heart of Darkness*, he crosses the line between political and *political* political a hundred times over.

Besides *Death of a Politician*, the same period brought two other Condon political thrillers: *Winter Kills* (1974) and *A Trembling Upon Rome* (1983). The former is a literary fugue on the coverup behind the assassination of the thirty-fifth president of the United States. Each of the half-dozen subplots is a virtuoso thought-experiment connecting the dots of the lines of inquiry abjured by the Warren Commission. True to form, *Winter Kills* is also a *roman à clef* which goes after the head of the Kennedy clan, Joseph P. Kennedy. No charge is too big, no detail too small in the dramatization of his bootlegging years, dealings with the mafia, and the creation of a political juggernaut fed by money, intimidation, and reciprocal grooming.

At higher levels, shrugs Condon, organized politics is indistinguishable from organized crime. "By the time I reached the end of the novel's incredibly complex plot," concurred Christopher Lehmann-Haupt in the *New York Times*, "I was a Richard Condon fan once more."[4] A decade later, *A Trembling Upon Rome* forged from such political cynicism another masterpiece of historical fiction. From the rose-scented bordellos of Bologna to the purple chambers of the Vatican, Condon orchestrates a swashbuckling extravaganza of Douglass Fairbanks vintage. Beneath the cloak-and-dagger façade lies, once again, the marriage of convenience between organized religion, organized politics, and organized crime.

The sunlit streets and dark alleys of early Renaissance Italy are a fitting backdrop for a nobrow thriller that manages to cram in more history than the average PBS miniseries. As if wishing to turn political innocents into cynical seen-it-alls overnight, Condon takes on the Catholic Church at its most vulgar. *A Trembling Upon Rome* narrates the life of Baldassare Cossa – politician, soldier, lawyer, financier, whoremaster, and Pope John XXIII. But it is equally the story of his promoters, among them his banker and confidant, Cosimo Di Medici. If Condon's villains are an incarnation of a mob family (*la famiglia* Medici was the archetype behind Machiavelli's *Prince*), in *Death of a Politician* it is the thinly disguised Rockefellers who function "the way the Medicis functioned in the Renaissance."[5]

The similarities between *A Trembling Upon Rome* and *Death of a Politician* are far from coincidental. Underneath rapid-fire narration, both are case studies of some of the most unsavoury and, for that reason, the most fascinating periods of history. Both pound home George Santayana's warning – which graces the entrance to the United States National Archives – that those who airbrush history condemn themselves to repeat it. There is no doubt that Condon prefers his history warts and all, perhaps even warts before all. Despising myth-makers and makeovers, his motto (like that of the CIA) is set out in the Gospel of John: The truth will set you free.

Not that the public is always ready to believe the truth. Larry J. Sabato and Glenn R. Simpson's investigation of electoral *Dirty Little Secrets* (1996) – appropriately subtitled *The Persistence of Corruption in American Politics* – documents the enduring public naiveté about high office perfidy. Similarly, in *Death of a Politician* Condon draws attention to the fact that, even as they export their political system on the point of a bayonet, Americans choose to remain blinkered to the faults that taint it from within. In 1986 he told the *New York Times*: "Every book I've ever written has been about abuse of power. I feel very strongly about that. I'd like people to know how deeply their politicians are wronging them."[6]

In this goal he was preceded by a raft of *romans à clef* in the 1940s, all of which struggled to come to terms with the meteoric rise and fall of a charismatic Louisiana Senator and, on the international front, a charismatic Nazi Chancellor. Hamilton Basso's *Sun in Capricorn* (1942), John Dos Passos's *Number One* (1943), Adria Langley's *A Lion Is In the Streets* (1945), and Robert Penn Warren's

All the King's Men (1946) all track the rollercoaster careers of politi-
cians cursed with Faustian hubris. Dissecting the hooks and the
crooks by which the latter clawed their way to too much power, they
blazed the trail for *Death of a Politician*.

> He was to be formally indicted by the House of
> Representatives and driven from his high office
> in disgrace.
> • Upton Sinclair, *Boston*

In *Parliament of Whores*, P.J. O'Rourke's thesis is simple: between
conspiracy and incompetence in American politics, always go with
incompetence. Condon's thesis could not have been more different.
Political machinery may be inept in some ways, he concedes, but
it is lethal when its vital interests are at stake. The appearance of
bumbling comes only from the visible portion of its covert machi-
nations that, from time to time, bubble up to the surface. Conspiracy
and fraud, rather than rank incompetence, make American politics
go around. In Condon's world, there is one basic tenet: "when you
don't know the whole truth, the worst you can imagine is bound
to be close."[7]

Dubbing this Condon's Law, Leo Braudy praised its practitioner
as one of the most original creators of paranoid surrealism, *the* novel
style of the 1960s. Reviewing Condon's novels, other critics also refer
to paranoia in so many variations you might be excused for think-
ing it was a Latin verb. Most concede, though, that the writer's pre-
occupation with conspiracy never blunts his political sting. The only
difference, after all, between a crank who keeps looking over his
shoulder and a tenured historian is in the facts, and *Death of a Politi-
cian* is chock full of them.

In his classic disquisition on *The Paranoid Style in American
Politics*, Richard Hofstadter invested paranoia with its proper
rhetorical and historical resonance. Virtually from its birth, he
argued, American politics has been shot through with conspirato-
rial fantasy. As a result, nourished by a conviction of persecution
systemized in grandiose theories of conspiracy, most political
aspirants blur – and find it expedient to blur – the line between truth
and falsehood.[8] Hofstadter's thesis strongly vindicates Condon's

seemingly over-the-top suppositions and conjectures. With American politics shot through with paranoia – whether driven by communism, terrorism, xenophobia, or anything else – political satire is bound to resemble pandemonium.

Absence of proof of conspiracy is, after all, not proof of its absence. Logically, no one can ever disprove paranoia – one can only prove it right. No amount of negative evidence could ever quash a skeptic's conviction that, as with Oswald, Ruby, and the Warren Commission, you can peel layer after layer off this political onion and still get no closer to the truth. Contrary to first impressions, Condon's Law is simply a case of classical decorum that demands that the style fit the subject. In this sense, Hofstadter's professed aim of "using political rhetoric to get at political pathology" is a remarkably good description of *Death of a Politician*.[9]

In *Biography and the Postmodern Historical Novel* (2001), John F. Keener examines the representations of America's three criminal icons of the twentieth century. His troika, odd at first glance, is oddly fitting at the second. Together with Dutch Schulz, mob hit man with the vision thing about Vegas, and Lee Harvey Oswald, ex-CIA "lone assassin" of John F. Kennedy, it includes the thirty-seventh president of the United States, Richard Milhous Nixon. Keener argues that the trio personify the corruption of America's core myths. In the president's case it is personal corruption in politics – underwritten by the 1974 Supreme Court ruling that unanimously found Nixon guilty of gross abuse of political office for partisan gain and personal revenge.

Gleefully dissecting the paranoia that, by all biographical accounts, Nixon personified, Condon joins Lord Acton in teaching that political power tends to corrupt all norms of civilized/ethical conduct. *Death of a Politician* is prefaced, in fact, by an extract from the British historian's letter to the Bishop of Peterborough and London. "Great men are almost always bad men," Acton summed up decades of magisterial study, "even when they exercise influence and not authority; still more when you superadd the tendency or the certainty of corruption by full authority."

Scratch paranoia. The absurdity of Condon's plots is a mere exaggeration of the absurdity present in the real world.[10]

Can anyone really tell where realism ends and surrealism begins when it comes to Condon's Washington – or, for that matter, Nixon's Washington? Watergate, with Crédit Mobilier in the 1870s and the

"I Want You" to stop asking questions about Watergate!
Richard Nixon as Uncle Sam: dark circles under his eyes,
dark political clouds on the horizon.
Businessweek.

Teapot Dome in the 1920s, ranks as one of the three worst scandals in American political history. The break-in and the bugging of the Democratic National Committee, although foremost in the public mind, were after all only the proverbial tip of the iceberg. *All the President's Men* is correct when Deep Throat (eventually revealed as the then FBI's no. 2, W. Mark Felt) warns Woodward that the coverup had little to do with the break-in but everything with the submerged partisan "ice."

When the paranoid, quasi-totalitarian White House conspiracy began to swim into focus, it was at first inconceivable. The list of offences compiled by the House Judiciary Committee ran from burglary, forgery, illegal wiretaps, and destruction of evidence to bribery, witness tampering, obstruction of justice, and conspiracy to involve government agencies in illegal activities. As the two-hundred-hour trove of secret tapes confirmed, the CIA, the FBI, and even the IRS were all complicit in incriminating Nixon's political rivals and all sorts of imagined adversaries. Investigators uncovered a network of illegal and criminal actions funded by concealed donations, some – in a script from *Get Smart* – delivered by briefcase in cash. All to re-elect the president and destroy his "enemies," with a special spot reserved for Edward Kennedy.

Although the intervening years saw more than their share of ignominy, Watergate remains the political and moral watershed by which other scandals are measured. In Sabato/Simpson's investigation of dirty electoral secrets it gets top billing with Crédit Mobilier and the Teapot Dome. The 2004 political prophylactic from John Dean – Nixon's White House lawyer during Watergate – puts the secrecy and paranoia of the Bush II administration in perspective with a telling title: *Worse Than Watergate*. Even Victor Lasky, a Nixon ally keen to exonerate his fallen idol by detailing the electoral fraud, illegal phone tapping, and other abuses authorized by Democratic presidents, titles his attempted whitewash *It Didn't Start with Watergate*.

> A "contemporary historical novel" is an unusual art-form, and may call for explanation.
> • Upton Sinclair, *Boston*

A dead man slumps, fully dressed, in a red plush chair placed incongruously in a hotel bathtub. The scene of the crime is New York's Waldorf Astoria and the political setup is pure Semtex. The apartment belongs to America's most powerful political broker, Dick Betaut, employed by the Felsenburshe family, who have Rockefeller-type wealth and clout. The blood-soaked body is that of the ex-vice president of the United States, Walter Slurrie. The police, led by Lieutenant Galagher, are staggered by the forensic reconstruction. No sooner was Slurrie shot dead than the murderer must have picked up the bleeding corpse, dragged it back to the armchair, executed it for the second time, then re-seated the mangled shell to restage the execution all over again ...

Death of a Politician is a book-length riddle about the death and, even more, the life of a politician modelled in remarkable detail on Richard Milhous Nixon. Corruption segues into full-fledged conspiracy with the liquid celerity of animator's cels, leaving readers grasping for a gauge on which to recalibrate their bearings. Wartime requisitions, fraud, and post-war defence-contract scams are punctuated by communist baiting at home and abroad, all manufactured

The American flag for a figleaf.
A literary monument to political corruption:
Death of a Politician.
By permission of Random House Archive & Library

to misinform the public, fleece the taxpayer, and keep outsiders away from the political trough. Among these byzantine goings-on, a venal plot to invade Castro's Cuba in order to "liberate" the lucrative casinos seems like an oasis of sanity.

If *Death of a Politician* reads at times like a summation from the prosecutor, it is because the nonfiction novel provides a perfect medium for the writer to take on his perennial bêtes noires: organized politics, organized crime, and organized money, all jockeying for power under the protection of America's secret police. Condon's revisionist history is at times alternative history, too. Castro's revolution takes place a decade earlier than in real life. Slurrie's children are fathered by his bosom friend, Eddie Cardozo.[11] Such plays of imagination make it even more imperative to wrest historical fact from speculative fiction.

To reinforce the gravity of Condon's accusations, *Death of a Politician* is styled as a documentary and typeset to convey that idea visually. Office memos in plodding bureaucratese, police blotter prose, and interview transcripts alternate with dry official reports from the chief investigating officer. Signed and countersigned at the bottom, the opening report is even set in roman numerals, like the preface in a nonfiction work. Reminiscent of the police procedurals of Ed McBain, sections are prefaced by typewritten headers and reproductions of Arrest and Crime Coding Section forms or Secret Police institutional stamps.[12]

Yet *Death of a Politician* is a procedural with a difference. Far from being a pretext for dispensing forensic lore and gore, the ghastly assassination is a summons to a moral trial in the manner of *Citizen Kane*. Indeed, recalling Orson Welles's classic, the narrative is chopped into a mosaic of debriefing reports taken from individuals who used to consort with Slurrie. Even the untouchables, Governor Beteaut and *capo di capi* Danzig – both exempted from the drug-enhanced interrogations administered by the Semley (Langley) goons – go on record. Gradually, as with Charles Foster Kane, the postmortem collage coalesces into a complex and incongruous picture of the dead man.

Condon's literary skill has never been more in evidence, for even if the reports were left unsigned, each would be identifiable by its speaker's verbal tics. Danzig is all slang, always looking for an angle. Beteaut is brusque to the point of contempt. Cardozo's thick Latin accent hides the easy-going manner of a born mixer and raconteur. Hinds's non-sequiturs meander in and out of reality. Slurrie's wife and mother chattily defend their crusading hero. Still, for all their idiosyncratic mannerisms, they, like a Greek chorus, speak in the same voice, laying a political myth to rest with the man. Where Horatio Alger's hero Ragged Dick owed his fortune to pluck and luck, Walter's confreres leave no doubt that this Tricky Dicky lookalike was nothing but a con job.

When it comes to the linchpin of the *roman á clef* – the key with which to decipher the political allusions – different writers resort to different means to help readers reconstruct real life from the clues in the text. Few fictions, for instance, can match Al Franken's nonfiction for chutzpah. To help readers map pseudonyms onto real people, early on in *The Truth (With Jokes)* Franken turns to the true and tried weapon of scholarship: the footnote. When the humourist receives a message from his secret source, Mark Felt, the footnote sends the reader to the gloss at the bottom of the page: "Mark Felt is the alias I'm using in order to protect the identify of my real source, Judith Miller"![13]

An only marginally less ostentatious way to give the game away is by allegorical name-tagging. No one will have trouble cross-referencing the cast of Philip Roth's *Our Gang (Starring Trick E. Dixon and His Friends)*: John F. Charisma, Robert F. Charisma, J. Edgar Heehaw, General Poppapower and, of course, Trick E. Dixon. Condon himself is not averse to employing giveaway names. His pairings of Cardozo/Rebozo, Horace Hind/Howard Hughes, Huggems/Kissinger, Nils/Nelson (Felsenburshe/Rockefeller) are as suggestive as the Polish assonance of Danzig/Lansky. It is the welter of biographical detail, however, that makes identification foolproof.

Condon can play the self-referential game as well as anyone, and his allusions run not only from fiction to life but from fiction to fiction. Often his intentions seem merely ludic, as when he gives the name Kullers to diverse characters in several novels (*Winter Kills, Death of a Politician, The Emperor of America*). In a similar vein, Partanna, a mere extra in *Death of a Politician*, becomes the centre-piece of the entire *Prizzi* saga. A more interesting example of such hyper-referentiality is the Pickering Commission. Here Condon alludes – this time consistently in all novels – to both the Warren Commission and, tongue-in-cheek, his mother, whose maiden name was Pickering. A riddle within a riddle, the device alerts readers to look for the real world in the fiction.[14]

Opening with a close-up of a dead body, and reconstructing a life story in a drawn-out flashback, *Death of a Politician* may be alluding to that great cinematic tragedy *Sunset Boulevard*. Indeed, although darkly comic moments abound in the book, it is darkness and not comedy that dominates the tone. How could it be any different, when the fatal character flaws of the politician-with-a-mission illumine the character of the nation? In Condon's *The Whisper of the Axe*, an anarchist reviles America's "masochism, re-fusal to reflect, hypnosis by self-interest, dependency upon instant gratification (as a way of life), passion to conform."[15] In *Death of*

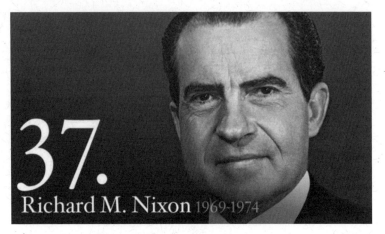

a Politician the same description could apply to its thirty-seventh
president.

> There is one simple rule for guidance in reading
> the novel: the characters who are real persons
> bear real names, while those who bear fictitious
> names are fictitious characters.
> • Upton Sinclair, *Boston*

Like every genre, *roman à clef* is an invitation to a literary game.
In Condon's case, it involves mapping fictional characters and events
onto Nixon's political retinue. Unlike the star system of Hollywood,
where a couple of leads usually overshadow a truckful of extras,
Death of a Politician showcases a prodigious cast of dramatis per-
sonae. A virtual panoply of Walter's controllers, fixers, sponsors,
spinners, movers, shakers, and other members of his den of thieves
enter and exit this biographical faction. Even though all hide be-
hind fictitious names, the novel leaves enough clues to decipher their
true identity.

Abner Danzig, for example, is Meyer Lansky, Miami's Jewish
crime boss (a prototype for Hayman Roth in Puzo's *The Godfather*).

Touted as the best business mind that organized crime has ever produced, he is notorious for – and, in the novel, instantly identifiable by – the remark that the American Mafia is bigger than the US Steel. Historically, Lansky's covert financing of Richard Nixon has been traced at least to mid-1940s, casting a deep shadow on the relation between the godfather, the future president, and the latter's confidante, Bebe Rebozo.[16]

In *Death of the Politician*, this grey eminence of the mob underworld and behind-the-scenes politics is Slurrie's puppet-master. Together, they rake in massive profits from a Cold War arms race carefully orchestrated to keep the nation scared and compliant. Condon knew exactly what he was talking about – in real life, Nixon's red baiting and John Foster Dulles's brinkmanship were, indeed, extremely profitable. Research shows that throughout the 1950s investments in firms specializing in defence contracts brought nearly twice the return of any others. Watching Danzig mastermind his tithe, it is difficult to resist a feeling that the same unholy alliance has been raking it in from the war in Iraq.

Naturally, when graft is not enough, there is always theft. In November 2006 no less than eight billion dollars were reported "missing" from Iraq's reconstruction fund. To the midterm-election vows of a new era of accountability, one can only echo Stevie Wonder: "I'll believe it when I see it." In *Death of a Politician* the jackpot is not Saddam's oil but Danzig's casinos, shut down by Castro's revolution. But the fictional course of action is not that different from the historical 1950s when, to get the Cuban dictator out of the way of profits, Lansky turned for help to then Vice President Nixon.[17]

Back in the novel, Eddie Cardozo is a charismatic Latino wheeler-dealer. He is also a protégé of Danzig's and a partner in graft of the OPA procurer-Congressman-Senator-Vice-President Walter Slurrie. In real life the threads lead to the Cuban real-estate dealer turned banker, Bebe (Charles G.) Rebozo, famous for being mixed up in the $100,000 cash "gift" from Howard Hughes to the president. Curiously, Nixon kept this business partner and confidant – the only person to participate in intimate family celebrations – out of the limelight from their first encounter in the early 1950s. Whatever their personal relationship, when Bebe's mob connections surfaced in the 1970s, in an effort to stifle exposure he sued *The Washington Post* for libel – and lost.[18]

Another of Condon's factional rogues bears the peculiar name of Horace Riddle Hind. According to his autobiographical sketches – which echo Dos Passos's biographies from *USA* – he is a self-made inventor, aviator, Hollywood starlet collector, and a defence-contract magnate. There is only one historical figure who fits the bill: Howard Hughes, paranoid tycoon notorious for using money as a passkey to both sides of the political aisle. In *Death of a Politician*, his money buys him Walter Slurrie. In real life, his handwritten entry in his agenda for 1968 speaks for itself:

> I am determined to elect a president of our choosing this year and one who will be deeply indebted ... who knows the facts of political life.

As if his own and Nixon's venality were not explicit enough, Hughes continues with the following (also handwritten) remark:

> If we select Nixon, then he, I know for sure, knows the facts of life.[19]

News of Nixon's hush-hush slush funds first began to surface in 1952, during his nomination as Eisenhower's running mate. Billionaires like Hughes as well as still undisclosed public corporations donated sizeable sums not just for his campaigns but, despite his hat-over-the-heart act, for personal expenses. To get an idea of who may have been so generous, we can turn to *Death of a Politician*. In the novel, the chief source of these contributions is the richest family in the world who, among others, subsidize the New York State Republican Party to the point where it is little more than a family subsidiary. Their scion – who thrice lost the Republican presidential nomination – is Nils Felsenburshe, alter ego of Nelson Rockefeller (a staunch Nixon ally).[20]

"Pre-lecting" presidential candidates might sound like one of Condon's conspiratorial fantasies were it not for the secretive Bilderberg Group. Since 1952, this covey of the world's richest and most powerful has been meeting annually to promote the integration of transnational business and politics. Its flexible membership has included the heads of the World Bank and the European Central Bank, chairmen of the biggest multinationals, MPs, cabinet ministers, high-ranking senators, European commissioners, military brass, even royalty. Bilderberg unerringly invites politicians to its congresses just before they make the big leagues. Bill Clinton was invited a year before he became president, Tony Blair a year before becoming Labour leader, on his way to 10 Downing Street. All recent presidents of the European Commission attended Bilderberg sessions before being appointed.[21]

Coincidence?

Of course, empire builders never wash their linen in public – they just buy a new set of sheets. For that the Felsenburshes hire political kingmakers, like the novel's Richard T. Beteaut. The pint-sized Beteaut is a former gang-busting DA, governor of New York, two-time presidential election loser, and the most powerful Republican in the 1950s. In real life, he is Thomas E. Dewey: DA, crimebuster, New York governor, and Republican kingmaker, equally admired and feared for his "when in Rome" courtroom and boardroom tactics. A close ally of Nixon's, he was pivotal in strong-arming the 1952 Republican nomination for the Eisenhower/Nixon ticket, thereafter moving in the White House's innermost circles and frequently shoring up the beleaguered veep.[22]

Beteau's righthand man is another factional enabler, Charles Coffey. Son of a Tammany Hall Democrat, he is a brutal political fixer, also on the payroll of the Felsenburshes. Condon makes sure to give the devil his partisan due. Tammany is synonymous today with political corruption but in Charley's mind it stands for clothing and feeding the immigrant masses, not to mention child-labour and sweat-shop legislation. Charley's political education comes straight from his Tammany Hall father: "You know and I know that it makes no difference which party we work for, any more than it makes any difference which party is elected" (74).[23]

Characterized by Condon as the vice-president's law-school roommate and campaign manager, Charley is part Murray Chotiner, Nixon's smear-artist extraordinaire. But he owes almost as much to the fictional Jack Burden in *All the King's Men*, another unlicensed trouble shooter with a flawed moral compass. A man divided, he is talented and not intrinsically evil, just rotten to the core. His account, together with Cardozo's, dominates the story and is more personal than anyone else's. At one point, Charley recalls a World War II beach assault in which he meets a nurse who becomes his

wife and conscience. In passages of lean prosody that bring to mind
Farewell to Arms, the couple bring each other back from the brink
of death to forge a separate peace.

Coffey is a tragic figure, a traitor to his party, to his principles,
and to the woman he loves. When his wife denounces him and his
world, it is hard to shake off the feeling that she is, to some extent,
her creator's mouthpiece.

> The gangrene that infects history was put there by politicians.
> They seek havoc for personal gain. They serve only a handful
> of masters and abandon all the others to die of the gangrenes
> they fostered – the wars, the inflations, the unemployment,
> the suffering, the corruption, the shame. (73)

Only when she leaves him and tragically dies in an accident does
Coffey flip into belated repentance ...

Slurrie and Beteaut are dyed-in-the-wool Republicans. Coffey
– before he joins them – a three-generation Democrat. But all that's
beside the point. In politics there are no permanent allies or enemies,
only permanent interests, and the latter do not care who is in the
driver's seat as long as they hold the wheel. Condon is an equal-
opportunity prosecutor. Corruption, he points out, has no ideology
and no partisan coloration. And, to repeat after Victor Lasky, it cer-
tainly did not start with Watergate. It was not the Republicans but
the Democrats who pioneered the clandestine tactics later adopted
by the Christian Coalition – using chartered nonpartisan organi-
zations to run covert partisan campaigns.[24]

> America had ceased to be a republic, it was an
> absolute monarchy, its ruler the Prince of Lies!
> • Upton Sinclair, *Boston*

In astronomy ellipses describe the shape of planetary orbits. In
literature, they are something altogether different. Much as in
the riddle about chess in Borges's "The Garden of Forking Paths,"
ellipses are an absence. Think of them as a synecdoche stood on
its head – whereby the whole narrative stands for the missing part.
Death of a Politician is structured around the riddle of a death of

Political basketball or political basketcase?
Richard Nixon orating in the post-"I am not a crook"-era.
By permission of Nixon Presidential Library

a man who is himself not only the greatest riddle but the greatest ellipsis of all. Much as in Alan Pakula's *All the King's Men*, the procession of informants and interviewees makes the narrative absence of the protagonist – be it Richard Nixon or Walter Slurrie – only more glaring.

Bisexual, asexual, masochistic, and grotesque, Walter Bodmor Slurrie is a pathetic figure in both the English and the classical Greek sense. Like a champagne cork, he rides the murky currents and riptides of history, buffeted by forces outside his control. This schmo with a killer instinct and the morality of an alligator epitomizes what Hannah Arendt called the "banality of evil." Needless to say, Condon's portrayal of America's thirty-seventh president as a frontman for big-league financial and political mafias proved too much for some of the novel's political and cultural critics. Sounding like they relished the thought, others simply noted that Slurrie "matches Nixon's political career almost event after event."[25]

The historical record proves, in fact, that Slurrie is Nixon incarnate. He is a self-appointed anti-communist crusader who grinds his way through law school and disastrously bungles his first case before getting a job in the tire-rationing division of the Office of Price Administration (OPA). In 1943 he is shipped by the Navy as an operations officer to the Pacific, where he sharks other soldiers in poker.[26] Retired as a lieutenant commander, he is raced by the Republican Party for Congress, clinching victory with smears, lies, and an eleventh-hour anonymous and slanderous phoning by proxy.

In 1950 he joins the Senate after another campaign that breaks new ground in mudslinging. Two years later – backed by a diminutive New York governor *cum* Republican kingmaker – he begins an eight-year stint as vice-president under an ex-general with a German name, who has to be wooed to run for president in his headquarters outside Paris. Like Ike Eisenhower, the fictional Dad Kampferhaufe keeps his number two at arm's length until 1960, when the latter runs for president himself, losing by a whisker to a charismatic Catholic president who is shot dead in Dallas before his term is up. Despite this setback, the former veep is poised to run again in 1968.

Even when their lives diverge, they are the same. Slurrie has two sons, Nixon two daughters. Slurrie is from Texas, Nixon from California, but both launch their political careers in 1947 in their home states. Checkers, the cocker spaniel from Nixon's infamous "I am not a crook" telecast, becomes Chessie the pet raccoon. Where Nixon laid it on thick with his wife's "respectable Republican cloth coat," Walter gets maudlin over his mother's "four-dollar Republican shoes."[27] Slurrie's career screeches to a halt on 9 August 1964, when he is triply executed in a Waldorf Astoria bathtub. Nixon's political death came on 9 August 1974, when the House Judiciary Committee voted to accept three of the four Articles of Impeachment.

If it is hard to tell their red baiting, corrupt anti-corruption campaigns, financial frauds, and other crimes apart, it is because Condon's disdain for politics is isotropic. *Death of a Politician* has this to say about candidates:

> they don't get inside one mile of the nomination unless they make their deal with the people who are putting up the money which the system makes the candidates spend to get elected. (111)

About an ideal politician:

> ambitious, cold, cruel man who would not hesitate to exploit mass fear under a banner of national security. (149)

Death of a politician.
Beleaguered but unrepentant: Richard Nixon resigns.
By permission of Library of Congress

About anti-communism:

> this is the first completely organized shot to scare the shit out
> of the people and keep them manageable, grateful and buy-
> ing. (110)

About Slurrie and the Cold War:

> He nourished fears: fears that the peace wouldn't last. He filled
> the vacuum created by the disappearance of the Nazis. (115)

About his character:

> as shallow as a whore's kiss. (217)

Though Nixon swore that he never profited from public
service, he stole almost as liberally as Slurrie did.[28] Among other
things, he diverted seventeen million of taxpayer's dollars for security
upgrades on his private estates in San Clemente and Key Biscayne
(drowned in this largesse were items for "the president's personal
benefit"). He got more than half a million in tax reduction for some

of his papers, diverted the leftover $1.6 million from the 1968 campaign into his own covert political fund – and still got a full presidential pardon from Gerald Ford. *Plus ça ne change pas, plus c'est la même chose.* If more proof is needed, to date, in more than half-century on the statue books, the federal Corrupt Practices Act has not led to a single successful prosecution.

The 1971 file named "Political Enemies Project" included 575 names on Nixon's black-list, among them newspaper critics and presidents of Yale and Harvard Law School.[29] The president then okayed a one-million dollar budget for Gordon Liddy, the chief legal counsel for the Committee to Re-elect the President (CREEP), who began to target the people on the list. Liddy also launched operations Target and Gemstone, elements of a wider sabotage and disinformation campaign known as the Liddy Plan. One part of the plan was to hire gangs to disperse demonstrations at the Republican Convention and hijack their leaders to Mexico. Another was to use expensive and "politically aware" hookers to seduce Democrats onto yachts equipped with hidden cameras.

All fun and games in the name of statesmanship.

What elevates *Death of a Politician* from a mere biographical thriller to a work of art, however, is the psychopathology of the protagonist. Condon charted the inner catacombs of his politician years before the appearance of Fawn M. Brodie's exhaustive monograph, *Richard Nixon: The Shaping of His Character.* One can judge the acuity of the novelist by the footnotes of the historian. Walter Slurrie looms from the pages of the *roman á clef* in every trait documented by Brodie: tortured, divided, insecure, assiduous, obsessive, fantastically frugal, and fanatically greedy – a puritanical moralist, a social outsider, a prodigious organizer, a consummate politician, and a Hall of Ill-Fame liar.

There is a curious similarity between Charles Coffey, a man rent by his angels and his devils, and Walter Slurrie, a man rent by his aspirations and his character. In a moment of insight, perhaps even epiphany, Coffey gets the measure of the vice-president and, unwittingly, of himself:

> He dreamed enormous dreams but he seemed to understand that, no matter how close he might approach them, the malevolent thing which would always stand in the way of his ever finding them would be himself. (47)

Low comedy and high entertainment.
The Man meets the King: Richard Nixon and Elvis Presley.
By permission of White House Photos Gallery

As for the real-life Richard Nixon, his Dr Jekyll, Henry Kissinger, admitted that "he'd never known another man who combined such great gifts with such a capacity for depravity and such a drive toward self-destruction."[30]

In the tradition of *Doctor Faustus*, in *Death of a Politician* the final redemption must be bought with life. In murdering the politician three times over Walter's executor may also be his saviour. Three is the magic number, an exorcism against evil, and one can only imagine the killer wishing for a silver bullet. What wrenches this scene from emotional overkill and puts it on par with Aeschylean tragedy is Walter's reaction. "When he knew what I was going to do," confesses the shooter, "he seemed happy about it. He asked me if he could be seated in the bathtub when it happened so that he wouldn't make another mess of his life" (308).

Condon's villain is horribly flawed but in the end shows a measure of dignity, perhaps even remorse. Not Nixon. As Harry Truman said, he "not only doesn't give a damn about the people; he doesn't know the difference between telling the truth and lying."[31] As if on cue, Nixon demurred: "I was not lying. I said things that later on seemed to be untrue." This megalomaniacal, almost narcissistic complaisance may perhaps explain the results of a fanciful poll conducted by the firm of Widgery and Associates. Asked about Richard Nixon's ultimate fate, only 35 percent of Americans said he went to heaven. 59 percent said he went ... somewhere else.

> Most political rings in America are financed by
> the local corporations, and exist to carry out
> their will.
>
> • Upton Sinclair, *Boston*

"Politics is a form of high entertainment and low comedy," Condon wrote. "It has everything: it's melodramatic, it's sinister and it has wonderful villains."[32] The villains, he might have added, are influential because they are legally invested with power and authority: with the ability to reach certain ends and the legitimacy to do so. But to get there, first they need to sell themselves to the highest bidder. The former House speaker "Tip" O'Neil made no bones about it. "There are four parts to any campaign: the candidate, the issues ... the campaign organization, and the money. Without money you can forget the other three."

In the twenty-nine presidential elections between 1860 and 1972, the winner outspent the loser twenty-one times.[33] This does not mean, of course, that the victors had no other cards to play. The race doesn't always go to the richer, or else the Republicans would have won every time since the Second World War. But statistically the cat's out of the moneybag. Spending does correlate significantly with who wins elections (in 2008 Obama outspent McCain), and American politics remains the playground of the rich. But the influence of money does not stop there. Corporate donors who ply candidates with donations do not part with these enormous sums merely to express their political convictions, expecting nothing in return.

Corruption and campaign finance have always been two sides of the political coin. Even though Watergate brought about a series of anti-corruption measures, in the years since – much as in the years before – candidates and contributors have displayed great ingenuity in skirting legal restrictions. Cartoons aside, corruption is not about men skulking in the shadows of the Capitol clutching briefcases under sweaty arms. Political scandals that ring out with the regularity of Big Ben often involve America's best known corporations violating public contracts, public property, public funds, zoning and land use, tax assessment and collection, the legislative and elective processes, law enforcement, and the administration of public services.

There are three types of election funding: hard, soft, and slushy. Hard money, regulated by the Federal Election Campaign Act (FECA), demands, among other things, that the recipients of these public funds refuse contributions from other sources. However – and it's a BIG however – FECA allows national and state party committees to spend soft money on behalf of candidates. Given that soft money is the sworn enemy of political integrity, it is hardly surprising that, in the four years between 1992 and 1996 alone, soft spending by both parties skyrocketed by 200 percent.[34]

Despite being amended in 1974, 1979, and 1991, FECA has loopholes big enough for an elephant (and a donkey) to waltz through. To take but one example, sales of ambassadorships are proverbial cash cows, especially those in classy, non-Third World locations. For his 1972 re-election campaign, reports George Benson in *Political Corruption in* America, Nixon got no less than $1,324,442 in donations from those he appointed to head embassies in Western Europe. After his re-election, "Nixon made ambassadors of a further eight individuals, each of whom had given no less than USD$25,000, and in aggregate USD 796,000."[35]

No need to stop at Nixon. Following campaign contributions from Big Oil, Reagan deregulated gasoline prices.[36] Thanks to millions in oil companies' contributions between 1997 and 1999, in 1999 Congress turned its back on the Kyoto Protocol. Bush I favoured oil corporations with special dispensations on regulatory and legal matters. Bush II gave the green light to the automobile industry for the Freedom Car, which would release more toxins into the air than existing cars. What works for the oil industry also works for arms makers. Lockheed Martin, the biggest military manufacturer on earth, donated $1.1 million to Republican committees in 2000 alone. It got it back a thousandfold: $1.1 billion in Pentagon contracts for military operations in the Balkans (not to mention $2.3 billion in government loans) in 2001.

One can only wonder how many promises Barack Obama must have made in order to amass his record-breaking electoral war chest, and how many of these promises will be called in now he is in office.

American politics, Condon would argue, is the epitome of free-market enterprise in which the desired commodity (preferential treatment) goes to the highest bidder, though not in any open and equitable auction. This cynical view, from a writer who made cynicism the backbone of his artistic success, is consistent with his novels, in which corruption and ideological sellout are not a matter of a few rotten apples but part of a system which turns integrity into a liability. Never mind the alleged fail-safe checks and balances, such as the watchdog function of the fourth estate (exemplified by the *Washington Post* during Watergate). Counting on them to serve as an effective watch over the judiciary, legislative, and executive branches presumes a press unconstrained by the ideological and business interests of its owners – a tall order indeed.

The more astute literary critics linked Condon's abiding interest in history to his nobrow aesthetics. Intent on bridging highbrow and popular culture, he mined a formula in which historical fact and historical fiction often add up to a whole greater than the sum of its parts. As if in anticipation, late in his life George Bernard Shaw wrote in a letter to Upton Sinclair:

> it is my considered opinion, unshaken at 85, that records of fact are not history. They are only annals, which cannot become historical until the artist-poet-philosopher rescues them from the unintelligible chaos of their actual occurrence and arranges them in works of art.[37]

This is, in essence, why we continue to read historical fiction even when histories abound, and why we ought to read *Death of a Politician*.

> There is such cynicism about the orthodox forms
> of government as they are offered to the public
> that we believe almost nothing at its face value.
> (1978)
>
> • John le Carré, *Conversations with John le Carré*

Chapter Three   1980s

The Whores R Us:
P.J. O'Rourke's *Parliament of Whores*

In the day when the average attention span does not exceed the average sound bite, gimmick is a *sine qua non* in the bookselling business – and controversy makes for a good gimmick. The proof is in the revenue from *The Satanic Verses* or *Stupid White Men*. Exploitation has become so cynical that not too long ago the Jordanian Islamic Action Front exploded in denials that it had issued a *fatwa* on Khalid Duran for *Children of Abraham*. Controversy spells S-A-L-E-S, a fact not lost on the American Jewish Committee, the book's publisher and the source of the allegation. And the only controversy to match sex or religion for column inches is political controversy.

As an elitist enclave monopolized by powerful insiders and rich outsiders, politics can hardly be bettered as a satirist's piñata. Take, for example, vote buying. However democratically distasteful the notion may be, American electoral finance paints a less than Horatio Alger–perfect picture. In 2004 the two would-be presidents combined for almost two-thirds of a *billion* dollars to get elected, saturating the airwaves with visual "bites" financed by Kerry's wife's Heinz empire and George W's oil fiefdom, Arbusto. Little wonder that, in a country so zealous about democracy as to inflict it on others, political elitism is what political satirists have for breakfast with their cereal and cup of acid.

Quartering America's political theatre in the name of common sense has a proven bestseller potential with the commoners. So has the fusion of political reportage and fictional narration – or, if you like, factual *gravitas* and stylistic *levitas*. Fiction and nonfiction have always run close in the American literary tradition, most conspicuously since the 1960s and the rise of New Journalism (and its crasser cousin, gonzo). But the historical roots of New Journalism go back to the other '60s – the 1860s of Mark Twain and his early pieces in *Enterprise*. Outraged and frequently outrageous satire was one of the hallmarks of the Gilded Age, guaranteed to make you laugh until you cried.

The parallels between Samuel Langhorne Clemens and Patrick Jake O'Rourke – humourists, satirists, essayists – are difficult to overlook. This is not to say that readers can expect from O'Rourke anything close to Huck Finn or even Tom Sawyer. But, like Twain, some of his travel essays are miniature masterpieces of barstool reportage on the quirks and whimsies of other cultures. And, like Twain in *The Innocents Abroad*, the author of *All the Trouble in the World* blends with the authorial persona in a gonzo cocktail of sober reportage and editorializing. Amid political sniping and ironic broadsides, it is anybody's guess how much of Twain's flamboyant libertarianism gnaws at the root of O'Rourke's masterpiece, *Parliament of Whores*.

With the subtitle *A Lone Humorist Attempts to Explain the Entire U.S. Government* – just because no one at Picador thought of *Federal Politics for Dummies* – the book had a good gimmick, as proven by contemporary exposés of America's power and finance elites. Paving the way for O'Rourke were books such James Stewart's 1992 *Den of Thieves*, whose anatomy of Wall Street scandals sold through the roof. Irreverent, political, with promise of an instant cure for political blues and liberal leanings, *Parliament of Whores* tapped the same vein and struck gold. In the first two months alone readers snapped up more than 150,000 copies, eventually voting it on to the list of Modern Library's 100 best-ever nonfictions.[1]

The ink was hardly dry, though, when the book came under fire. What could be more clichéd, panned the critics, than a lone penslinger riding into Capitol City to take its bosses to the cleaners? With indictments of banality and crowd-pandering, few accorded

Funny *and* conservative.
Iconic preppy tie, suspenders, cigar: Patrick Jake O'Rourke.
By permission of Southern California Public Radio, Lauren Osen

it any staying power. But, fortified by a foreword from political columnist Andrew Ferguson, in 2003 a new edition of *Parliament of Whores* took America by storm. Whether it was intended to cash in on the partisan/satirical revival sparked by Michael Moore or to check the popularity of the latter's *Stupid White Men* is an open question. Whatever the case, rock'n'roll conservatism was back in combat for the hearts and wallets of the American public.

Editor-in-chief of the *National Lampoon* in the late 1970s, O'Rourke is said to have turned to journalism when, like Will Rogers, he realized that jokes could never measure up to politics in comic quotient. With a more rational lampoon, in no time he had carved out a reputation as a Republican *enfant terrible*, cementing it with

Parliament of Whores, a book whose "main argument is that politics are boring" (v). Boring is not, of course, how the public perceives the author. With umpteen bestsellers to his credit, O'Rourke rates more entries in *The Penguin Dictionary of Modern Humorous Quotations* than any living writer except Fran Lebowitz.

The first edition of *Parliament of Whores* vaulted to the penthouse of the *New York Times* bestseller list and made the *Publishers Weekly* hardcover list for more than six months. Not bad for a collection of essays that tackles perhaps the most boring subject in the world: the government. Jonathan Lynn, co-author of *Yes, Minister* and *Yes, Prime Minister*, found this kind of triumph nothing short of miraculous. "Three elderly men sitting around, talking about politics," he marvelled at the success of his show, "I don't know how it ever worked." Yet, as he and Anthony Jay had shown, watching politicians and bureaucrats in assorted stages of self-empretzelment can be as hilarious as edifying.

This is not to say that everyone who bought *Parliament of Whores* did not begrudge the expense. For every Genevieve Stuttaford boosting it with "very funny and on target, a purgation of the Augean stables of American politics," there was a David Brock with "not terribly funny, at least by O'Rourke's standards, and it does not explicate anything new about the ways of Washington."[2] Other critics were, if anything, even less amused. Thomas Grant found it, "full of sweeping and unsupportable indictments of the system yet is so conspicuously short on particular cases or culprits. Such blanket attacks focus maximum attention on the humorist himself, who exercises his talent for facile hyperbole."

Perhaps trying to reconcile both parties, James Fallow gave with one hand and took away with the other, claiming that O'Rourke did a thorough job of reporting on Social Security, even as he kept falling back on wisecracks and pat attitudes. Whether *Parliament of Whores* really does a top job on Social Security or other aspects of American life remains to be examined. But it is difficult to see why any humourist should be blamed for taking on the Potomac industry. Given the ignorance and apathy that dominate America's attitudes to politics, getting people to read about the affairs of the government is no mean undertaking by any standard.

And if, as Brock and Grant would have it, the book is really a failure, at least it's a grand failure – and a wildly entertaining one to boot.

> This is not history, which has just been written.
> It is really what would have occurred if this
> were a novel.
>
> • Mark Twain and Charles Dudley Warner, *The Gilded Age*

Those who accused O'Rourke of not having much new to say were right, in a way. More than half of his two-hundred-plus-pages had appeared previously in *Rolling Stone*, for which he used to work as a White House correspondent. No one, on the other hand, has ever accused O'Rourke of dull reporting on the protection racket that goes by the name of taxation-by-government. Indeed, his gift for riotous oratory has never been more in evidence. Subchapters such as "The Three Branches of Government: Money, Television and Bullshit," or "Our Government: What the Fuck Do They Do All Day, and Why Does It Cost So Goddamned Much Money?" keep readers coming for more.

Parliament of Whores is equally remarkable in other ways, not the least of which is its disavowal of credibility. "The numbers in this book are correct to the best of the author's ability," states the author. "But the statistics presented here are for illustrative, not statistical, purposes" (xii). This is odd. Either you get your statistics from reliable sources, in which case you do not need to hedge your bets, or not, in which case your statistics are unreliable. The disclaimer does not stop there. "Some figures are disputable, some will be out-of-date by the time this is published and a few were probably wrong from the get-go" (xii).

Unremarkable in a work of comedy, such dodges are remarkable in a work of journalism, even if from a gonzo humourist. Non-fiction from the left – look no further than Michael Moore – habitually draws flak for its alleged statistical, illustrative, and interpretive errors.[3] To be sure, foolish consistency may be the hobgoblin of little minds (even if Emerson never spells out how it differs from sage consistency). Still, for a writer of nonfiction, especially one who dissects the Alpha bureaucracy in the land, absence of self-contradiction, to say nothing of consistency with fact, ought to be the bottom line for being taken at his word.

This dieter's dilemma – I want to have my partisan cake and eat it too – permeates *Parliament of Whores*. The unreliability of gonzo has, of course, received its share of attention over the decades, notably in Joseph Nocera's archetypal essay "How Hunter Thompson

Killed New Journalism." Nocera cogently argues that first-person narration, self-projection (not to say promotion) as a character, attribution of dialogue, novelistic tropes, and blurring of fact and commentary sell copy at the expense of the reporter ethic. This is why gonzo may have hit if off with the slicks, writes Nocera, but not with the dailies, which for the most part take fewer liberties with the truth.[4]

Still, the gonzo devil may not be as black as painted. On occasion, at least, the payoff may be worth the tradeoff. In *The Armies of the Night* Norman Mailer refers to himself in the third person as Aquarius precisely to forestall charges of dressing up personal storytelling as history. Of course, between hyperbole and self-projection, Aquarius will stop at nothing to hype up the narration and himself. Far from being maligned as new-journalistic publicity stunt, however, Mailer's novelistic history-in-the-making is required reading in the postwar canon. There is no point, it seems, in blaming a writer for poetic licence as long as he gets to the heart of the matter.

So, what about O'Rourke? Should one dismiss his book as the antic of a public entertainer or take note of his partisan rants? By his own admission, *Parliament of Whores* was "written, of course, from the conservative point of view" (xxi). To clarify what this portends, O'Rourke marshals a touchstone definition. Conservatism, he writes, is "a philosophy that relies upon personal responsibility and promotes private liberty" (xxi). One has to wonder, though, how being liberal is incompatible with reliance on personal responsibility. For every Chappaquiddick Democrat there is a Watergate, Irangate, or Iraq-gate Republican. And, unlike Congressman Mark Foley (R), when Bill Clinton (D) dallied with an intern, at least she was of age.

O'Rourke's dice are no less loaded when it comes to private liberty. Freedom for gays to marry, freedom for women to control their bodies, freedom for the have-nots to fight for social conditions befitting the wealthiest nation in the world, freedom for nonwhites to live in dignity and equality, freedom to live without the menace of assault rifles and submachine guns, and dozens of other freedoms and liberties are promoted by decidedly non-conservative types. To fit O'Rourke's rhetorical cloak, a conservative would have to be a strange kind of political animal: half ass, half elephant, and rarer than the yeti.

All this does not mean, however, that rhetorical legerdemain afflicts only funny, provocative, and thought-provoking nonfiction

You can't be neutral on a moving train.
Historian, lecturer, activist: Howard Zinn.
By permission of Howard Zinn

writers like P.J. O'Rourke. It can also afflict serious, provocative, and thought-provoking nonfiction writers like Howard Zinn. A celebrated historian and anti-war activist, Zinn is perhaps best known for his magisterial *A People's History of the United States* (1980). With over a million copies sold, reprinted as a Perennial Classic, and featured on high-school and university curricula, it is considered – together with its offspin, the *Twentieth Century: A People's History* – a high point of social liberalism.

This is not to say that Zinn does not have detractors who berate these studies as leftist and biased. "If you've read Marx, there is no reason to read Howard Zinn," maintains his self-styled nemesis, Dan Flynn, in "Master of Deceit."[5] In *Declarations of Independence* (1990) Zinn confronted his detractors head-on with élan that matches O'Rourke's. Contending that you cannot be neutral on a moving train, he wrote: "It is a world of clashing interests – war against peace, nationalism against internationalism, equality against greed, and democracy against elitism – and it seems to me both impossible and undesirable to be neutral in these conflicts ... I do not claim to be neutral, nor do I want to be." With the manifesto came the pledge. "I will try to be fair to opposing ideas by accurately representing them."

With two admittedly biased – but fairly biased – contenders in the ring, let us compare their partisan scorecards. Although O'Rourke writes in the main from the perspective of the 1980s (with especial venom reserved for George Herbert Bush's 1991 budget), Zinn's sweep, even in *The Twentieth Century,* is nothing short of panoramic. To make the comparison fair, let us examine what the humourist and the historian have to say about the decade that, right or wrong, belonged to Ronald Reagan. As the lightning rod I take two issues that continue to arouse as much passion today as they did in the last decade of the Cold War: poverty and military spending.

> The eight years in America … uprooted institutions that were centuries old, changed the politics of a people, transformed the social life of half the country, and wrought so profoundly upon the entire national character that the influence cannot be measured short of two or three generations.
>
> • Mark Twain and Charles Dudley Warner, *The Gilded Age*

With the largest economy and one of the highest per-capita incomes on the planet, the United States epitomizes the immigrant dreams of rags-to-Rolls-Royces. That is also why poverty, a hot topic in any country, is doubly so in America. Looking at the miscellaneous indices of economic performance, it seems inconceivable that anyone could be mired in poverty, especially during the prosperous 1980s. Yet, assessing Reagan's tenure, Zinn states flatly: "At the end of the eighties, at least a third of African-American families fell below the official poverty level" (351). O'Rourke contradicts him as flatly: "there is no poverty in America" (125).

Before sorting out these contradictory claims, let us rewind the clock on the decade and on the actor-turned-president whose eight years in office are virtually synonymous with its triumphs and fiascos. Ronald Prescott Reagan's claim to the presidential Hall of Fame comes principally from two sources. He was one of the most popular and charismatic leaders in history, elected and re-elected with landslide margins. Secondly, he engineered a radical overhaul of the national socioeconomic policy, the legacy of which reaches into all corners of Bush the Elder's, Clinton's, and Bush the Younger's administrations.

Broadly speaking, there were four cornerstones of this conservative makeover. Notwithstanding the Cold War enemy's hunger to find a face-saving exit from Afghanistan, priority number one was an unprecedented expansion of defence spending. Combined with domestic priority number two, tax breaks for the rich and deregulation of big business, it formed the keystone of Reaganomics. The third leg of the platform, as prescribed in Milton Friedman's neoliberal (today we would say neocon) *Capitalism and Freedom*, consisted of across-the-board cuts to social programs. Finally, there was the quest for smaller and therefore, in conservative axiomatics, better government. In the end, the enterprising president failed to implement only one part of this quartet.[6]

During his first five years alone Reagan more than doubled military expenditures, from $144 billion to $295 billion.[7] With the exception of the peak of the Korean and Vietnam wars, this made for the highest military budget since World War II. For all intents and purposes, the commander in chief put the country's economy on a warpath, while resisting a barrage of Soviet proposals for armament cuts and caps. In his first term the C in C authorized armed incursions in Libya, El Salvador, Nicaragua, Lebanon, and Honduras. This is not counting the *cause célébre* of 1983, Grenada, where, in violation of international law but to bipartisan hurrahs at home, the US invaded an island whose population could fill the Rose Bowl.

Much ink has been spilled on the effects of Reagan's tax cuts on wealth disparity in the nation – poverty in oldspeak. Kevin Phillips, a Republican analyst, documents that while the top twenty percent of Americans reaped a bounty, the fortunes of the bottom twenty percent – 45 million in all – took a dive, exacerbated by the slashing of social programs. The plight of children became especially dire. In 1984 one in four children under six lived in poverty. For black children, it was one in two. Penury shot up, with 33 million (including nearly twenty percent of fulltime workers) sinking below Reagan's poverty line, mocked by Art Buchwald in a 1984 skit, "Living on the Line."[8]

Only recently, however, has is it been *publicly* acknowledged that the beneficiaries of these tax reforms were the country's richest.

Nothing brings this home like the stunning demand from 150 of America's billionaires for a more socially just taxation system. In a 1999 "Tax Fairness Pledge," the billionaire lobby actually donated money from their capital-gains tax cuts to campaigners for economic justice! Their rationale? "The wealthy are doing too well in America."[9] Indeed, having doubled between 1976 and 2001, the wealth of the top 1 percent of American households now exceeds that of the bottom 95 percent. Strikingly, 80 percent of all political contributions now also come from only one percent of the population. Coincidence?

Beguiled by the Laffer Curve – a supply-side thesis conceived by one of his voodoo economists – Reagan pushed through immense tax cuts for upper-tier businesses and taxpayers. The "trickle down" rationale was that in the past – the past during which the United States became an economic superpower – progressive taxation had deterred economic growth. To further help corporate America, Reagan's team passed labour legislation that drastically restricted the number and type of cases admissible before the National Labor Relations Board. Not to stop halfway, it also deregulated many business and banking safeguards. Today you and I, along with the rest of the world, are paying for this folly.[10]

In the 1980s the stock market responded with a leap and a bound, and Wall Street began to crawl with Gordon Gekkos. But the downstream effects of these policies proved disastrous, from scarce inspection staff and laughable penalties, to clipping the wings of workplace and environmental safety. To take one example among many, enforcement of strip-mining violations shrank by two-thirds, while FDA controls plunged by almost ninety percent. The news for those at the bottom of the American social pyramid was especially grim. Interest rates spiked under the inflationary pressure of the tax cuts, recession kicked in, unemployment passed ten percent for the first time in half a century, and secure full time jobs went the way of the dodo.

Finally, the conservative grail: smaller government. The Gipper's first shopping spree clocked in a deficit of $130 billion (Carter's last deficit came in at less than $80 billion). So much for Republican tight-fistedness. Reagan's first budget also brought the accumulated national debt within putting distance of a trillion dollars. If this sounds like a lot, it was – until his last budget, which pumped the debt up to three trillion (today the federal debt weighs in at well

Pinocchio presidents.
O'Rourke's stance is diametrically opposite to Condon's:
between incompetence and corruption, always choose
incompetence.
By permission of Affordable Political Items

over twelve trillion, or $12,000,000,000,000). When Reagan as-
sumed office, the US was the world's greatest creditor. By the time
he ceded it to Bush Senior, the world's greatest economy was also
the world's greatest debtor.[11]

Even with the massive diversion of funds from social spending,
most of the shortage was the result of military expenses. Despite
his vaunted goal of cutting the budget, Reagan handed over
1,300,000,000,000 dollars to the Pentagon in his first five years in
office. That was roughly what Nixon, Ford, and Carter spent in the
twelve years of their presidencies combined.[12] One way to cover up
this largesse was to "trim" the overall by taking regular expenses,
such as the Post Office, off-budget. Such book-doctoring is not
illegal. It couldn't be – it's too common. The taxpayers still foot the
bill, only the bill doesn't show in the ledgers. Talk about crooks who
know their business. Even O'Rourke was impressed: "you have to
admire the brazenness of the thing" (96).

In the end, the Reagan second-term recovery cranked up the
economy faster than you could say Savings & Loans bailout ($1.4
trillion). But not for long. On Black Monday of 19 October 1987,
the bullish stock market took a nosedive, wiping out twice as many

savings as the Black Monday of 21 October 1929.[13] That fiscal melt-down flushed the country from the jazz age into the blues age known as the Great Depression. That the S&L blowout didn't snowball into a financial pandemic like 2009 was largely because of trading reg-ulations (decried as anti-entrepreneurial when first put in place), a massive intervention by the Federal Reserve, and social programs that had not succumbed to the conservative restructuring.

```
I tell my wife, that the poor must be looked to;
if you can tell who are poor - there's so many
impostors.
```
• Mark Twain and Charles Dudley Warner, *The Gilded Age*

Most debates over poverty boil down to what poverty means, which boils down to how it is measured. Let us take a measure, then, of the definition employed by the US Census Bureau. Starting with *before-tax* incomes, federal statisticians use income thresholds (which vary with family composition and size) to fix the baseline. If a family's *total income* falls below this baseline, then every person in it is taken to live in poverty. Total income covers a lot of ground, including Social Security, Supplemental Security Income, public assistance, veteran's payments, child support, alimony, educational assistance, assistance from outside the household, and a slew of other categories.

On the other hand, incomes as calculated by the feds do *not* in-clude non-cash benefits, such as subsidized housing, Medicaid, food stamps, or capital gains.[14] Moreover, poverty thresholds are *not* ad-justed from region to region – even though Manhattan's upper east side will set you back more than rural Iowa – but they *are* adjusted for inflation. And if the bureaucrats cannot verify your poverty status, you are excluded from their "poverty universe." Such is the case, for example, with armies of the homeless not in permanent shelters (i.e., most of them) who do not leave a trace on the sta-tistical charts. As far as the welfare system is concerned, it is not concerned at all – they do not exist.

Now, let's look at poverty in America through the right eye. O'Rourke does not deny that, as per the government's own statis-tics, there were more than 32 million Americans in poverty in 1991. Instead, he attacks the manner in which such statistics are compiled. The numbers are awry, he says, because they exclude huge sums

Not another talking head.
Late night on PBS: P.J. O'Rourke takes his message to America.
Public Broadcasting System

pumped annually into welfare. In the year in question, for example, the government spent almost $22 billion on Food Stamps, Head Start, and the Special Supplementary Food Program for Women, Infants and Children. "None of this counts as income in the Census Bureau poverty statistics," points out O'Rourke, "because it isn't cash" (126).

Like most everything in America, poverty is a relative term. On the authority of economist George Gilder, O'Rourke argues that 80 percent of America's poor have telephones and colour TVs. In fact, he grumbles, "a poor American family had an income twenty-nine times greater than the average per capita income in the rest of the world" (127). Never mind for the moment if the numbers are correct. But is coming out ahead of the world's wretched anything to brag about? Does owning a colour TV – an abysmal necessity for single parents raising children – vitiate being poor, especially when TV sets sell for chump change? Is heaving citizens above the poverty

line with food stamps anything for the richest nation on earth to
be proud of?

O'Rourke's rant crumbles before housewife logic. "I've got a
big, technical, chart-and-graph laden academic paper," writes the
humourist, "to prove that America's poor feed themselves on 19 per-
cent of their cash income – as compared with 18 percent for all Amer-
icans" (127). This, he says, proves America's poor aren't. In fact,
it is just the reverse. The less you make, the bigger the percentage
of your income that goes towards necessities such as food. If you're
poor, in other words, your food bill will be proportionately larger
than Steve Forbes's (though puny in absolute dollars). The fact that
the national percentage is almost the same as that for the poor is
actually a worrisome sign, implying that most of the country may
be living perilously close to poverty.[15]

Far from shoring up O'Rourke's thesis, the fact that percentage-
wise the poor spend more on food actually mitigates *against* it. The
essayist who claims to have proven mathematically that there is no
poverty in America is, in truth, a professor of mythomatics. This isn't
the end of the smoke and mirrors. *Parliament of Whores* squeezes
every satirical mile it can out of the bloated, inefficient, wasteful,
uneconomical, incompetent, bungling, and inept monster that is the
federal government. Then entropy disappears. By the time O'Rourke
divides government handouts by the number of recipients, he gets
all that money to the people. Nothing wasted, nothing frittered away,
nothing spent on greasing the administrative wheels.

But just being inconsistent isn't as bad as counting the same pork
barrel *twice*. First O'Rourke calculates the average income deficit
for poor families by balancing their needs against the cash coming
in: "paychecks, welfare payments, veteran's benefits, Social Secu-
rity, etc." (125). But there cannot be poverty in America because
his data shows that "combined federal, state and local antipoverty
spending is $126 billion per year" (126), i.e. more than the deficit.
So, here is how you get rid of poverty. First you count the poor's
total income *including* welfare, then top it up with *the same* welfare,
and presto – no deficit.

O'Rourke is right that there may be less poverty than the sta-
tistics suggest if you count every dollar spent on social programs.
Yet he is wrong to claim that the poor get the dole they need. In
American Poverty in a New Era of Reform (2000), Harrell R. Rodgers
documents that only some of the poor receive the welfare they are

entitled to. According to the 1998 Census, less than 70 percent of Americans in poverty received means-tested assistance, less than 45 percent food stamps, and less than 35 percent cash-assistance. Similarly, only one in four of eligible families receive housing assistance, in part because the program is advertised only sporadically, leaving those in need unaware.[16]

Indeed, under Reagan's 1981 budgetary fat-trimming, 70 percent of the savings came from programs for the poor. Job training was cut by 81 percent, means-tested assistance by 54 percent, housing assistance for the elderly and handicapped by 47, and legal services for the poor by 28 percent.[17] Throngs of Old Age, Survivors, and Disability Insurance recipients were "decertified" and 43 percent of new applicants denied eligibility in the president's first six years in office. Only in 1986 did the uproar reach the Supreme Court, which ruled that the administration's secret and systematic denial of benefits to those eligible violated the Social Security Administration rules.

Where does this it leave the Republican Party Reptile? His claim that the US census figures are skewed is dead right. His claim that there is no poverty in America is dead wrong. No matter what numbers the conservative calculator spits out, not all Americans who qualify for help get it. And despite vast sums going into the pot, like the repo man, poverty refuses to go away. Worse, it grows. In 1989, in the wake of Reagan's economic miracle, there were almost 32 million (or almost 13 percent) of Americans living in poverty. In 1994, during Clinton's economic miracle, there were 38 million (or 14.5 percent).[18]

That year Michael Jordan was enjoying his first retirement, the Houston Rockets carried their first NBA title, and unemployment among whites slunk to 5.3 percent. But Jordan's astronomical salary and endorsements hid overall black unemployment of 11.5 percent, 35 percent for blacks under nineteen.[19] High as these official stats are, the real figures are almost certainly higher still. Lila Lipscomb, executive assistant for Career Alliance, made no bones about it when interviewed by Moore for *Fahrenheit 9/11*.

At the end of January of '04, the unemployment rate in Flint was actually 17 percent, but you have to take into consideration as well, that when your unemployment runs out, you're no longer counted. I would say we're probably close to at least 50 percent. Not working or underemployed, because underemployment is just as dangerous."

This is for those already in the federal poverty universe. The homeless or newly arrived immigrants, for example, get nothing. No Medicaid, no food stamps, no job training, and either no work at all or the kind of work that comes with a ticket to the slums.

The situation is exacerbated by the regressive (flat) Social Security Tax, which takes a thin slice off the rich and a big hunk from the working stiffs. Moreover, it is docked from your pay cheque whether you pushed the mop for just one week a year or made $76,200 (no SST is collected above that level).[20] Worse still, the income tax (progressive because the more you make, the more they take) continues to be reduced, while the one-size-fits-all Social Security tax is boosted. Ironically, owing to the difference in life span, many nonwhite Americans die before collecting Social Security, although they pay into it all their lives.

If someone told you to bootstrap yourself out of poverty by tipping yourself until you collected enough to pay the debts incurred by borrowing for the tips, you would put him in a straitjacket. But that's exactly what the federal bureaucracy does. Welfare payments do hoist many people above the poverty line. But the tax system – which collects a disproportionate cut from low earners to fund programs such as welfare and the military – pushes even more people back below it. That is why throwing money at the poor fails to erase poverty. Even as the government does just that, it taxes poor Americans until they sink to the bottom of the economic pool where they fail to find fulltime permanent employment.

I said to the President, says I, 'Grant, why don't you take Santo Domingo, annex the whole thing, and settle the bill afterwards.'
• Mark Twain and Charles Dudley Warner, *The Gilded Age*

So, it looks like the liberals were right all along?

Yes and No. There is one category of the federal budget that draws the partisan adversaries together, after a fashion. Surprisingly, it is defence – or, less euphemistically, war – spending. On the subject of the federal war budget O'Rourke is disarmingly candid: "I like having lots of guns and bombs" (102),[21] His problem with extravagant government spending is not with the Pentagon. "The problem is an American public with a bottomless sense of entitlement to federal money" (104). His solution? Nix all the money-pits like Social Security, Medicare, Medicaid, et al., before they bring down the house of cards called government finance.

The view from the left could not be more anthithetical. Extrapolating from *The Twentieth Century: A People's History*, it is: put the generals on a fiscal crash-diet and use the savings to help those in need. Thus, reflecting on Reagan's terms in office, Zinn protests: "welfare took a tiny part of taxes, and military spending took a huge chunk of it."[22] We may debate either writer's moral values, but there is no debating the numbers. And here the score is O'Rourke 1: Zinn 0. For comparison, let's tabulate the respective budgets: Carter's last, Reagan's mid-office, Clinton's last, and George W.'s mid-office. Side by side, the table lists money for social welfare, money for the Pentagon, and all the money the presidents got to play with.[23]

Year	Social welfare in billions of dollars	National Defence (+ Veteran Benefits) in billions of dollars	Total federal outlay in billions of dollars
1980	263	134 [+21]	591
1985	394	253 [+26]	946
2000	1117	295 [+47]	1,789
2005	1446	495 [+70]	2,472

For every year in question, as well as for all the years in between, the federal outlays on welfare far exceed those on defence. Zinn's heart is in the right place, but his rhetoric in this case is inflated. Clearly, what he intends to say is that welfare spending was a tiny part of the *discretionary* spending, in which he is absolutely correct, and that the military outlays took almost half of the *discretionary* budget, which is also correct. The difference is crucial. Discretionary spending covers that part of the annual budget that is left to the discretion of Congress. Entitlement programs such as Social Security, Food Stamps, and the like do not count in that category.

Liberals will object that the tabulated data looks only at Mona Lisa's smile instead of the whole picture. The Pentagon budget is *much* larger than shown if you count in the NASA, industrial, and academic R&D outlays that benefit the military. And it is larger still if you include appropriations for waging open and covert wars as well as intelligence and propaganda ops. The price tag on wars in Afghanistan and Iraq alone is estimated to exceed two *trillion*. The tabled figures must therefore be taken with a grain of salt (and, as O'Rourke would add, tequila and lime). But, even as the Pentagon takes a huge chunk out of the annual budget, welfare's chunk is huger still.

Why mention defence and welfare in the same breath? For liberals they are zero-sum antitheses slugging it out at the federal counter. For conservatives they are kindred efforts to give Americans work and income. Politically, the latter outlook wins hands down, insofar as cuts to the military are decried as cuts in employment, striking at the core of the liberal value system. On this picture the US Army is really a Salvation Army, saving many black and poor Americans from joblessness – precisely why Democrats and Republicans compete to cloak themselves in patriotic hues and military hardware.

No one can afford to be left behind the bandwagon of patriotic defence. No one can afford to be remembered as the party that left America weak and defenceless or, worse, as the party that killed so many jobs. Much as O'Rourke says in his 1993 follow-up to *Parliament of Whores*, everyone prefers to give war a chance. The humourist himself harbours few illusions: "defense spending in America is not so much a matter of Americans sacrificing to keep their country safe as it is a matter of Americans telling their government to give them defense contracts and defense-industry jobs" (175).

As usual, part of what he says is true, part is a snow job. It is not true that Americans explicitly demand military or defence-industry jobs. They demand jobs period. If the government began to shovel money into education, for example, Americans would clamour for jobs in education because that's where jobs could be had. It is only because mammoth sums go to the Pentagon – which has been known to lavish them on $800 toilet seats, $500 coffee makers, and $400 wrenches – that army and satellite-industry jobs (computers, aviation, telecommunications, etc.) are so plentiful and alluring.

A Republican at a conservative think-tank.
Goldwater Institute (named after the 1964 Republican
presidential candidate, Barry Goldwater): an independent,
nonpartisan research and educational organization dedicated
to the study of public policy in Arizona (self-description).
By permission of Goldwater Institute

It is here that the political adversaries begin to see eye to eye.
"Defense spending is immensely wasteful. Even if defense spend-
ing were managed by honest, clairvoyant geniuses (and this is not
the case), it would still be immensely wasteful."[24] This is not a sen-
timent you would pin on a conservative who likes having lots of
guns and bombs. Soldiers and weapons do not do much of anything,
after all, unless there is a war. "Can we count on Saddam Hussein
to come along every year and resolve our defense-policy debates?"
asked O'Rourke in 1991. In 2003 the Bush and Cheney adminis-
tration provided an eloquent answer.

In the same vein, Zinn quotes a Rand Corporation analyst
who, in a mid-1980s review of the politics of American defence,
acknowledged that the enormous number of weapons bought by
the Pentagon was unnecessary from the military point of view.[25]
In 1984 the CIA actually admitted "that it had exaggerated Soviet

military expenditures, that since 1975 it had claimed Soviet military spending was growing 4 to 5 percent each year when the actual figure was 2 percent." The same misinformation, propaganda, and outright deceit were at work during Vietnam, Nicaragua, Kuwait, the Balkans, Afghanistan, and the hysteria-whipped invasion and occupation of Iraq.[26]

In America, the relation between the military and the poor are more umbilical and circuitous than many people realize. Indeed, it would be hard to find a more poignant example than the Social Security Trust Fund (SSTF). As it happens, it would be also hard to find a more egregious one. Created in 1939, the SSTF was envisaged as an independent trust fund, whose earnings would be earmarked for the Social Security Retirement program. The government was entrusted not to roll the SSTF into its general operating fund, which then would become usable for any program the administration might see fit.

Trouble is, the Social Security funds were invested in non-marketable *national* bonds rather than in the private market, as in most countries. Given how much of America's credit goes to the Department of Defense, the Social Security Fund was, in effect, invested in support of the military without public consent. The system began to creak in the joints under the voodoo economics that boosted the military, while taking in less in taxes. When the pressure got too big, something had to give, and it was the Social Security Trust Fund. In a denouement that stunned the nation, in February 2005 George W. Bush went public with the news that "Social Security's $1.8 trillion trust fund doesn't really exist."[27]

> The publicans and their retainers rule the ward
> meetings (for everybody else hates the worry of
> politics and stays at home).
> • Mark Twain and Charles Dudley Warner, *The Gilded Age*

Winston Churchill said that if you're under thirty and not a liberal, there is something wrong with your heart, but if you're over thirty and don't vote conservative, there's something wrong with your head. As a litmus test of partisan identity, this piece of folk politics is as good as the Beefeater-dry quip from Will Rogers: "I'm not a member of any organized political party. I'm a Democrat." O'Rourke's

Nothing wrong with his head.
Voting conservative: P.J. O'Rourke is over thirty.
By permission of Joplinindependent.com, M. Taylor

partisan labels are no less witty. "God is a Republican and Santa Claus is a Democrat, because while Santa might be nice, God, while harsh, is just." In fact, "Santa Claus is preferable to God in every way but one: There is no such thing as Santa Claus." (xxii).

Before we look at partisan identity in more detail, let us take a moment to examine O'Rourke's equation in the spirit it was written. The major premise is: Santa Claus is a Democrat. Minor premise: there is no such thing as Santa Claus. Conclusion: Santa Claus cannot be a Democrat. Since the conclusion contradicts the major premise, one of them must be wrong. Since it is true that there is no Santa Claus, it must be the major premise, leaving us with Santa Claus is not a Democrat. The lone humourist has entertained us with another example of pretzel logic.

By polarizing the identities of the two parties, O'Rourke obscures the fact that they are, largely, two sides of the same political coin. The reasons behind this uniformity are at once ideological and historical. Jealously guarding their turfs, both parties have continuously conquered smaller blocs by cannibalizing them, drawing them into the fold, or if necessary, merging. In the process, they inexorably merged their political identities. In 1857 Frederick Douglass put it in words reminiscent of Orwell's last words of *Animal Farm*: "The silver-gray whig shakes hand with the hunker democrat; the former only differing from the latter in name."[28]

In the 1890s alone, the Democrats allied with the Populist Party and amalgamated with the Greenback Party, absorbing much of their farmer and blue-collar base and removing potential vote-splitters. Decades later they used the same tactics to neuter the New Deal Democratic Coalition founded to carry forth FDR's platform.[29] In that case it was not too difficult, since Roosevelt cared more for pushing through his reforms than for the party he represented. During the epic 1932 election for the governorship of California he even sold Upton Sinclair (former Socialist running as a Democrat) to the Republicans in a backroom deal that left his legislation intact.

The results of such realpolitik are plain to see. Even as they eliminate political rivals, mergers of convenience dilute both parties' ideological capital. Drifting towards a homogenous middle, modern Republicans and Democrats are both centre-right establishment. Lampooning their 1988 conventions, even O'Rourke was hard-pressed to find any difference. Today's Democrats are, indeed, respectably gentrified, reifying the economy as a shorthand for profit while leaving their old-time power base in the lurch. Scarcely anyone pays heed to critics who argue that the party cannot represent average Americans when its leaders "accept the myths of Corporate America as if they were gospel."[30]

The drift towards the centre is not helped by the fact that congressmen (and, in the 109th Congress, seventy women) are willing to follow voters anywhere. Liable to recall every couple of years, the representatives seldom hesitate to cross party lines when those conflict with other interests.[31] Partisan identity evaporates almost entirely when it takes up residence in the White House. Although selected by their party, presidents change their philosophies as a matter of course to massage approval ratings. Republican Nixon ("We are all Keynesians now") passed progressive legislation, upped minimum wage, and bolstered social security. Democrat Carter cut inflation by cutting welfare. The deficit expanded under Reagan, shrank under Clinton, only to grow again under the younger Bush.

With no alternative between Tweedledum and Tweedledee, American voters largely abstain from politics controlled by one or the other branch of the Tweedle party. Gone are the days of 1876, when eighty-five percent of those eligible cast the presidential ballot. In 1988, the US ranked second-*lowest* in election turnout among twenty-eight leading democracies.[32] The leader of the West lags behind the rest. On average, 92 percent of Austrians, 90 percent of Swedes, 88 percent of Danes, and 86 percent of French go to the polls. In the US, only 40 percent of the electorate voted in 2004. This is to say that George W. Bush governed with only twenty percent of the country behind him. Or, if you like, eighty percent of Americans did not vote him into office.

Apathy and a sense of disfranchisement prevail. At the 1988 peak of Reaganomics, when the figures were actually at ebb, Americans at large subscribed to the following series of policy assessments. Sixty percent – with O'Rourke in the lead – polled positive on: "The government wastes a lot of money." Fifty-five percent agreed that: "You cannot trust the government to do right most of the time." And almost sixty-five percent affirmed that: "The government is run for the benefit of a few big interests." Whether Lincoln actually said it or not, clearly you can fool most of the people only some of the time.[33]

While interest groups buy political influence left and right, legislators favour policies that benefit not the public but the donors. To keep the spotlight on the 1980s, let us look at what Elizabeth Drew, Washington correspondent for *The New Yorker*, documented about the links between donations from Political Action Committees – lobby groups – and the laws that govern the nation. To take one example out of many, in 1982 used car dealers persuaded the House and the Senate to kill a niggling regulation of the Federal Trade Commission – a regulation that mandated that all known defects of an automobile had to be listed for the benefit of the buyers. Eighty-five percent (242 out of 286) of the Representatives who voted to scrap the regulation had taken donations from – you guessed it – the concerned lobbyists.

Elected officials do not often find it easy to refuse those who ply them with generous donations. That's why, when it comes to choosing between the interests of the donors and those of the constituents, the decision is often a no-brainer.[34] The magnitude of the problem can be gauged by the fact that, during the 2006 general elections, it occupied the top spot on the Democratic Party's legislative agenda. In their profile on Nancy Pelosi, the BBC reported on her schedule

for the first 100 *hours* as a House Speaker. The top priority? "Bringing in rules to break links between lobbyists and legislation."[35]
     Interest groups aside, it is not true that majority rule is the answer. O'Rourke himself brilliantly explains what life would be if we all joined in the stampede. "Every meal would be a pizza. Every pair of pants, even those in a Brooks Brothers suit, would be stonewashed denim. Celebrity diet and exercise books would be the only thing on the shelves in the library. And – since women are a majority of the population – we'd all be married to Mel Gibson" (5). Of course, the government does not make dough for Pizza Pizza, sew Brooks Brothers pants, or tell you who to marry (unless you are gay). The government makes social policy and, in all fairness to those who do not like it, it's not hard to imagine where "obey as you please" libertarianism would get us all.

> We do not object to criticism; and we do not
> expect that the critic will read the book
> before writing a notice of it.
> • Mark Twain and Charles Dudley Warner, *The Gilded Age*

To some *Parliament of Whores* was replete with cheap jokes, conservative sophistry, and prejudicial statistics. For others those were the very reasons for buying it, only in their eyes they became vitriolic satire, incomparable non sequiturs, and oodles of common sense. Some found O'Rourke's main thesis – incompetence always trumps conspiracy in American politics – sophomoric. Others, relishing his proofs of the government's mission statement, "if it ain't broke, break it," thought the lesson terrific. "*Parliament of Whores* may not spark a revolution," cheered *Time*, "but it is one of the few books on civic affairs worth reading from cover to cover."[36]
     Ironically, civic affairs is where boomer conservatism meets left-wing grassroots democracy. On the political antipodes from Patrick Jake O'Rourke, Noam Chomsky has long deplored public apathy about the political process. If only people cared as much about politics as they care about sports, he argues, America could take a political step forward. Some of his contemporaries have put his words to action. On his 1988 tour, Frank Zappa set up voter-registration booths on his concert grounds, while on stage he skewered equally

Grassroots politics.
One size fits all: turning couch potatoes into political animals.
By permission of Zazzle and Howard Zinn

the right-wing moral majority ("When the Lie's So Big") and the adrift left ("Rhyming Man").[37]

Chomsky's own "Quartet," a collection of short political abece - daries, is another cure for political apathy. As is *Parliament of Whores*. Being tutored in the tricks of the trade, while laughing at every page, is a perfect way to turn a couch potato into a political animal – especially if the satirical lessons carry from politics to real life. The government is greedy, mendacious, and unaccountable, but so were Enron's investors and executives. The White House is authoritarian, grandstanding, and out of control – but so are the media. Self-serving politicians march to the beat of the latest opinion poll – but so do the voters. The whores, jeers O'Rourke, are us.

Even as one hopes that *Parliament of Whores* will not be the end of readers' political education, as a starting point, one could do far worse. Not all book critics agree, however. Thomas Grant, for one, argues that there is a world of difference between dilettantes like O'Rourke and bona fide satirists. Some writers are regarded as satirist by their admirers, he maintains, only because they mock the admirers' enemies. They have no principles, other than those that support their right to sound outrageous in order to entertain. They elevate "style over substance, attitude over conviction, the quotable insult over telling wit. What a shame O'Rourke has squandered the opportunity to unmask actual knavery and folly with the ferocious impartiality of a true libertarian. Instead, he has become the Republican Party hit man.[38]

As a real-life hit man, it must be said, O'Rourke's career would not last long. After all, he hits his own gang too, in a display of what others might see as a show of impartiality. Conservative down to his socks, it is not the case that the lone humourist is always pro-Reagan or pro-Republican. Much of the time he is simply anti-anti-Reaganites and anti-anti-Republicans. Buried under his *Republican Party Reptile* outpourings about getting drunk, soused, and inebriated, O'Rourke's reflection on the Philippines, "Goons, Guns, and Gold" shows that, on occasion at least, he has his heart in the right (as opposed to Right) place.

Still, the lone humourist does live down to Grant's critique whenever his funny boiler runs out of steam. Trading in stereotypes that descend to the level of quotable insult, O'Rourke's thrusts are sometimes indistinguishable from petulant name calling. As a marketing tactic, shrugs Danny Goldberg in an otherwise sympathetic review, it may endear him to readers whose views happen to coincide, but it strikes a discordant note when he tries to elevate his discourse to grown-up levels. In a 2001 online interview for *Washington Post*, O'Rourke tried to leap over the partisan trenches he himself had dug, demurring that America's problem is not political affiliation. Rather, it is "the fact that bad politicians make this debate between left and right difficult to conduct and often deeply dishonest."[39]

Unfortunately, even as fans cherish their rhetorical irreverence, O'Rourke's ad hominems are little more than shrewdly calculated political and personal caricatures, which are then derided with impunity. His battle plan is clear and effective: distort the opponent's views until there is no choice but to agree with his derisions. Conscious of his past excesses, in the *Washington Post* interview the humourist struck a rare penitent note. "One of the problems with being a writer is that all of your idiocies are still in print somewhere," he admitted, adding "I strongly support paper recycling."

Sooner or later, all debates about culture gravitate towards questions of artistry, of which paper recycling forms a proper subset. Though not all things about *Parliament of Whores* can be maintained with the same degree of certainty, its success with the reading public is beyond debate. Extolled from *Presidential Studies Quarterly* in the US to the *Spectator* in the UK, this brain-tickling humoresque for the politically challenged citizen is also a sage tutorial on the American *res publica*. Fiercely rhetorical and fiercely partisan, it may be, first and last, a publicity stunt from a Republican Party Reptile. But, agree with O'Rourke or not, don't ever start *Parliament of Whores* if you have to go to work the next morning.

I always vote Socialist – with misgivings. (1980)

• John le Carré, *Conversations with John le Carré*

━━━━━━━━━━

Chapter Four   1990s

That Dirty Word, Socialism:
Warren Beatty's *Bulworth*

July 4th is a date fraught with significance in the American political calendar. It is the birthday of a nation, a celebration of its independence, and a photo-op bonanza for the Democratic and Republican political machines. No different in pageantry from any other year, 4 July 2004 was, however, a celebration apart. Left and right, the nation flocked to see a partisan broadside from a writer/director who, with a verve that harked back to Irving Wallace's sixties, made political waves from Hollywood to Washington. The filmmaker was, of course, Michael Moore, his target, George W. Bush, and his weapon of mass attraction, *Fahrenheit 9/11*.

Never reticent when it comes to commandeering media spotlight, on 4 July 2004 Moore fired off an open cyber-communiqué that celebrated the sundry ways in which he was making American film history. Entitled "My Wild First Week with *Fahrenheit 9/11*," the email revelled in the fact that, in its first weekend alone, the picture was seen by more people than had gone to see *Bowling for Columbine* in nine months. It had broken *Rocky III*'s record for the best opening in less than a thousand theatres. Most astounding, it beat the opening-weekend receipts of *Return of the Jedi*. George Lucas, eat your heart out.

Writing on 4 July, Moore could not have known that his Cinderella story would continue unabated. In two more weeks *Fahrenheit 9/11* would break the $100 million landmark in box office receipts, becoming the highest-earning documentary in Hollywood's history. In the process, it smashed the box-office record set two years earlier by *Bowling for Columbine*, which clocked in under $30 million. This is not to even mention winning the coveted Palme d'Or for Best Film at the 57th Cannes Festival, the first such laurels for a documentary since Jacques Cousteau's *The Silent World* (1956).

One can hardly blame the writer/director for exulting over his success. In a nation addicted to Hollywood features, few documentarians ever cross over from art-houses and rep theatres to nationwide popularity or stardom. Beside Errol Morris, director of *The Thin Blue Line* and *The Fog of War*, or Morgan Spurlock, noted for his sleeper hit *Supersize Me*, only Ken Burns has carved a similar place for himself in the public's heart. Here, however, all similarities end. Renowned for his *Civil War*, *Jazz*, and other epics, America's film-historian laureate is not known for taking partisan sides. Although no stranger to sociopolitical critique when warranted by his material, Burns's histories are unapologetic in their evocations of the United States' patriotic myths.

If the difference between David Letterman and Michael Moore is that between a satirist and an activist, the difference between Burns and Moore is between an a-political and a political artist. With *Roger & Me*, *The Awful Truth*, *Bowling for Columbine*, *Fahrenheit 9/11*, *Sicko*, and *Capitalism: a Love Story*, Moore has almost single-handedly rekindled interest in political movie-making, making it almost hip. What makes this turnaround even more extraordinary is the virtual absence of partisan feature films in America's mainstream. Like hip-hop and bluegrass, party politics and commercial blockbusters just don't seem to mix.

This is not to say that the studios have never evinced interest in politics or never churned out a picture with the White House as a backdrop. Only a few years after the birth of Hollywood there was, after all, *The Birth of a Nation* (1915). Only a few years after the birth of the American welfare state there was *Mr. Smith Goes to Washington* (1939). There were the First World War and the Second World War bond-sale campaign films, not to mention the election of one of Tinseltown's own to Washington in 1980 and 1984, and to Sacramento in 2003 and 2006. And of course there was, is, and forever shall be, the Dream Factory's aptitude for political fund-raising.[1]

Actors as dissimilar as Will Rogers, Humphrey Bogart, Ronald Reagan, John Wayne, Barbra Streisand, George Clooney, Susan Sarandon, Sean Penn, Tim Robbins, Arnold Schwarzenegger, and Warren Beatty – to name but a few – have been known for their political opinions and, equally, for not shying away from airing them in public. So where, one is compelled to ask, *are* the movies? "I don't think there's enough political films here or anywhere," confided Sean Penn to BBC News at the 2004 Cannes Film Festival, the same that crowned Michael Moore. An outspoken critic of the 2003 invasion of Iraq, Penn was in town to promote *The Assassination of Richard Nixon*, a film that, while not ostensibly about politics, promised to inflame passions left and right.

The fact is that, after a century of releasing so-called political movies – documented by Kevin Brownlow in *Behind the Mask of Innocence* (1990) – Hollywood is no closer to partisan politics than Groucho Marx was as the president of Freedonia in *Duck Soup*. While it is possible for a dedicated partisan like Warren Beatty to push through a radically political feature, such as his 1998 rapping comedy *Bulworth*, an event of this nature is about as common as a politician with a stutter. Whence the reluctance to dip more than a toe in the partisan waters of the Potomac? The reluctance to invest in political films that, at least in Moore's and Beatty's savvy hands, have proven to be both lucrative and critically acclaimed?

```
There is the word. It is the king of words -
Power. Not God, not Mammon, but Power. Pour it
over your tongue till it tingles with it. Power.
• Jack London, Iron Heel
```

Robert Altman nailed the issue in the opening scene of his 1992 autopsy of Hollywood, *The Player*. "Does political scare ya?" asks a wannabee producer before he even starts his pitch. "Political doesn't scare me. *Radical* political scares me. *Political* political scares me," comes the reply from the mogul. This fictive scene of self-censorship better explains the dearth of *political* political writing in Hollywood than pointing to regulatory agencies and practices – from the Hays production code and the House Un-American Activities Committee to the industry's own rating system. Political is okay, it seems, provided it's not radically so, especially from the point of view of a studio producer.

Communication Reports, the critical study released by William McIntosh and his group in 2003, empirically confirms this political-yet-apolitical bias. Guided by the working hypothesis that studios were "more invested in producing entertainment that is politically generic and palatable to a general audience," the researchers investigated forty-seven of Hollywood's popular political films, spanning the last fifty-plus years.[2] Their goal was to look for correlations between, on the one hand, the depiction of characters from either end of the partisan spectrum and, on the other, the political climate at the time of the film's making.

The selection criteria were straightforward. A film must not have been a documentary – thus instantly ruling out Michael Moore, except for *Canadian Bacon* – and must not have been be made for television. It had to contain at least one major character who was political and include American political characters.[3] Finally, it had to have been released after 1945 and have a rating of at least 2 (out of 6) as a box-office success. This last stipulation was no accident. Assuming a link between levels of attendance and levels of affective response, it eliminated obscure flops not seen by anyone.

The findings would not have surprised Robert Altman.

Oddly enough, it turns out that liberal characters do enjoy more happy endings while the Democrats are in power and fewer during Republican terms in office. Yet by far the most striking finding was that political films were ambiguous in terms of partisan politics. This is to say that, even in the most political of scripts – which, by default, should push party agendas, partisan loyalties, and legislative platforms – there were virtually none. "Most political films present commentaries on the American political system," conclude the analysts, "but pointedly avoid the riskier business of commenting on partisan political issues." As if with Beatty's *Bulworth* in mind, they add: "Partisan politics was especially difficult to determine in star characters."[4]

These findings hold even for the apparent exceptions, such as Martin Ritt's 1976 dramatic comedy *The Front*. Fronted by Woody Allen in a rare acting-only role, this comedy-with-a-cause fits the pattern. To be sure, *The Front* does not lack a political dimension. Its director, writer, and many cast members had been blacklisted

Meet the Reds.
In conversation with Nancy Reagan: Warren Beatty and
Diane Keaton, stars of the Oscar-winning film about the
Russian people's revolution.
By permission of White House Photo Office

during the 1947–57 witch-hunts by the House Un-American Ac-
tivities Committee. The first commercial picture to lift the veil of
silence thrown by the studios over the fate of the Hollywood Ten,
The Front is not, however, a political film according to the criteria
employed by McIntosh. Even as it ardently defends America's con-
stitutional liberties, it skirts anything resembling partisan politics.

The same absence of partisan involvement is evident even in
films that plant themselves squarely in the world of politics, from
Robert Rossen's 1949 *All the King's Men* (remade in 2006 by Steven
Zaillian) to Alan Pakula's 1976 *All the President's Men*. It would
be difficult to find better testimonials to the edge-of-the-seat thriller
quotient present in political cinema. Both films pour scorn on abuse
of power and perversion of democracy, taking evildoers to task
without a moment's hesitation. But while they give no quarter, they
take no partisan sides either. Party politics and the current power
structure remain strictly off limits.

This is not to take away from the moral courage of these pic-
tures and their makers – the courage made salient by the 1975 docu-
mentary *Hollywood on Trial*. As the producers reveal, most of the

studios personnel approached for comments on the persecution of the Hollywood Ten *still* refused to talk for fear of endangering their jobs. And rightly so, scoffs the ultimate insider, Irving Wallace.

> Studio heads were always mounds of Jello when it came to standing up to the kind of small monsters represented by Senator McCarthy, Martin Dies, Richard Nixon ... That gang on the Un-American Committee was far more dangerous than any cadre of Communists.[5]

But by the time Hollywood is ready to tackle a political subject, it is guaranteed that the result won't threaten viewers or the powers that be. So it was with *The Front, All the King's Men*, and *All the President's Men*. By the time the three films came out, McCarthy's ideological terrorism, Huey Long's pork-barrel populism, and Nixon's criminal machinations could all be dismissed as isolated warts on an otherwise wholesome body politic. Long was, of course, a lifelong Democrat, while McCarthy and Nixon were card-carrying Republicans. But, with party colours suppressed, all that remains are politically correct censures of manqué politicians – not of the system.

Hollywood may have been liberal leaning when it was the provenance of first-generation Jewish émigrés. Today's tycoons, like Rupert Murdoch (owner of 20th Century Fox), are far from fostering left-of-centre liberalism. The consequences of this for American partisan expression are as weighty as the novel forms of censorship applied to Movieland. One of latter is, oddly enough, the Pentagon, which exerts backstage control over a large and mounting number of blockbusters in need of military hardware. The Air Force alone receives about a hundred scripts every year to consider – so much so that a dedicated liaison officer is on active duty in LA to peddle the force in Hollywood.

Unbelievable as it sounds, producers and directors are actually invited to demonstrations of new weapon systems to entice them to make another war film. Of course the bargain is nothing but Faustian, reports Jonathan Turley in the *Los Angeles Times*. The devil's cut is the director's integrity – "the right by the Pentagon to vet films produced through such collaboration and veto anything in them." Phil Strub, the head of the Pentagon's liaison office, is on record explaining the military's ground rule for giving approval to a movie as accurate. "Any film that portrays the military as negative is not realistic to us."[6]

All these incarnations of political censorship lead back to Warren Beatty and his unapologetically partisan *Bulworth*. Significantly, Beatty's film is not a documentary, is not made for television, features a major political character, includes American political characters, was released after 1945, and did well at the box office. In short, it meets all the selection criteria of the McIntosh study and yet stands apart from its findings like a solar-powered oil rig in Texas. Critics like Richard Alleva may put Beatty's brainchild down, questioning whether it really is daring. Yet, given how openly *Bulworth* defies the powers that be with a *political* political script, this is one critical salvo that misses its mark by a country mile.

> But, outside the realm of business, these men
> are stupid. They know only business.
> • Jack London, *Iron Heel*

The ingredients, it must be said, were tailor-made for Oscar contention. The film boasted a provocative if not downright controversial theme, a great cast that included a past and a future Oscar winner, and an entertaining, hard-hitting, partisan script. Once released, it attracted heaps of critical praise, nation-wide reviews, and interviews with Beatty in trend-setters like the *New York Times Magazine*. Yet in spite – or, more likely, because – of its frontal assault on the American political hierarchy, Beatty's tour de farce seems destined to remain an underground classic.

From the start, *Bulworth* defied all rules. Made in complete stealth, it was released by a major studio, but only after protracted contractual wrangling, only for a brief period of time, and practically without publicity.[7] The consequences were predictable. Despite the attention from the media and academic panels, not to mention a radically political subject, it died almost without a trace. Today, only *Wag the Dog* (1997) and *Primary Colours* (1998) are remembered as Hollywood ventures into politics before the infamous 2000 election – even though, instead of taking political sides, they merely lambaste politics as usual.

The back story was as riveting as the movie itself. After 20th Century Fox backed out of producing *Dick Tracy*, Beatty used the

Mr. Hollywood.
In 2008 Warren Beatty was passed over for the role of Richard
Nixon in *Frost/Nixon*: ten years earlier he gave the Fox studio,
the Democratic party, and the then president of the United States
the middle finger.
Belfast Telegraph

leverage of a lawsuit to wangle unprecedented artistic freedom for
his next project. Disclosing only the barest sketch of the plot, while
demanding – and obtaining – complete control, the writer-actor-
director essentially duped Fox into bankrolling the project. The story-
line that got thumbs-up from the executives said only that a man
hires someone to kill him, then falls in love and tries to call off the
hit. What the audiences saw was a brazenly *political* political com-
edy that gave the studio, the Democratic Party, and the president
the middle finger.

"I thought it was a good idea," rued Joe Roth (then chairman
of Fox). So long as Beatty didn't exceed the budget of thirty-two
million, "he could do what he wanted."[8] Beatty corroborated his
subterfuge in the same *New York Times Magazine* interview. "I
wanted to have complete freedom to do what I wanted to do ... I
didn't want to be influenced by commercial considerations." And
he wasn't. The finished cocktail of badass comedy and inflammatory
politics was as much a triumph of the medium as of the message,

featuring a United States senator in a gangbanger getup, rapping the socialist mantra of redistribution of wealth.

The script opens on a dark and stormy night in 1996, days before the primaries. In the opening shot the camera ignores a "No Entry" sign to steal into the opulent but impersonal chambers of an aging, lonely powerbroker at the end of his rope. Beatty's allusions to the opening scene of *Citizen Kane* – and through it, to the corrosive effects of political power – are reinforced later on through an allusion to Frank Capra's *Meet John Doe*, when power is cut to disrupt one of Bulworth's revolutionary orations.[9] Much like Welles, the actor playing Citizen Bulworth was also the film's writer, director, and co-producer, a black culture buff, and a lifelong Democrat (active on the RFK, McGovern, and Hart campaigns).

Wordlessly, two close-ups follow. First, a physical one of the ravaged, sobbing Democratic senator. Then a spiritual one of his betrayed liberal past. As the credits roll by, the camera pans over framed photographs of Dr King, Malcolm X, Rosa Parks, Huey Long, and RFK arm in arm with Bulworth's real-life alter ego, Warren Beatty. Depressed and self-loathing after looping through his own neocon TV spots, the Senator first arranges a $10 million policy from big insurance and then a suicide-by-assassin by putting out a contract on his own life. The dice cast, he flies back to California to garnish his re-election campaign with more sanctimonious sound bites – and the proverbial shit hits the fan.

With literally nothing to lose, the Senator throws image control to the wind in a series of politically incorrect rants that leave his entourage slack-jawed but his poll figures soaring. He affronts a Hollywood fund-raiser with verbal jabs about rich Jews and lousy movies. He disses black churchgoers for not laying off malt liquor, chicken wings, and the wife-stabbing OJ. He insults Democrats by calling them the party of the left – the left pocket of corporate bagmen. Liberated by these devil-may-care salvos, he ends up bodyslamming in a nightclub in Compton where, in a dig at Clinton's "I did not inhale," he savours every toke of the good weed. And, all through that seemingly endless night, the white Senator soaks in the ABC of rhyme from gangsta-rap vinyls.

It may be the pot, it may be the fly girl, Nina – raised on Huey Newton and the Panthers – or it may be the haunting exhortations from Amiri Baraka, who plays a homeless mystic (á la *Julius Caesar*).

The flag and the apple pie.
Blowing sanctimonious gas: Senator Jay Billington Bulworth
poses for a photo-op.
Fox

One way or another, the Senator gets the bug. Exit sixty-year-old
WASP honky; enter sixty-year- old WASP homey, complete with a
gangland outfit, unprintable language, and reformist zeal. And as
the knockabout farce shifts into high gear, slogans of the disparity
of wealth, socialized Medicare, and public ownership of the air-waves
roll off Bulworth's tongue in inner-ghetto verse – the only script using
heroic couplets outside cinematizations of Shakespeare.

Needless to say, the film flummoxed reviewers, who could not
figure out if it was a political drama, a political comedy, a politi-
cal drama-comedy, a tragic farce, a satire, a black comedy, or even
a 'hood film rooted in the same aesthetics as John Singleton's *Boys
in the Hood*.[10] Predictably enough, the storm of commentary brought
the usual mix of raves and pans. "A terrific movie," applauded the
Nation. A "hard cocktail to mix or drink," dissented the *National
Review*. "A Load of Bulworth," thundered the *New York Post*.
"Politically sound and theatrically glittering," countered the *New
Republic*. In the midst of critics who appeared only to agree to dis-
agree, *Newsweek* held the middle ground: "Overstuffed, excessive,
erratic – and essential."[11]

What followed continues to be the subject of intense speculation
and controversy. First, Fox refused the film any pre-release publicity,
including the lifeblood of contemporary box-office success, television

ads. Then, in what Beatty described as an "effort to bury it," they proceeded to release *Bulworth* opposite the summer blockbuster *Godzilla*. Although they were the only studio to compete against Sony's monster flick, and opened in only two thousand theatres as against the competition's six thousand, Fox denies the charge, claiming "creative counterprogramming" behind this suicidal David-vs-Godzilla scheduling.[12]

Beatty himself had few illusions about where artistic freedom ends and the bottom line begins when it comes to the business of making movies. "I don't think anyone would have financed this with anyone in it if they'd known what it was," he said. "Fox hated it, though at least they were honest enough to say so."

> This reference is to the socialist vote cast in the United States in 1910 … Its voting strength in the United States in 1888 was 2,068; in 1902, 127,713; in 1904, 435,040; in 1908, 1,108,427; and in 1910, 1,688,211.
> • Jack London, *Iron Heel*

What could account for the studio's hatred? What could drive them to deny the film any publicity, which practically ensured its fadeout from theatres and from the public eye? Although in one of the early scenes the Senator gleefully savages Tinseltown and its tycoons for political timidity and artistic sellout, it does not seem likely that Bulworth would be held culpable for biting the hand that feeds him. The Dream Factory is not known for holding grudges against mavericks as long as they take care of the bottom line and, with $10.5 million gross in the first week alone and fourth place overall behind the leader, *Godzilla*, the movie proved anything but a financial washout.

Could it be the vignettes from how the other side lives, melodramatic and pat as some of them are? Or the fact that, even as the Senator raps sociopolitical revolution and straddles racial divides, his perspective on ghetto drug-lords is nothing if not politically incendiary? He makes clear, after all, that it is they and not the police who control the inner cities, and that it is they and not the feds who are the source of employment and grassroots authority. But Beatty might once again be forgiven. After all, he is hardly the first man to expose the federal war on drugs for the sham it is, and hardly the first white man to pass himself off as what Mailer glorified back in 1957 as a White Negro.

No. The real issue seems to be Beatty's mention of the unmentionable in America's political mainstream: Socialism. That, together with the call for a fullscale political and socioeconomic reform, pretty much guaranteed that Murdoch's Fox would go into conniptions. Asked by the *New York Times Magazine* what's wrong with America, Beatty could not have been any more explicit:

> The profits go to the upper class, whose advertising money has itself formed public opinion. And the classes are pushed farther and farther apart.[13]

"The real issue," he went on, "is the disparity of wealth in this country. And that gets unattended and unacknowledged."

What also gets unattended and unacknowledged is that this disparity of wealth goes against the precepts of the founding generation of Americans who inscribed the political compacts on which the United States rests to this day. At the end of the eighteenth century the economic depression that followed the War of Independence spread in the former colonies, stagnating mercantile New England and ravaging the ill-prepared American nation. The response from the legislators – so dramatically at odds with the laissez-faire rhetoric of the centuries that followed – reveals a different vision of a great republic. Hard as it may be to believe, they "sponsored bills favoring debtors, on the grounds that *republican government required a general equality of property.*"[14]

There may be officeholders today, presumably in the Democratic wing of the Democratic Party, who would find this platform congenial. But for the 1990s right-of-centre Clintonites, who had taken so many political right turns they were looking at the backs of their own heads, Beatty's provocation was the equivalent of a front-page editorial in the *Vatican Gazette* agitating for the abolition of Christianity. In the end, it is hardly surprising that, although the socialist message drives the entire film, most reviewers prefer not to mention it by name, while those that do manage to sound like they wish they hadn't.[15]

Rapping like it is.
Politically incorrect: "C'mon, let me hear that dirty word:
Socialism!"
Fox

Rapping time and again about the accumulation of national
wealth in the hands of the privileged elite, Bulworth (or is it Beatty,
Oscar winner for his 1981 *Reds*?) goes after the foundations of the
American political catechism. Baiting big-money audiences at one
of the Senator's fund-raisers, he is baiting the audiences that flocked
to see the film: "C'mon, let me hear that dirty word: Socialism!"
For those who miss the point the first time around – or, more to the
point, for those who'd rather ignore it – the film loops into a sly
reprise. At the end of the reel, when the Senator's wife and her lover
lounge in front of a TV tuned to a political broadcast, in a true rap
fashion the director samples his own movie, replaying that taunting
clip with "that dirty word: Socialism!"

Although socialism is the crux of the matter, the limits of this
chapter preclude a full discussion of the issue. Let me, therefore, limit
myself to a few salient facts. After the assassination of JFK, Lyndon
Johnson, a much more skilful negotiator and more experienced
operator in Congress, pushed through the backlog of the domestic
Democratic agenda. Known as the Great Society legislation, it made
provisions for free medical aid and free legal aid for the poor, man-
power retraining, New Deal style public works for the employment

of the unemployed, the Housing Act for public housing and urban renewal, aid to education, reform of immigration laws, the Civil Rights act, air-quality act, minimum wage increase, extension of social security benefits, and many others – more than four hundred bills in all.

Yet, in one of the supreme political ironies of the twentieth century, the programs passed by the Johnson administration had been branded as un-American, subversive, and acts of high treason only five decades earlier, when they were advanced by the Socialist Party of America. In an unacknowledged political debt, America's welfare state from the 1960s was, in effect, a socialist utopia from the 1910s. Indeed, before Reaganomics and the 1994 GOP reformation dismantled many of the liberal gains, successive administrations implemented most of the Socialist platform from the first decades of the twentieth century.

For the Socialist Party itself there was no such happy ending. Although vilified in the state media as communists under a different name, they never had to toe the Comintern line and were in fact heirs to homegrown, made-in-USA progressivism. Under political siege, they were eventually suppressed with the help of Wilson's 1918 precursor to the Patriot Act – the Sedition Act. Before then, however, under the banner of populist reform, in 1911 Socialists carried eighteen American cities, coming within a whisker of winning Los Angeles and Cleveland. A year later, no less than thirty-three cities were run by Socialist mayors, from Berkeley in the West, through Butte in Montana, to Michael Moore's hometown of Flint, Michigan.

During the presidential election in 1912, under the perennial leadership of Eugene Debs – a conservative union leader who became the heart and face of the Socialists – the party polled 6 percent of the national vote, their highest ever. This was, however, the beginning of the end. Under wartime rule, rapid measures were passed to suppress organized labour and the progressive left. Unconstitutionally suppressing free speech, the Sedition Act fixed a penalty of twenty years for anyone deemed disloyal to America, the war, the flag, the government, or the constitution. Over two thousand people were immediately arrested, among them Socialist Congressman Victor Berger and Debs himself who, imprisoned for ten years for condoning draft-dodging, ran for president in 1920 from jail![16]

> William Randolph Hearst - a young California mil-
> lionaire who became the most powerful newspaper
> owner in the country.
>
> • Jack London, *Iron Heel*

Although hardly victorious in the political sense, the Socialist Party's legacy would appeal to a political satirist like Beatty. It's not about victory but about leadership, sniped the writer/director in an undisguised barb at Bill Clinton's electoral "triangulation" and the Republican-lite makeover of the Democratic Party. Pointedly, he added: "let's just stand for something and let's lead. It's better to lead than to win."[17] In a reciprocal bow, Debs himself was deeply appreciative of the power of fiction to mobilize fencesitters to political action. Few things can match popular art that appeals to millions as an instrument of political enlightenment, he wrote in "The American Movement."

> Although not an exposition of scientific Socialism, Bellamy's social romance *Looking Backward*, and its sequel, *Equality*, were valuable and timely contributions to the literature of Socialism and not only aroused the people but started many on the road to the revolutionary movement … Thousands were moved to study the question by the books of Bellamy and thus became Socialists and found their way into the Socialist movement. (89)

Bearing this in mind, it is easier to understand why, in the Indian summer of his career, Beatty put everything on the line with such a caustically *political* political film. Senator Bulworth himself led, rather than won, his campaign to do the right thing. Presaged by the opening shots of Malcolm X, Dr King, and RFK, and by the red food stain that sits for most of the film on the Senator's heart, the populist politician ends up being assassinated in cold blood. *Bulworth* the movie also led, rather than won, the partisan rebellion in the Demublican 1990s. Despite a robust first week at the box office, this most innovative and entertaining comedy of the summer of '98 was pulled by Fox as soon as it failed to eclipse *Godzilla's* blockbuster appeal.

A casualty of Hollywood's safety-first economics and economics-first politics, denied a fair shake in publicity and at the movies, *Bulworth* vanished from American theatres in less than a month. It was pulled in spite of being a good draw in the theatres, the talk of the town, and the topic of countless – and for the most part enthusiastic – reviews. It was pulled in spite of the Oscar nomination for the best Original Screenplay and the Best Screenplay Award from the LA Critics Association. Lamented Pat Dowell and other New York critics: "like the mid-list books of major publishers, the film was pulled," though "like most mid-list books, *Bulworth* deserved better" (6).

Even lions don't kill their own, reserving the ultimate solution for the offspring of their rivals. Yet, in a town in which the biggest compliment is to tell people they look like a million dollars, Beatty's Fox backers gave their own thirty-plus-million production a premature burial. Curiously, even though the story of that burial tantalized with a promise of a hundred succulent headlines, there was no journalistic stampede to the scoop. Could that have had to do with the fact that Rupert Murdoch owns not only the Fox studio but the Fox News network and a thousand other print, cable, and satellite media companies?

There is nothing new or even newsworthy in the "urge to merge," the end product of which is multinational multimedia corporations. These mass-media behemoths operate in every nook of the globe, playing everyone's – including Bond's in *Tomorrow Never Dies* – favourite villains. But the perils inherent in the control of information, and thus in the control of the public, escalate in proportion to the concentration of these communication giants in the hands of any one group or person. The advance of modern-day electronic media may have lulled the public into believing that it is better informed than of yore. It is only when one looks more closely at news coverage that its systematic discrepancies begin to appear.

Fox's own partisan bias was recently dragged into the sunlight by a muckraking documentary, *Outfoxed* (2004). Subtitled *Rupert Murdoch's War on Journalism*, the picture parades a roster of former Fox News producers, bookers, writers, consultants, and reporters, all grimly testifying as to how they were pressured as a matter of course "to push a 'right-wing' point of view or risk their jobs."[18]

Rapping like it is.
Air strike: "Telecommunications is the name of the beast."
Fox

A few employees – in a poignant analogy with the fears of those interviewed for *Hollywood on Trial* – even opted for anonymity for fear of putting their livelihoods in peril. All this in a nation that guarantees freedom of speech in the constitution.

After months of monitoring Fox News programming, *Outfoxed* reveals what lies behind the network's "fair and balanced" self-promotions. Selective reporting, biased consulting, event doctoring and interview bullying are almost routine and corroborated by all echelons of the network's former staff. Robert McChesney – who relates some of the backstory in the documentary – himself investigates the nature of the beast in *The Problem of the Media*. Although the media like to shroud themselves in bromides about being a private profit-making enterprise that serves the public, they serve one public only.

Media companies and the staff in their employ work first of all for the corporate owners who pay their salaries, second for the financial interests who sponsor the programming, and finally for the higher-income-bracket audiences targeted by the advertising. The consequences are plain to see. On the scent of the ultimate scoop, the media today rewrite the standards on tolerance and excitement in an effort to exorcise the vestiges of "traditional" journalism. Mundane reporting is out, extreme journalism is in. The demands of the marketplace dictate that consumers should not be bored by the product they pay for.

The Internet, television, newspapers, and magazines compete for the public's scant time and attention, rising above such quaint and old-fangled notions as objective stenography of events. Forget assiduous reportage of the ins and outs of the political process or of the complexities of multicultural eclecticism. Today the media's role is to provoke and titillate with hyperbolic headlines, exclusive covers, and flash-news story breaks, more often than not juiced up by bloody visual aids. No wonder that, at the mercy of workaday compromises, journalism-school ethics tarnish quicker than Tom Wolfe's suit in the LA smog. To sell more copy, infotainment thrives on exaggeration and embellishment, and even occasional out-and-out lies.

But while making it, some are caught faking it. In 1998 Stephen Glass, the *New Republic* point-man for sociopolitical analysis and commentary, was caught making up quotations, websites, faxes, and even organizations for his highly sought-after reports. He pleaded the pressures of extreme journalism as extenuating circumstance. So did Jayson Blair of *The New York Times*, after being caught plagiarizing quotes and fabricating outright fictions in dozens of articles. So did Janet Cooke, formerly of the *Washington Post*, Patricia Smith of the *Boston Globe*, and Jay Forman of *Slate*. Some say that these were the only rotten apples in the barrel.

It is a cub-reporter's truism that you cannot report everything. But who does the selecting, and who selects the selectors? Time and again, evidence demonstrates that corporate news media snap to the owners' heel. What passes for selectivity is, in fact, consistent media bias – consistent over a diversity of programs, news crews, and networks. The bias favours laissez-faire economics over social planning, well-to-do WASPs over low-income ethnics, officialdom over reformers, management over labour, and corporations over community critics. Given who owns the media, distortions are not innocent errors of omission but errors of commission perpetrated in the name of vested, suited, and cravatted interests.

> Rioting and mob rule reigned throughout the rural districts. Day and night the smoke of burning farms, warehouses, villages and cities filled the sky. Dynamite appeared.
> • Jack London, *Iron Heel*

Examples of how the media control, if not downright shape, public opinion abound. The best case in point is the 1992 Los Angeles

Telling like it is.
What happened after the 1992 LA ghetto uprising: "Well, what
happened is that we all knew it was gonna be big news for a
while so we all came down here: Bush, Clinton, Wilson, all of
us, we got our pictures taken, told you what you wanted to hear,
and we pretty much forgot all about it."
Fox

revolt that propelled black America into the headlines and Warren
Beatty to write his script. The flashpoint to violence was the acquittal
by a predominantly white jury of four white cops caught on camera
senselessly brutalizing a black motorist, Rodney King. The City of
Angels erupted with the fury of Mount St Helens. In three days more
than 50 people were killed, more than 2,000 injured, 17,000 arrested,
and more than $1,000,000,000's worth of property destroyed.

With the city on fire, the local networks found their reality-
TV hit. Yet even as arson, looting, and fighting began to be piped
to viewers almost round the clock, an invisible hand began to fiddle
with the tint controls. Not that the colour-coding of the media is
a secret. Stretching from the almost uniformly white ownership down
to the newsrooms, where only 11.5 percent are non-white, it stretches
equally into the past.[19] David Domke's examination of nineteenth-
century newspaper reports on black-and-white relations reveals a
clear pattern: American media systematically portrayed whites as
citizens and decision-makers and blacks as dependent and inferior.

But while America recoiled from scenes that could have been shot
in war-torn Bosnia rather than downtown LA, broadcasters began

to rally around a thesis. Far from being ignited by racism and clas-. sism, insinuated the coverage, the massive protests were the work of roving bands of thugs and lawbreakers. With the thesis as the word and image gatekeeper, the nature of this citywide unrest could be recast from a racial uprising to a rootless and senseless riot. In no time at all, and with team-tag efficacy, roaming crews began to shore up – and studio pundits to justify – the thesis to the captive audiences.

KABC Channel 7, for example, began to tag those who tangled with the police as "creeps," while KTLA Channel 5 cranked the hysteria higher still with the slogan "Look out for the Crips and Bloods." Working around the clock, KCBS Channel 2 branded the protesters as "hooligans," while KNBC Channel 4 pulled out all the stops, calling them "Thugs, criminals, and gang bangers."[20] The same invisible hand started to tweak the image so that, after the outbreak of clashes in South Central, reports zoomed in on the inner city to the neglect of other epicentres of unrest.

The focus was hardly innocent, but only postmortem statistics reveal a systematic bias. The April/May municipal records show, for example, that more arrests were made *outside* the South Central ghetto than in it.[21] Cynics may retort that the overwhelmed cops may have been too thinly spread to raid South Central for culprits. But the record paints a rather different picture. Among the riot hotspots that never made primetime television were posh areas such as Hollywood, where gay protesters were unceremoniously suppressed. There was also Huntington Park, where a number of Cuban businesses were burnt to cinders, and Long Beach, where the police slugged it out with wilding youth.

All these pleasant white residential areas missed out on their fifteen minutes of shame in the riot flash specials. Rioting in upper-class enclaves was simply incompatible with the thesis of thug violence. With the majority of news services in agreement, anyone questioning the status quo by looking into the deeper social causes quickly found himself part of a beleaguered minority. The whys and wherefores of this city-wide peristalsis could be kept at arm's length. The troubles that fuelled the riots – racism, non-representation, penury, and even the acquittal of the white assailants – receded into the background, obscured by the arsonists' smoke and the journalists' smokescreen.

In courts of law, witnesses are under oath to report the truth, the whole truth, and nothing but the truth, on the premise that suppressing information differs only in degree from sowing disinformation. Suppressing coverage of violence in upper-class districts, while denouncing gangsterism and subversion in the ghettos, the media buttressed their *thése de jour* while obscuring the historical recurrence of social revolt by America's dispossessed. The whitewash vitiated the need to scour the charred debris for the truth. It also furnished the media with the high ground from which they could reprove the troublemakers and even aid the law by capturing them on celluloid. What better shield to deflect accusations of coverage bias and racial typecasting?

But bias and typecasting were in plain sight. Arrest records reveal, for instance, that only a third of the incarcerated rioters were black. More than half of those who were apprehended were Hispanic and almost 11 percent white. In contrast, almost 60 percent of rioters depicted on LA television were blacks.[22] You don't need the Black Panthers to know that blacks and violence make for a surefire prime-time hit. The three day riot coverage boosted sales and ratings of the local papers and TV stations by more than a third. No wonder that Michael Parenti's acclaimed study of the Fourth Estate calls these self-appointed paragons of rectitude *Make-believe Media*.

Commercially, violence – especially sensational and senseless violence – trumps even sex in the ratings game. Politically, by playing on the public's fear of crime and black rampage, reports of violence incline the average viewer to trust the authorities, members of the same social elite that includes the media moguls. That old fox of political reportage H.L. Mencken had no illusions. "The whole aim of practical politics," he sniggered, "is to keep the populace alarmed (and hence clamorous to be led to safety) by menacing it with an endless series of hobgoblins, all of them imaginary."[23]

In *Boston*, Upton Sinclair described how the game is played at street level.

If you tried to argue as to the rights of people to use the streets, they would not argue back, but jab their clubs into your stomachs or your backs and run you along. If you failed to run fast enough, you would get a thump; and next day in the police-court you would be sentenced as a rioter, and newspapers would tell you how the mob was getting out of hand. (73)

In LA, while reports of black violence were hardly imaginary, the hype leaned heavily towards the racial cartoon of rogue outlaws. Overwrought Angelinos were led to believe that anything on the screen could happen to them in the next moment. The instinct at such times is to put your faith in the authorities, stay put in front of the TV, and let it reinforce the lopsided picture it helped create.

Among the deluge of gritty helicopter videos, one would look in vain for the grassroots causes of the flare-up. In reality, not that different from the Watts uprising, 1992 was simply an incendiary phase of another generation of unaddressed grievances. Far from a black thug riot, argues Cornel West in *Race Matters* (1993), the insurrection was ultimately rooted in the economic decline in the wake of the aeronautics and defense industries leaving the Los Angeles region in the 1970s. Add sharply rising poverty, the indifference of state and city governments to the poor, racism in the criminal justice system, and the police brutality against non-whites. Shake and ignite. A surefire recipe for a Molotov cocktail.

> Even as late as 1912, A.D., the great mass of the people still persisted in the belief that they ruled the country by virtue of their ballots. In reality, the country was ruled by what were called political machines.
>
> • Jack London, *Iron Heel*

So, why fork over the rental fee to see *Bulworth* more than a decade after its release? The answer goes far beyond the political irreverence, not to say iconoclasm, that make Beatty's script such a riot. It transcends the creative risks the writer/actor/director took in this off-the-wall comedy without a happy ending. It transcends even his embrace of black culture in search of the rhyme to the partisan reason. "Rap ... is the language of social protest," observed the maverick director, resurrecting the memory of the Los Angeles unrest. "He who fails to listen, fails to hear at his own peril."[24]

The answer, at once more personal and more political, transcends the issues of race and goes to the heart of big-money political campaigns. Will Rogers was right when he quipped that these days you have to be loaded just to get beat. With governor races in New York or California easily topping $60 million for television ads *alone*, and with election finance reform in shambles, today only the richest can afford to run for high-profile public office. By far the most expensive item on the campaign menu is TV advertising which in senatorial or presidential bids can soak up in excess of three-quarters of total budgets.[25]

For all the talk about the Internet changing the ground rules, television spots are the life blood of American politics. It seems almost beyond belief that Eisenhower, the first presidential campaigner to use boob tube commercials, had to be sold on the idea. "I think the American people will be shocked by such contempt for their intelligence. This isn't Ivory Soap versus Palmolive," scoffed his equally unimpressed rival, Adlai Stevenson.[26] Well, it is. Disney's publicity team designed Eisenhower's ground-breaking "I Like Ike" campaign, broadcast it in front of "I Love Lucy," and started a trend in which presidential budgets for television advertising have doubled roughly every two years.

Times have indeed a-changed since the days of stump oratory. Facing a geographic and demographic leviathan, modern political campaigners rely on the media to generate interest in themselves and, a distant second, in the issues. Were it even endurable, a year-long cross-country blitz with several thousand listeners a night might connect a candidate with one or two million voters. A strategically purchased TV spot will multiply that number over and over – and over, every time it's aired again. After all, virtually all American households own a television, three quarters more than one. And, according to the Department of State, 40 percent of Americans turn to local television for election news.[27]

Election coverage can be a big hit with viewers, especially if it hits below the belt. The 1988 Gary Hart campaign will forever be remembered as the moment when the private lives of public figures became primetime material. In a textbook display of junkyard journalism, zealous media hounds stole the senator's garbage from the kerbside, combing it for clues to his extramarital life. In this simple way they solved the programming riddle of how to fill the gap between *Dallas* and *Night Court*. By now the technique is popular

Mid March, 1996.
The time of the California Primaries.
Robert Dole has secured the Republican
Presidential Nomination.
President Clinton runs unopposed by
other Democrats.
The populace is unaroused.

...and so it is with little fanfare
or attention that incumbent
Democratic Senator Jay Billington Bulworth
prepares to embark upon the final weekend
of his primary campaign to return to the
United States Senate for yet another term.

Opening frames.
Keywords: Dole, Clinton, Republicans, Democrats,
primary, campaign, United States Senate.
Fox

enough in political parlance to have acquired a technical term of
its own: dumpster diving.

The abiding result of this shift from issues to vaguely but
patriotically defined personalities is that today's political pundits
define, rather than merely report on, the candidates. Off-the-cuff
remarks, stripped of the context in which they are uttered, routinely
receive more airtime than canned speeches (which themselves come
off the shelf from a generic supermarket), under the pretext of
revealing the candidate's character – especially, it seems, character
flaws. The biggest winner of this state of affairs is the network com-
mentary. The biggest loser is the American citizen, a state of affairs
reflected in the shrinkage of the already humble sound bite.

In his critique of the news media's domination of America's
political process, Thomas E. Patterson documents the diminution of
the sound bite over two decades of presidential campaigns. In the
year RFK was shot, the average sound bite was forty-two seconds
in duration. Significantly, most of the time the candidate appeared
on the screen when speaking. By the time Bush *père* ran against

Michael Dukakis, the average political statement had shrunk to less than ten seconds, while candidates became wallpaper for reporters' commentary. So much so, writes Patterson, that commentaries were six times longer in length than candidate's speeches![28]

Talk about putting the cart ahead of the donkey and the elephant.

And yet, if you were to open any of the glossy electoral pamphlets issued by the Department of State, you would find yourself in Disneyland. Presidential election coverage, suggests the official publication, ought to be objective, ought to report on the positions the candidates take, and ought to reflect what the voters take to be the biggest issues. In the words of John King, CNN's senior correspondent to the White House, the mass media should "just tell. Tell what they [the candidates] say. Don't try to tell people what to do. Don't try to influence people. That's not our job."[29]

In reality, today's news reporter is the news maker, having replaced the candidate as the chief communicator of political issues. This shift in power consolidates the move away from "mere" reporting to more analysis-oriented coverage, in which news is interpreted by journalists. Reporters analyze more and more, describe less and less, and give candidates fewer opportunities to speak in their own words about matters of importance. By 1992, for instance, more than 80 percent of *Times* articles analyzed candidates' words and actions *entirely* in terms of how they were calculated to advance their electoral careers.[30]

Also in ascendance are campaign polls, despite the fact that many are hardly accurate at all. Even though polls often come out in black and white, placing one political horse ahead of the other, this authoritative look is highly deceptive. Even when the media conduct their own polls, which is not often, they seldom cross-check or correlate them with those obtained from other groups or sources. The impression that the scientific sampling ensures reliable results is just that: an impression. Many polls are dead wrong: look at Obama's vaunted twelve percent lead over Clinton in the 2008 New Hampshire primaries. The 1996 Clinton-Dole presidential race and the 2000 presidential primaries both ended in landslides, even though polls had predicted a photo-finish only hours before.[31]

Inordinate focus on horse-race polls only attenuates coverage of policy issues. These are already so negligible that, according to the Department of State itself, in January 2004 less than five percent of network reporting covered candidates' positions on the issues that mattered most to the public.[32] This is why, in an electoral tradition that mystifies non-Americans, would-be presidents, senators, and governors air their views not through the network media but on popular talk-shows. Ironically, these bastions of easy entertainment let them speak at greater length of matters of sociopolitical importance than the newscasters do.

In a report on the political advertising in the 2002 general elections, researchers under the aegis of the Wisconsin Advertising Project reveal that, between the Senate, House, and gubernatorial races, American viewers were exposed to more than a million airings worth over $0.6 *billion*. More to the point, up to a staggering 90 percent of such airings tend to be not issue ads, i.e., those addressing a specific policy, but rather name-tagging or image-fixing ads, aimed at introducing the candidate to viewers. This is crippling, to say the least, for any candidate whose war chest is not well stocked – unless, that is, you can obviate the need for the image-fixing spots.

Candidates with no need for nation-wide exposure ads are those who are already familiar to the voters through the film roles they portray and their off-screen publicity. The case in point: the Austrian *Terminator* as a man of action, or the artist behind *Bulworth* as a liberal man of the people. Stars who are by default photogenic, who know how work the teleprompter and ham up to the camera, who are almost by definition outsiders to the political machine – and who, like the former Minnesota Governor, Jesse Ventura, know how to play that card – may paradoxically be well equipped to vie for appointment *inside* the political machine.

No better case in point than film stars like Schwarzenegger or Beatty himself. The former became the governor of one of the largest states in the union, with an impressive 60 percent approval rating after his rookie year in office (by now the honeymoon is long over). The latter was at one point touted to run for president in 2000. Despite persistent media rumours, Beatty chose not to throw his hat into the ring then, nor in the 2006 gubernatorial elections. Still, the $64,000 question remains: will he reprise the political risk he took in co-writing *Bulworth* and stage an artistic comeback with another *political* political script?

Where we often fail – and this may be one of the qualities of real tragedy – is in the disproportion between the dream we had and the reality when we meet it. (1966)

• John le Carré, *Conversations with John le Carré*

Chapter Five   2000s

Truth or Dare?
Michael Moore's *Stupid White Men… and Other Sorry Excuses for the State of the Nation!*

"Political language – and with variations this is true of all political parties, from Conservatives to Anarchists – is designed to make lies sound truthful and murder respectable."[1] More than half a century after the publication of "Politics and the English Language," George Orwell's words ring as true as ever. For eight years the political language of the Bush II administration was a fig leaf held in place by a Pentagon general. As the coalition of the willing violated international laws to secure American access to Iraqi oil, hundreds of thousands died, millions were terrorized in the name of eradicating terrorism, and the use of torture was sanctioned by the White House in the name of waging peace.

Ironically, while the ostensible *casus belli* was to free Americans from the menace of weapons of mass destruction, the only country to use weapons of mass destruction in Iraq (white phosphorus) was the United States.[2] On the domestic front, the Bush-Cheney-Rumsfeld-Ashcroft-Powell axis suppressed civil liberties in the name of a fight for freedom, instituted nationwide spying in the name of national security, and passed tax breaks for the rich in the name of creating national wealth. Turning war into peace, freedom into slavery, and ignorance into strength, it proved once again that

Nostradamus without equivocations.
As Barack Obama sends more troops to fight neocolonial wars
in Asia, Moore's message rings clear: the more things do *not*
change, the more they stay the same.
By permission of Cox and Forkum

political language is a more powerful weapon than a bomber fleet.
But, with the Bush administration out of the White House, the time
of reckoning is at hand.[3]

The longterm consequences of political disinformation may prove
to be most catastrophic when it comes to environmental damage.
For years the administration insisted that climate change was fear-
mongering science fiction, leaving individual states and cities to
opt *into* the Kyoto Accord. Drilling in Alaska was said to reduce
dependence of foreign energy supplies, but legislating auto makers
to make more fuel-efficient vehicles was not. It would take Barack
Obama to put an end to this particular self-deception, even as he
sustains another by pouring troops into America's unjust and un-
winnable wars in Asia.

But no need to look that far. The evidence of how political lan-
guage rewrites common sense into uncommon nonsense is all around.

Some of it comes straight from the American statute books, parts
of which read like the script to a never-seen episode of *Saturday Night
Live*. To wit: it's against the law to look at moose from an airplane

in Alaska, to have more than two dildos in the house in Arizona, and for pigeons to eat pebbles from composite roofs in Alabama. In Florida, it's against the law to have sex with a porcupine. It's illegal to say "Book'em, Danno" (Hawaii), or give a box of chocolates that weighs less than fifty pounds (Idaho). It's against the law for kisses to last more than five minutes (Iowa), for chicken thieves to work in daytime (Kansas), and to use a reptile in religious services (Kentucky).

In Louisiana, you cannot legally rob a bank and *then* proceed to shoot the cashier from a water pistol. In Michigan there is a law that forbids putting a skunk under the boss's desk. (There must have been a rash of this to spur state lawmakers into action.) Moving on, you can't hang men's and women's underwear on the same line in Minnesota, or look up while peeing in New Hampshire – but only on Sundays. And how is this for a crime against logic: in New York State there is a law that makes it against the law to do anything against the law!

In Oklahoma, it's against the law for three dogs or more to congregate on private property without the signed consent of the mayor. In Pennsylvania it's illegal to sing in the bath. In Texas it's against the law to own the *Britannica* (it tells you how to make beer). In Utah it's against the law to detonate nuclear weapons (there's nothing against possessing them). You can't legally tickle women in Virginia, or have intercourse with an animal weighing more than forty pounds in West Virginia. And, rounding up this trip through the outbacks of common sense, if you live in Wyoming, you can't take a picture of a rabbit during the month of June.[4]

It is easy to ridicule these laws, insofar as few of them (one hopes) are actually enforced. But what about countless porkbarrel giveaways that make a mockery of federal legislature every year? In 2003 these pet handouts, known on the Hill as earmarks, set taxpayers back twenty-two *billion* dollars. Passed with little fanfare and even less debate, the earmarks tacked onto the 2004 Omnibus Bill alone ran to eleven billion. Crucified by Taxpayers for Common Sense, these acts of oinkmanship ranged from two million for exotic-pet diseases research (California), to two million for the First Tee program using golf to teach "life skills" to kids (Florida). The top prize goes, however, to the Rock and Roll Hall of Fame in Cleveland which received federal pork to educate young people about rock music.[5]

Fed up, one writer thought he saw a pattern: "stupid white men are always the problem. That's never going to change."[6] Never is a long time, but historically he had a point. Ninety years after American women got the vote, the dearth of female representatives, senators, governors, cabinet members, and top judges makes men accountable for the state of the nation. Nor do they have to be white – Clarence Thomas or Colin Powell aren't – though most are. Jobs vanishing, stocks crashing, air polluted, deficit mounting, prisons overflowing, drugs and guns on every corner, unpaid overtime everywhere, perennial welfare at home and perennial warfare overseas.

"How did all this happen?" mocked Michael Moore in his 2002 smash seller. "Three little words: Stupid White Men."[7]

Documedian extraordinaire, Moore known the world over for his prize-winning movies *Bowling for Columbine* and *Fahrenheit 9/11*. But amidst the barrage of publicity, critics, biographers, media analysts, and political pundits have largely overlooked his career as a writer. Although each year more and more critical studies attempt to come to terms with his cultural and political presence, the lion's share of attention is lavished on Moore's films – as if he had never written a political book in his life. *American Dissident: The Political Art of Michael Moore*, to take the first example off the shelf, discusses five films and two television shows – not one word about the books.

More than the toast of Hollywood and Cannes, however, Moore is a writer *par excellence*. It is not just that his script for *Bowling for Columbine* won the Writers Guild Award for Best Original Screenplay – the first documentary to accomplish this in fifty-five years. Like Swift and Twain, he is a prolific journalist, syndicated columnist, humourist-essayist, and even writer of fiction (script for *Canadian Bacon*). More to the point, he is the author of a string of bestselling nonfictions, from *Downsize This!* and *Dude, Where Is My Country* to *Stupid White Men... and Other Sorry Excuses for the State of the Nation!*

Whence the source of this publishing success? *Publishers Weekly* put it down to a Moore formula: "provocative writing, nice timing and the foibles of political leaders."[8] Nothing to it, in other words, except for the old-fashioned virtues of good writing, good timing, and a good nose for politics – as good a definition of good

Roasting Bush.
Temperature: 911 degrees Fahrenheit.
By permission of Cox and Forkum

investigative journalism as any. Formulaic or not, Moore's politi-
cal writing continues to hit a nerve across the world, igniting a war
of words between his admirers and detractors. But even as Amer-
ica's cultural wars may have reached a new partisan peak with *Cap-
italism: A Love Story*, their earlier flashpoint from this popular artist
cum agitator was not a film but a book: *Stupid White Men*.

> Remember our war hysteria, when we called sauer-
> kraut "Liberty cabbage" and somebody actually
> proposed calling German measles "Liberty
> measles"?
> • Sinclair Lewis, *It Can't Happen Here*

With Lincoln's stovepipe and Chaplin's bowler, Moore's baseball
cap and in-your-face political satire are American icons. Yet there
is something mystifying about this popularity, not to say stardom.
How did he ever win over the TV/ADD generation with such mind-
numbing issues as blue-collar unemployment, corporate tax rebates,
voting irregularities, or even literacy and education? How did he

break through the apathy measured by library shelves of untouched nonfictions and documentaries?

Recognizing that partisan politics are too serious to be tackled without humour, the writer/filmmaker fashioned his own brand of firebrand activism, calling it "a consumer's guide to raising hell and having fun while doing it."[9] Having fun indeed. Some of the chapters from *Stupid White Men* sound like they came from O'Rourke's cutting-room floor: "A Very American Coup," "Kill Whitey," "Idiot Nation," "One Big Happy Prison." Oh, and don't forget "Democrats, DOA." As for hell-raising, Moore charges the leader of the free world with illiteracy, corruption, and high-office larceny before calling him a "drunk, a thief, a possible felon, an unconvicted deserter, and a crybaby" (48).

By any reckoning, *Stupid White Men* was a publisher's dream. Like *Bulworth*, released with almost zero publicity and a virtual boycott in the mainstream media, in its first two years it sold five million copies, becoming a byword in the United States and overseas. Rapidly translated into dozens of languages, it ruled the bestseller charts in Canada, the UK, Australia, Japan, Ireland, New Zealand, and Germany.[10] With one in eighty Germans owning a copy, it commandeered the *Nr. Eine* spot on the *Der Spiegel* bestseller list for eight months running – the only English book besides Harry Potter ever to do so. Not bad for a book that nearly wasn't.

Stupid White Men came close to being another casualty of 9/11. On 10 September 2001, HarperCollins had 50,000 copies bound and ready. The next morning – the gag order. "We feel the book is no longer in keeping with the political climate in the country," announced the publisher, which is "now very positive towards Bush."[11] It's not difficult to understand their cold feet. While America rallied behind the president – who, in the meantime, finished reading *The Pet Goat* – they were going to drop an incendiary device in every bookstore in the country. There was no politically correct way to spin Moore's thesis: the unelected president and his junta were taking the country for a joy ride through unchartered territory.

A tug of war ensued. HarperCollins demanded that Moore drop the title, rewrite half the book, and go easy on the president. The writer shot back with *Bring Me the Head of Antonin Scalia* as a new title and "The Sad and Sordid Whereabouts of Bin Cheney and Bin Bush" as a new chapter.[12] With the tiff threatening to become a *cause*

Media mogul as urban rebel.
A Tiananmen Square moment: *Stupid White Men*, slated for
release on 11 September 2001, was delayed by events.
Orfilms

célèbre, *Stupid White Men* was finally released in February 2002
– uncut. In the months that followed, more than any other book
in print, it highlighted the fissures between blue and red America.
While Bush's post-9/11 ratings shot into the ionosphere, Moore's
Bush-bashing book shot to No. 1 on Amazon on the day of its re-
lease. By March 2003, when the United States attacked Iraq, it has
been raising hell from the *Times* bestseller list nonstop for forty-seven
weeks (eight of them at number one).

Stupid White Men consists in equal parts of riotous rants on
the state of the nation and fiery philippics against the Bush regime.
Released in the days when, cloaked in the mantle of a victim of ter-
rorism, the president sponsored the suppression of sections of the
Bill of Rights and the WMDs fraud, it dared say in public what many
thought in private. Predictably, the shockwave of its reception rip-
pled around the world like the 2004 tsunami. For many, *Stupid
White Men* reaffirmed Moore as *the* voice of the anti-capitalist,

anti-imperialist anti-Bushidos. During a book speaking tour, the London *Times* lionized him as "the most influential performer-cum-activist of our times."[13]

Not all Europe, however, spoke with one voice. Even as the US declared hostilities on food groups, renaming French fries "liberty fries" and pouring *le vin* into gutters, some French critics proved ambivalent toward their favourite American dissenter. True, in "Paris Dispatch" Pascal Bruckner honoured the freshly anointed Cannes winner with a spot between Vaclav Havel and Andrei Sakharov.[15] But, echoing charges past and future, he charged that Moore's omissions and oversimplifications undermined not only the credibility of *Fahrenheit 9/11* but the *raison d'être* of his partisan activism. Are Moore's caricatures and cheap play for tears, he asked, that different from those of the Republican propaganda machine?

Love him, hate him, or love him *and* hate him, Michael Moore attracts controversy like a dog attracts fleas. Oddly enough, even as he stirs passions left and right, it's not always according to partisan labels. Part socialist, part green, part loose-canon independent, you would think Moore would draw nothing but hurrahs from self-declared liberals. Wrong. Christopher Hitchens condemns *Fahrenheit 9/11* as "a sinister exercise in moral frivolity, crudely disguised as an exercise in seriousness."[16] You would think he'd be uniformly crucified by the right-of-Rove Fox News. Wrong again. Roger Friedman lauds Moore's efforts as a tribute to patriotism which "all political parties should see without fail."

What complicates matters is that, as with Woody Allen, the analysis of Moore's work is often only a pretext to the psycho/analysis of the man himself. Not to look too far, in *Michael Moore Is a Big Fat Stupid White Man*, several members of the "Moore is less" school of criticism use his books and movies as a platform from which to blast the writer/director as a walking Narcissistic Personality Disorder. Even in the thriving discipline of anti-Moore studies, it would be hard to find a more ill-tempered and ill-argued attack. And yet, their character assassination notwithstanding, the assassins highlight a sore point with those who would defend Moore's documentary integrity.

Moore's persona can hardly be taken out of this cultural equation. The question of objectivity surfaces every time the writer/filmmaker subjectivizes the point of view by injecting himself into the proceedings.

Adored by lecture-circuit audiences, he has proven an indefatig-
able, personable, and humble showman who, taking potshots at
Dubya, is not above taking a few at himself. But even as he wins
people over by saying out loud what's on their minds, his attitude
to veracity borders at times on the frivolous. Given the gravity of
issues raised in *Stupid White Men*, how can he cast doubt on the
book with flippant question-beggars, such as: "How can there be
inaccuracy in comedy?"[17]

Herein lies the crux of the controversies that surround Moore
and his firebrand nobrow art. Everyone, from the writer/filmmaker
himself to his right-wing critics, is entitled to their own opinions –
but not to their own facts. The problem with Moore's facts goes back
to his cavalier approach to accuracy. One can hardly blame his crit-
ics for fearing that, like P.J. O'Rourke, Moore arrogates to himself
the high political ground of a truth-teller, while absolving himself
and his facts from the need for accuracy. And the stakes could hardly
be greater.

If his revisionist portrayal of the United States in *Stupid White
Men* is true, it is devastating in the extreme. On the other hand, if
what Moore tells us is no more than personal opinion, it can be
largely ignored – a fact that cannot but have wide-ranging reper-
cussions for his status as an artist and as a political voice of his
non-aligned constituency. While detractors pillory his work as ma-
nipulative propaganda, Moore's capacity for focusing nationwide
attention on issues that mainstream media fail to address is, arguably,
second to none. But even as he captures nationwide attention, the
doubt lingers: does he speak the truth or is it all just an elaborate
partisan dare?

> He, who understood himself abnormally well, knew
> that far from being a left-wing radical, he was
> at most a mild, rather indolent and somewhat
> sentimental Liberal.
> • Sinclair Lewis, *It Can't Happen Here*

Brushing political spinsanity aside, Ron Briley gets to the heart of
the matter in the special report for the *Historians Film Committee*.
The relevant issue, he writes, "is not whether Moore is partisan in
his politics, but how strong is his case against the President."[18] How

Larger than life, or full of hot air?
Standing up for the little man: Michael Moore salient.
By permission of Bongonews, Mike Pasternack

seriously, indeed, should we take his report on the state of the nation
and the sensational charges *Stupid White Men* levels against the Bush
administration? Not at all, clamour the would-be debunkers. The
right-wing's position, epitomized by David T. Hardy and Jason
Clarke, is staked with admirable pith in the title of their chapter 2:
"The Prophet of the Left Is Never Right."

If arguments were racehorses, this one would never win the Ken-
tucky Derby. First, if "right" means something like "conservative,"
the claim is tautologically true but not worth the ink needed to print
it. If, on the other hand, "never right" means "always wrong" – and
the book leaves no doubt about *that* – the rebuttal could not be easier.
Find one thing Moore gets right, and he is no longer always wrong.
Let's see. On the very first page of *Stupid White Men*, Moore tells
us that Pluto is no longer a planet. This is true. Ergo, Hardy and
Clarke are wrong. *Quod erat probandum.*

But no one remembers the last time reason and logic carried the day in a political, or for that matter cultural, forum. Besides, far from proving that Moore is necessarily right, this elementary application of propositional logic demonstrates only that the right-wingers' "holier than thou" hyperbole isn't. Crucially, it leaves the question posed by Briley and the rest of the American reading and viewing public unanswered. Is Michael Moore to be trusted? Where does comedy stop and nonfiction begin? How much truth is there in *Stupid White Men*, this statistics-filled volume of journalistic flash?

Since a full answer would take a book in itself, a partial one will have to suffice. In chapter 5, "Idiot Nation," Moore's opening gambit is entirely characteristic of his rhetorical style – grab the reader by the lapels and fire off the Big Bertha: "Do you feel like you live in a nation of idiots?" (87). The question is just the opening salvo in a textbook display of guerrilla journalism. Before you can catch your breath, he is two pages ahead, capping the torrid rant with a whopper: "There are forty-four million Americans who cannot read and write above a fourth-grade level – in other words, who are functional illiterates" (88). It is with verbal stunts like these that the writer grips the attention of all Americans – those who can read, that is. And he then points an accusing finger at the "Idiot in Chief," the same who had signed the milestone No Child Left Behind education act.

The richest country on earth – home to the Ivy League, hit-parade of Nobel Prize laureates, fanciest gizmos, most option-loaded SUVs, smartest bombs – taxed with being an Idiot Nation. How could this be? Hardy and Clarke's assault on what they condemn as un-patriotic humbug is two-pronged. First, they underscore what Moore does not: a full one quarter of America's functional illiterates are immigrants, and the next nineteen percent have visual disabilities that affect their ability to read. Second, to demonstrate that "functional literacy is a worldwide phenomenon" – by which, I gather, they mean functional *il*literacy – they cite a UNESCO survey that pegs literacy scores in the UK slightly lower than even those in the US.[19]

Notice that, even as they cry foul, the critics do not dispute Moore's numbers. Matter of fact, they concede that his facts are right – because they are. National adult literacy surveys of the Department of Education show that almost a quarter of all American adults (40-44 million) perform at the lowest of five skill-levels on literacy tasks related to daily life. What's more – and what Moore does not mention either – the next fifty million adults score at the second lowest level. Like father, like son: fifteen percent of highschool graduates cannot read above the sixth grade level. Like son, like father: almost half of American grown-ups cannot follow a bus schedule, and twenty-one percent cannot follow the front page of a newspaper. Like citizen, like president: on 22 September 2003, Associated Press reported that Bush scans headlines but seldom reads newspapers, relying instead on staffers' digests.[20]

For a writer who is supposed to never be right, Moore's facts are remarkably accurate. His sin, therefore, is not one of commission but of omission. While using accurate statistics, he didn't see the need to provide a breakdown of the categories that fall under the rubric of "functionally illiterate." Does that alter the accuracy of his facts? No. Does it affect the poignancy of his "Idiot Nation" thesis? Here a one-word answer may not suffice. If you confine yourself only to the single set of figures in the study, as Hardy and Clarke do – maybe. If you correlate and cross-reference this data with other figures and other studies, as I just did above – no.

Now, the second half of the alleged rebuttal. The fact that the English, the Welsh, and the Irish scored even worse than the Americans is not just cold comfort but completely beside the point. Moore's point is *not* that there aren't other nations who do even worse. His rant is directed at the fact that the leader of the post-industrial world falls far short of being a leader in education policy, education funding, and world knowledge. It is directed at the nation in which not only millions can't read but millions more can but don't. A nation, in short, that "not only churns out illiterate students BUT GOES OUT OF ITS WAY TO REMAIN IGNORANT AND STUPID" (89)."[20]

The case study of illiteracy is representative of Moore and his nonfictition. Did he lie? The answer is a clear and unequivocal: No. Was he manipulative, or just careless, or just more interested in flagging a festering problem than writing an academic dissertation about it? You decide. The sad part is that what always gets lost in the ideological diatribe is the root problem. One does not, for instance, have to condone the manner in which Moore pans politicians who decry public education, while refusing to fund it. But his facts are once again right on the money. The teacher "who cares for our child every day receives an average of $41,351 annually. A Congressman who cares only about which tobacco lobbyist is taking him to dinner tonight receives $145,100."[21]

So, how strong is his case against the misunderestimated "idiot leader of the idiot nation" (89)? Although Bush paid lip service to education from the first day in office, his solutions were like New Year resolutions, made with no expectation of being kept. The No Child Left Behind Act was signed with fanfare in 2001 to salvage failing primary and secondary education. Since then, the administration has neglected the act, especially when the president failed to fully fund even its core provisions. Strapped by wars in Asia, in 2006, for example, Bush requested only 55 percent of the already authorized budget. The result of these and earlier cuts, deplores the American Federation of Teachers, is grist for Moore's mill: critical shortages in many local schools.[22]

Bush's 2007 proposal to make his first-term tax cuts permanent made things even worse. By favouring the upper rungs of the social ladder, the gap between private and public schools is set to become more entrenched than ever. In addition, by calling for a $3.5 billion cut in discretionary spending on education, Bush put forty-two education programs – almost a third of all so targeted – up for elimination.[23] So long as The Man shortchanges schools to fund the generals, it is difficult to blame Moore for concluding that a nation that graduates illiterates should not run the world – "at least not until a majority of its citizens can locate Kosovo or any other country it has bombed on the map" (89).

> An honest propagandist for any Cause, that is,
> one who honestly studies and figures out the most
> effective way of putting over his Message,
> will learn fairly early that it is not fair to
> ordinary folks - it just confuses them - to try
> to make them swallow all the true facts.
> • Sinclair Lewis, It Can't Happen Here

Far from being always wrong, Moore is in fact quite right. After all, he says, "I have a staff of researchers, and I have two lawyers consecutively go through the entire book and movie, tear it apart, try to find something wrong with it. If I say something is a fact, it

Going head to head.
The court of public opinion: Michael Moore vs George W. Bush.
Bint Jbeil

is a fact."[24] Bush the Father may upbraid Moore as a slimeball and his Cannes winning documentary as a vicious personal attack on his son. But, given a White House crawling with lawyers, you can bet that the writer would have been dragged to court long ago if his satire had no basis in reality.

But facts are one thing. Sloppy presentation or plain misrepresentation is another. You can be entirely correct in your figures, and entirely misleading in how you string them together. Among the rightwing attacks on the artist as a con artist, few, however, appear prepared to make this distinction. Bernard Goldberg's book *100 People Who Are Screwing Up America (And Al Franken Is #37)*, which pegs Moore at #1, and Michael Wilson's documentary, *Michael Moore Hates America*, are echoed in cyberspace by Ben Fritz's "One Moore Stupid White Man" and a muckraking orgy of websites such as Moorelies.com, Moorewatch.com, Mooreexposed.com.

Among this barrage of partisan flak, Hardy and Clarke's book stands out, though not by virtue of rigorous application of argumentative logic. Its value is in being representative of its subgenre. Not only does it rehash all the cardinal charges made against the writer/filmmaker over the years but it includes contributing chapters from fellow Big Mike bashers. One of them is Tim Blair, whose solo attack on *Stupid White Men* was published by FoxNews.com in March 2002. The aim of that earlier piece, as far as one can tell, was to attack Moore's credibility by exposing alleged contradictions between his words and deeds.

On the subject of gun control, for example, Blair conclusively proves that "Michael despises guns" and "Michael is a member of the NRA, and grew up using guns."[25] The author of *Stupid White Men* is accused, in other words, of violating his documentary integrity by being for gun control but not against sports hunting. The juxtaposition proves, of course, nothing of the sort. Another of Blair's master arguments ran as follows: "Michael has an unusual manner of breathing." After this non sequitur comes the next one: "Moore was ... normal. He was heavy. He obviously combed his hair simply by running his fingers through it. He breathed through his mouth."

If such "refutations" from a member of Hardy and Clarke's hand-picked team leave one underwhelmed, let us suspend judgment and inspect a few nuts and bolts in the case of *Hardy, Clarke, Hymowitz, Sullivan, Blair, Zoubek, and Range vs Moore*. In their opening gambit, the authors of *Michael Moore Is a Big Fat Stupid White Man* claim to advance their case "based on a decade and a half of the best and brightest analysis."[26] This, in other words, is the real deal: the most punctilious and unassailable prosecution of the documedian's deceptions. The evidence against him, we are told over and over again, is ironclad and watertight, and the findings beyond any doubt, reasonable or not.

Putting *Stupid White Men* under the microscope, Hardy and Clarke quickly conclude that the book's polemics "are almost too simpleminded to dignify with a rebuttal."[27] Still, in chapters such as "Dude, Where's Your Integrity?" and "Michael Moore's Truth Problem," they press on with the attack on the man and, a distant second, his work. I won't dwell here on the *ad hominem* part of this brief, largely immaterial to the appreciation of Moore's brand of partisan artertainment. Instead, let us take a look at the charges of fabrication and falsification, rolled out in a comparison with Hitler's "Anybody will believe a lie if it is big enough."

Ouch! – even for a writer/filmmaker who's had to endure more than his share of bad press (and whose favourite director *is* Leni Riefenstahl).

Hardy and Clarke open with an example of argumentative logic more fuzzy than a Georgia peach. "Assume the opposite of anything Michael Moore says," they declare, "and you've got your finger on the pulse of the future."[28] This is allegedly established by juxtapositions of statements such as:

> 1989: Moore releases *Roger & Me*, an attack on General Motors.
> 1989–1995: GM's annual profits soar by 1.6 billion.

What does that prove? Nothing at all. The would-be prosecutors provide not a shred of evidence that *Roger & Me* was made to bring GM to fiscal ruin. The implied link between the company's profits and the film's release is equally nowhere in evidence. If anything, plant closures and layoffs – precisely the events deplored in the film – likely contributed to GM's profits. In short, Hardy and Clarke's attack on the view they attempt to pin on the filmmaker is a paradigmatic case of category error.

More wonky reasoning is in evidence. Incensed by what *Stupid White Men* says about the 2000 election, the best and the brightest thunder:

> Moore continues, shamelessly using the race card for maximum dramatic effect: "31 percent of *all* black men in Florida are prohibited from voting because they have a felony on their record."[29]

Their counterevidence? None whatsoever. The case is dismissed out of court with: "that number sounds absolutely ridiculous." That's right: brand someone a liar simply because something sounds wrong to your ear. Unfortunately, the last (and sad) laugh goes to the documedian. In 1998 the Sentencing Project and Human Rights Watch jointly reported that thirty one percent of Florida black males – the very number cited, though not referenced by Moore – were indeed so disenfranchised.

If this might seem like a good time for the defence to rest its case, things are not so simple. The fact that so many of the prosecution's arguments are flawed does not necessarily mean that the defence is above reproach. Even though Moore's facts are, on the whole, remarkably accurate, sometimes his research can be remarkably sloppy. Here, Hardy and Clarke lean for support on Ben Fritz who, in a web post, has drawn the critical spotlight to this passage from *Stupid White Men*:

$250 billion the Pentagon plans to spend in 2001 to build
2,800 new Joint Strike Fighter planes.[30]

Moore's raw figure of a quarter trillion is correct, but the budget
in question is the five-year total – *not* the amount to be spent in 2001.
In the next line Moore writes: "The proposed increase in monies
for the Pentagon over the next four years is $1.6 *trillion.*" Again,
his raw figure is unimpeachable. But the budget in question is not
the *increase* but, as per "Fiscal Year 2001 Military Budget at a
Glance," the Pentagon's then proposed *cumulative* spending.

For a man said to play fast and loose with facts, Moore does
something strange, however. He carefully references the above-cited
data, which allowed Fritz and me to look them up and correct the
slip. Nor is this an isolated gesture. In fact, marvels Ken Nolley on
the *Historians Film Committee* forum, "Moore takes the highly un-
usual step for a documentary filmmaker of providing the sources
for a large number of his claims – on his website, eventually in a
book, and even by references in the film."[31] Indeed, in addition to
supplying footnotes, correcting errors, and expanding the whole
reference section, the 2004 edition of *Stupid White Men* updates
its numbers and URLs, offering readers a chance to evaluate its fac-
tual claims.

The crucial word here is "factual," for the writer is entitled to
his point of view as much as anyone else. You may take exception
to his interpretation of international affairs, such as his solution to
the Palestinian conflict through mass non-violent civil disobedience.
It worked for Ghandi, King, and Mandela, Moore advises the Pales-
tinians, so all you need to do is sit your ass down. True, he says, "a
number of your people may get injured or killed. Still, don't move.
Just sit" (185). Call it simplistic, call it simple-minded, call it simply
naive. But you do not get from difference of political opinion to prov-
ing that Moore is a liar.

Cure the evils of Democracy by the evils of
Fascism! Funny therapeutics. I've heard of their
curing syphilis by giving the patient malaria,
but I've never heard of their curing malaria by
giving the patient syphilis!
• Sinclair Lewis, *It Can't Happen Here*

On balance, Moore's ideological opponents are frequently less interested in nailing the truth than in nailing the man they love to hate. Their hyperinflated rhetoric gives plenty of reason to suspect that if the writer/filmmaker did not exist, he would have to be invented. But what about Moore's ideological confederates on the left? Here, among the welter of positions and oppositions, the most sustained critical effort to date has been Jesse Larner's *Forgive Us Our Spins: Michael Moore and the Future of the Left* (2005). Replete with biographical fact and personal commentary, the book is structured as a digest of shortcomings of what it calls a "political clown with an edge."[32]

Curiously, Larner has very little to say about what, on paper at least, is the best researched of Moore's projects. Among the bevy of bones the critic picks with the writer/filmmaker's person, lifestyle, and politics, *Stupid White Men* gets barely four pages of desultory discussion. Adding insult to injury, Larner gives the book's title incorrectly – twice in the space of one paragraph![33] This negligence is consistent with the overall direction of his critique, which occasionally borders on misplaced, if not absurd. Moore is taken to task, for instance, for failing to offer a stable and effective "pole of attraction" in American politics. Never mind that this goal has also eluded Ted Kennedy, Al Gore, John Kerry, Nancy Pelosi, Hillary Clinton, Barack Obama, and other Democratic heavyweights.

Still, when it comes to raising questions about Moore's methodology, Larner is unrelenting. Does Moore mislead and manipulate? You bet. The rap sheet is extensive, although again it sidesteps *Stupid White Men* and other books altogether. Take *Roger & Me*. The whole film is built on the premise that Moore was stonewalled in his attempts to speak to the chairman of GM. Yet, as even Ralph Nader noted, Moore and Smith did meet and talk on at least one occasion. Next, contrary to what the film implies, two-thirds of GM's layoffs in Flint took place over a decade and not in 1986. Similarly, plans to reinvigorate the city's economy, daft as they were, were not in response to the layoffs. They had been in place since the 1970s and had largely fizzled out by 1986.

In a pattern that has not changed since, Moore loves to cut and paste – never mind the chronology. Reagan visited Flint as a presidential candidate, not as president. Televangelist Robert Schuller visited it four years earlier than the narration implies. All this mystification, Larner rightly points out, could have been easily avoided.

All that is needed is a preamble that Moore belatedly makes in the voice-over to the special-features of 2003 DVD edition: "This film covers essentially the entire decade of the 1980s. It's meant to present this mosaic of what happened in Flint during the 1980s, so we'll be going back and forth – there are no dates in the film."[34]

Bowling for Columbine remixes two clips of Charlton Heston, shot a year apart, into a single "NRA forever" bluster to intimate defiance of the suffering community. Even the opening "guns in a bank" sequence is partly staged. Moore had to call ahead to arrange for a rifle pickup during his filmed visit, which is not normally done (the background check can take several days). Furthermore, the reference to five hundred guns in a vault is to a central storage vault, miles away from the bank – a detail left in the editing room. As for *Fahrenheit 9/11*, Dave Kopel contends that there are no less than fifty-nine deceits in the film, all posted on his website for scrutiny. The majority hinge on semantics and point of view and, as such, are a matter of interpretation.[35] A few, however, conclusively show what we already knew: on occasion the film stage-manages context for effect.

The secret of Moore's success is that, for all the humour, posturing, and rhetoric, viewers and readers trust that his documentaries and nonfictions are true. Otherwise, his exposés of Big Business hypocrisy and federal corruption could not draw the kind of emotional and political response they do. Going after the bad guys, Moore sets himself up as a good guy and, to the extent he takes his audiences for a ride, he hurts not only himself but the rest of us. With each report of a fudged fact or faulty time sequence, one can almost hear a collective groan: can he be trusted? Imagine the uproar in Nottingham if Robin Hood was found to prey on the gullibility of the commoners. No one likes to be duped and, once burnt, the public may find it harder to believe the rest, no matter how true and poignant.

But is that really what happens? Strikingly, most film experts shrug off the evidence of Moore's liberal handling of time and context. Writing from the Sundance Festival shortly after the release of *Roger & Me*, Roger Ebert noted the unanimous support for the film from other documentary directors. "There is no such thing as a truly objective, factual documentary," ran the consensus. "All documentaries ... manipulate factual material in order to make a point, and they imply by their style and tone what kind of a point they are making. Some hope to give you an accurate view of a situation, and you can tell that while you're watching them. Others might be poetic, elegaic, angry or funny. You can tell that, too." Fully in agreement, Ebert concluded: "Parts of 'Roger & Me' are factual. Parts are not. All of the movie is true."[36]

His argument is simple. What the documentary has to say about General Motors and Flint is more significant than the bare facts, insasmuch as it supplies "poetry, a viewpoint, indignation, opinion, anger and humor."[37] This sympathetic interpretation is, however, contested by Larner. "If a film claims legitimacy as a documentary," he writes, "'poetry' can't trump sequence." The problem with the latter claim is that *all* representations of reality are deformed in one way or another. Even the most profound models of the world, such as $E=mc^2$, are at the same time colossal deformations. But without them, neither scientists nor artists could hope to compress the world into the experiential orbit limited by our finite processing resources.

All art, no matter how representational or mimetic, necessarily deforms reality, if only by virtue of selecting aspects of experience on which to focus. John Grierson, the father of documentary cinema, stressed this very point in his definition of the genre as "the creative treatment of actuality."[38] His stance has been echoed a hundred times over since. In *Documentary:Tthe Margins of Reality* (2005), Paul Ward takes it as a given that "staging is an unavoidable part of the filmmaking process." Stella Bruzzi argues that "documentaries are a negotiation between filmmaker and reality." Bill Nichols agrees: "the poetic mode sacrifices the conventions of continuity editing."

Denigrated for allegedly cheapening documentary filmmaking, Moore makes the same point. "All art, listen, every piece of journalism manipulates sequence and things. Just the fact that you edit, that certain things get taken out or put back on."[39] Of course, the crucial – if invariably contingent and contextual – question is how far the film can go before it goes too far. But it is a sobering thought that, even if disputes about the documentary ethic became inflamed with *Bowling for Columbine* and *Fahrenheit 9/11*, they have been raging at least since *Nanook of the North* (whose igloo had to be made twice the normal size to accommodate the filming crew and equipment).

A skeptic like Larner, who wants his reality raw and unedited, should watch 7-11 surveillance camera footage for two hours and see how he likes it. "The reason why people don't watch docu-

mentaries," observed Moore, "is that they are so bogged down with
'in '82 five thousand were called back ... in '84 ten thousand were
laid off ...'"[40] In short: dry facts and tedious statistics. Nothing to
grab your heart strings and tie them in a knot. That's why, rather
than objectively and soberly, the documedian prefers to tackle his
material emotionally and rhetorically. If America is too serious a
topic to be tackled without humour, it may also be too big to be
tackled without hyperbole.

> We don't want all this highbrow intellectuality,
> all this book learning.
> • Sinclair Lewis, *It Can't Happen Here*

Moore is a purveyor of rhetorical nonfiction, a mode of narration
with its own conventions and practices. Although accentuated in
films, the same rhetorical mode underlies *Stupid White Men* and
his other books, all the way down to his unabashedly activist *Mike's
Election Guide 2008*. The goal of rhetoric is to convince, and
Moore will endeavour to convince in every way he can. One of
his strategies of suasion is a successive return to his leading theme
– in chapter 5 of *Stupid White Men*, education. Such periodic re-
turns, which progressively dish out more information to the reader,
create a sense of being eased into a complex topic of which the
narrator is in full control.

The many instances of repetition in *Stupid White Men* serve the
same rhetorical purpose. The cyclical return to an argument pre-
viously debated not only reassures the reader, who now feels on fa-
miliar ground, but creates an image of an author who knows his
subject intimately and makes the difficult parts progressively more
accessible to his audience. Another conspicuous feature is his penchant
for cataloguing, designed to confer an air of discursive fairness and
completeness. So enamoured is Moore of lists and inventories that
he actually lifts one of the best ones from the internet, leaving him-
self partially open to a charge of plagiarism.[41]

Another conspicuous stratagem is challenging readers with in-
quiries in the course of an argument. These can be purely rhetorical,
as in "Do you feel like you live in a nation of idiots?" More fre-
quently, however, Moore uses *hypophora*, posing questions only to
answer them immediately himself. Right after announcing that there

are forty-four million Americans who cannot read and write above a fourth-grade level, he asks: "How did I learn this statistic?" In comes the reply: "Well, I *read* it" (88). Or, later in the same chapter: "What kind of priority do we place on education in America? Oh, it's on the funding list – somewhere down between OSHA and meat inspectors" (104). The rapid Q & A fosters the impression that the answer given with such ease and immediacy must be the correct one.

Much as in his Oscar acceptance speech, Moore's homilies frequently crescendo to a comical (because incongruous) punchline, not unlike a conceit in metaphysical poetry. His humour may not be highbrow, but it rarely misses its mark. Among others, *Stupid White Men* regales with the following Prayer to Afflict the Comfortable.

> Dear Lord ... we ask that You inflict every member of the House of Representatives with horrible, incurable cancers of the brain, penis, and hand (though not necessarily in that order). We ask, Our Loving Father, that every senator from the South be rendered addicted to drugs and find himself locked away for life... We beseech You to make the children of every senator in the Mountain Time Zone gay – *really* gay. Put the children of senators from the East in a wheelchair and the children of senators from the West in public schools (236).

Another ingredient of Moore's rhetoric is a deliberate blurring of the truth – built-in sloppiness, if you will – that renders him less vulnerable to disproof by leaving room for interpretation. It would take relatively little time to tightenall the loose ends and render his films and books immune to critique. The fact that the writer/ filmmaker chooses not to suggests that this apparent laziness is a calculated – if less than responsible – rhetorical defense against detractors. It allows him to operate safe from conclusive refutation, while remaining provocative and thus commanding the spotlight on the cultural and political arena.

Much of the time, Moore's facts and his ability to weave them into the kind of book you devour in one sitting are nothing short of impressive. Other times, especially on celluloid, he will cynically blur the edges between fact and fiction, not least because – as Wallace, Condon, O'Rourke, and Beatty knew too well – controversy makes

for good publicity. Moore does not set out, however, to manip-
ulate facts as much as emotions. Only when forced to pick between
sober reportage and satirical punch, will he miscontextualize his
data – or remix his footage – to induce sympathetic harmonics in
the audience. Waxing rhetorical, he will exercise every clause in his
poetic licence to shake readers and viewers out of political complacency.

Take this scenario from *Stupid White Men*. "You're working two
jobs, and so is your wife, and you've got little Jimmy working down
at McDonald's too" (xiv). Then "you" get fired and suddenly face
a made-in-USA blank wall. How not to relate to this fellow, espe-
cially if he's you? Identification is not easy in political nonfiction,
but Moore pulls it off without breaking stride. His gift for hom-
ing in on the emotional correlative of any debate is uncanny and
was brought out in an exemplary fashion in the 2004 interview on
"The O'Reilly Factor." Defending Bush II's deceptions, O'Reilly tried
to defend the invasion of Iraq and the resulting sectarian bloodshed
in the name of jumpstarting democracy. Instead of arguing further,
the writer pinned his host with a single question and watched him
squirm: "would you sacrifice your child to remove one of the other
30 brutal dictators on this planet?"[42]

Moore plays with his audiences' heads by brilliantly playing
with their hearts. Getting people to listen, to empathize, and thus
to participate (if only vicariously) in the political process is one of
the lasting achievements of his trademark brand of artertainment.
You may frown on his rhetorical ploys but, for better or worse, they
are in keeping with the ways Americans today select and absorb
political information. Forget factual, evidentiary, ratiocinative,
argumentative. Forget the sober canons of cinematic mimesis or
narrative veracity. As one film critic sums it up, it is "auto-biog-
raphy and pop culture that move American consumers, not sense
or sensibility."[43]

When you reach out to your audience, emotion is essential. When
you talk politics, it is indispensable. "Al Franken's so clever, and
Jon Stewart's so good at what he does," observed one of Moore's
allies, "but Michael has an ability to touch people's hearts that
neither of them has. He's like a great blues singer."[44] In a veiled
reference to Chomsky, Janet Street-Porter seconded the sentiment,
marvelling at how the documedian makes politics as exciting as a
ball game. His great achievement, she concludes, "is to draw

Pitching low, hitting hard.
Michael Moore on a rally: "Slacker Uprising Tour"
in Albuquerque, New Mexico, weeks before the 2004
Presidential Elections.
By permission of Prognosic, GNU Free Documentation License

people who would never vote or read a newspaper to sit through
a film about politics. He aims so low it's extraordinary."

Whether lowbrow or nobrow, there is no doubt that Moore's
variety of artertainment is reformist and partisan. The former Re-
publican mayor of New York, Ed Koch, put down *Fahrenheit 9/11*
as a mere propaganda piece. In his rush to condemn it, however,
he failed to comment on how Moore hits out at the Democrats
(mocking Clinton as a model Republican president). One wonders
what Koch would say about Albert Maysles, a documentary director
cited by Hardy and Clarke, who slams Moore's films as dishonest
even as he admits that he had not seen *Columbine* for fear he "might
start believing some of Moore's total fabrications."[45] Or about Cathy
Horton who, with like-minded Republican activists, organized a
protest against *Fahrenheit 9/11*, although only one of the group had
seen it.

When Upton Sinclair declared that all art was propaganda, he
was essentially paraphrasing the definition of the term. According
to the OED, propaganda is any association, systematic scheme, or

concerted movement for the propagation of a particular doctrine or practice. As such, to the extent that all writing propagates a particular viewpoint in order to change the disposition of the readers, all literature is propaganda. This is not to gloss over dramatic differences in the degree or the kind of political engagement. But the most effective American writers of nonfiction, from Paine and Thoreau to W.E.B. Dubois and Milton Friedman, have all been propagandists in their own right.

> He was not only 100 per cent American; he exacted
> 40 per cent… interest on top of the principal.
> • Sinclair Lewis, *It Can't Happen Here*

"I am an American," shot back Moore when questioned about his acceptance speech at the 75th Academy Awards. He had just returned backstage, mobbed after a performance that matched in bravos and boos what Sacheen Littlefeather said on behalf of Marlon Brando in 1973. Second earlier, cameras rolling, Moore stunned the nation:

> I have invited the other documentary nominees on stage with me. They are here in solidarity because we like non-fiction. We like non-fiction because we live in fictitious times. We live in a time where fictitious election results give us a fictitious president. We are now fighting a war for fictitious reasons. Whether it's the fiction [sic] of duct tape or the fictitious Orange Alerts, we are against this war, Mr. Bush. Shame on you, Mr. Bush, shame on you. And, whenever you've got the Pope and the Dixie Chicks against you, your time is up.[46]

What could be more American than a working-class college dropout who, through luck and pluck, strikes it rich and famous? And yet, while *Stupid White Men* was scorching the charts, the writer/filmmaker found himself under attack for making money while standing up for the working poor. Exasperated, he lashed out: "I'm filthy rich. You know why I'm a multi-millionaire? 'Cause multi-millions like what I do."[47] It goes without saying that such retorts only inflame those who take him to task for violating the principles that drive his work. By these standards, of course, George W.

Bush ought to have been catching bullets in Iraq – a point the detractors never fail to fail to make.

Ironically, even as he rails against the fiction of classless society, equal opportunity, and economic justice for all, Moore's populist rhetoric is steeped in the mystique of the American Dream. Indeed, for some he has become the embodiment of the national myth whereby, by virtue of boundless ambition, industry, and self-reliance, everyone can bootstrap himself to peaks of wealth and power. Be that as it may, *Fortune* editorials do not dwell on the spiritual poverty of this quest for material affluence. Or, for that matter, on how its single-minded character is at odds with larger social objectives, embodied in Jefferson's endorsement of happy mediocrity.

Equally, Moore embodies the principles of liberal democracy, notably the freedom of expression. Historically, *Stupid White Men* – to say nothing of *Fahrenheit 9/11* – marked a Tiananmen Square moment when a solitary figure in a baseball cap stood up and heckled the most powerful politician on earth, armed with nothing more than anger at economic injustice, phoney war, and suppression of civil liberties. In the post-9/11 days, when "liberal" became a four letter word, Moore emerged as one of the few antidotes to the militant right-is-right of Rush Limbaugh, Ann Coulter, or Michael Savage. With guts and humour, he reminded the country the basic truth about any government, namely that – as Thoreau put it *Resistance to Civil Government* – it does not keep the country free.[48]

But the archetypal American trait may be Moore's identification with the common man. His books, films, TV series, blogs, and flannel plaids paint him as a homegrown David who confronts business and political Goliaths on behalf of the working stiff (one reason why the masses see him not as a media mogul but as Mike). What helps *their* identification with his point of view is not only Moore's masterful American vernacular but the homey contexts that never fail to trigger a sense of recognition. Run-ins with delayed flights, lousy fast food, small-print exemptions to "full" medical coverage, free-trade job losses – all from page two of the Introduction to *Stupid White Men* – are all too familiar to too many Americans.

Moore's evocation, and in many ways embodiment, of characteristics commonly associated with Americanness has undoubtedly contributed to his popularity. Having fashioned himself into the mouthpiece for the working Joe and Jane, it is no surprise that *USA*

An icon is born.
Jeans, baseball cap, camera and the American flag: Michael
Moore as a filmmaker – with nary a hint of his prodigious
literary output.
Portland Mercury

Today hired him in 2004 to speak to the nation. To be sure, the
editors disavowed that Moore's celebrity status had anything to do
with their decision. "Our sole interest is having him in the paper.
We're not interested in the show."[49] All the same, it is not often that
a maverick finds a forum for his partisan message in a mainstream
print outlet, a fact that raises Moore's stature to that enjoyed once
by Walter Lippmann or the Alsops.

This may be disagreeable to critics from Larner to McKibbin who
have accused Moore of offering neither an intellectual nor a polit-
ical solution to the problems he addresses – as if that were part of his
job description. Moreover, such critiques gloss over the awakening
among the non-voting and normally apolitical American public his
books and films have provoked. As if on cue, Moore contends: "I
don't want the public to think that I'm the one who's going to cor-
rect the problem. I am not going to correct it. I'm asking them to
do that. I'm asking them to join with me and I'll join with them. I
don't want them to sit there passively and watch me and vicariously

live through me, sort of a, 'Yeah, go get'em Mike!' Nuh-uh. I'm sorry. I'm not going to get them for you." [50]

In the end, inundated by information and disinformation, fans and foes alike continue to scratch their heads over his popular appeal, not to say art. Outside of crucifying Dubya, what are his political goals? How do they relate to the education of the public, especially the working-class public that he claims to speak for? How effective is his brand of political action and political comedy given that it failed in 2004 in his professed goal of preventing Bush's re-election? After all, jokes can mislead one to take the author and his level of commitment less than seriously.

Interviewed in the *People's Weekly*, Moore saw it differently: "The best humor comes out of anger, whether it's George Carlin, Lenny Bruce, Charlie Chaplin." [51] On reflection, there is much to be said for approaching Moore as the modern incarnation of Shakespeare's wise fool, with a licence to say things others might be afraid to. Only don't look to the jester for complex solutions to complex problems. In fact, you'd be a fool to do so. The abiding resonance of the court jester lies elsewhere. He is often the first to cry that, mad with power, the king has no robes, or that things are rotten in the state of Denmark.

In doing so he may, indeed, embellish the story. But, much as with Wallace's romance, Condon's *roman á clef*, O'Rourke's book of essays, and Beatty's script, you ignore his warnings at your own risk. So much so, in fact, that all five writers ought to be labelled by the surgeon general:

All I desire is that humane values be maintained in our institutions, codes of conduct and systems of thought. It is probably nothing more than old-fashioned liberalism. (1986)

• John le Carré, *Conversations with John le Carré*

─────────

Conclusion

Political Art, American Art

The United States occupies a unique place in history. Notwithstanding claims on behalf of the British empire, it is the first truly global pace-setter and trend-setter. Its firstness and foremostness extend to most areas of contemporary life, from telecommunications to popular culture, from (sub)urbanization to consumerism, from business to science, from weapons manufacture down to playing Globocop. For all nations caught in the world wide web of reciprocal entanglements, it pays to learn about the United States, whether to emulate its ideals or to steer away from its mistakes. Lessons learned from the global superpower are truly global in nature.[1]

But as far as learning about the United States goes, no one may have more remedial work to do than the Americans themselves, and nowhere more so than in the realm of politics. Armed with the experience of running large-scale surveys on military personnel, post-World War II pollsters set out – on a scale extrapolatable to the country at large – to calibrate what Mr and Mrs Doe knew about politics. The results were shocking, to say the least. The vast majority of respondents were found to be "nonideological almost to the point of intellectual disorganization, uninformed about government policies and the parties' positions vis-à-vis those policies, oblivious to congressional politics, and unable to comprehend, if not hostile to, basic democratic freedoms."[2]

Over the decades these attitudes, or more precisely non-attitudes, have been identified with regularity bordering on uniformity. Worse, in panel studies, respondents' views, hazy to begin with, have often turned out to be so unstable as to be indistinguishable from guessing. In one 1987 poll – after exposés of illegal military aid to Nicaragua's murder-squad Contras – after years of media airings and congressional hearings about the cover-up of the CIA operations Black Eagle and Supermarket (aka Irangate) that nearly toppled Reagan and his government – two-thirds of the country didn't even know that Nicaragua is in Central America.[3]

Even as he dilates on the spins and sins of Michael Moore, Jesse Larner does not worry too much about Americans who cannot place Nicaragua or Iraq on the map. One shouldn't make too much of such ignorance, he shrugs, because "non-Americans have many more practical reasons to study America than Americans have to study other countries, and, due to the dominance of American pop culture, many more opportunities to do so."[4] Other pundits are less sanguine about what passes for political culture in the country. American political discourse is stuck at the TV-ad level, derided Al Gore in 2006, in a masterful understatement branding the thirty-second electoral commercials as "not thoughtful statements of policy."

With the country polarized along partisan lines by tit-for-tat accusations of, respectively, creeping socialism or nascent fascism, hardly anyone is inclined to keep an open mind. The current presidency is the best case in point. In April 2009, a Pew opinion poll documented a countrywide fault-line. While almost nine in ten Democrats approved of Obama's first 100 days in office, less than three in ten Republicans did. Tellingly, even at the corresponding time in Bush's first term – which came in the wake of the divisive 2000 election – the numbers were not as far apart. Blinkered by partisan loyalties, today's Blue and Red Teams America tune out every preacher who does not preach to the converted.

The first casualty of every war, even if it is only a war of words, is truth. As if to prove the point, study after study, poll after poll returns the same verdict: American citizens have for the most part little notion of what goes with what in the country and in the world. By 2003, for instance, enough evidence has accrued from the International Atomic Energy Agency inspectorate to prove beyond any doubt, reasonable or not, that there were no weapons of mass destruction in Iraq. The evidence – supported later by admissions from members of the Bush team, including former Secretary of State Colin Powell – made it clear that the WMDs had been a red herring from the start.[5] Yet, thirty-six percent of Americans surveyed believed Iraq had WMDs when the United States invaded it in 2003.

The punchline? In 2006 this number went *up* to fifty percent.

The number of political myths in circulation is vast. Consider the bromide of American isolationism. According to the 2002 Congressional Research Service report, between 1798 and 2001 there were at least three hundred separate instances wherein US forces have been deployed abroad (for an average of about eight months). No one is prepared to admit the extent to which the American military tail wags the socioeconomic dog, even though the evidence comes from every administration, including the present. Why else would Congress earmark "billions of dollars to be spent on weapons systems that neither the White House nor the military actually want" – materiel that even the defense secretary finds simply obsolete?[6]

The optimists will argue that modern opinion polls have rendered citizens' political participation obsolete insofar as they have made public preferences public. The pessimists will point to *Yes, Minister* and *The West Wing*, popular hit shows that amply educated viewers on how polls get cooked to get the "right" results. And the reformists will point to Switzerland and to its municipal, cantonal, and national referenda that, quite literally, pluck most political choices out of politicians' hands and place them in the hands of the people. "Who said citizen participation and political action has to be limited to the politicians and the fat cats who subsidize them?" seconded Michael Moore and Kathleen Glynn in the opening pages of *Adventures in a TV Nation* (x).[7]

Most commentators agree that, during the 2000s, the need for citizen participation became more urgent than ever. Early in the decade, the United States transformed itself into one nation under surveillance, as prescribed by the 2002 (renewed in 2005 and 2006) Patriot Act. Propaganda and doctored spin ruled the airwaves, bamboozling captive audiences with made-for-TV dramas such as "Iraq and the WMDs." Political correctness ruled the day, books and ideas became monitored via library and credit card checks, and, with freedom fries on the menu, neocon ideologues argued that the American democracy must be defended at all costs and by all means, even the undemocratic ones.[8]

In 2003 Harold Pinter pulled no punches. "The US is really be-yond reason now. It is beyond our imagining to know what they are going to do next and what they are prepared to do. There is only one comparison: Nazi Germany."⁹ Not all artists, of course, have the audacity or, indeed, the cultural cachet of Pinter. Not all are given to outspoken political oratory like the late Arthur Miller. Not all are Eric Arthur Blair, who took up arms to fight in the Spanish War for the political principles he believed in. Not all are Mario Vargas Llosa, who ran for president of his native Peru, only to lose by a whisker. Not all are Upton Sinclair, who, putting fiction writing aside, clawed his way to within spitting distance of the EPIC (End Poverty in California) governorship of California.

But in a great triumph of American democracy, those who bear witness to injustice but cannot address it through action can speak out against it. Most artists and artertainers effect change not by changing social systems but by changing belief systems. Much of the time this involves asking a lot of awkward questions of the sort that never come up on political panels. One such inquiry has always been self-directed. Given their hit-and-miss advocacy, what is the role of political literature, film, and other forms of art and mass com-munication in shaping social attitudes and public policies? This is, indeed, where criticism can make its mark on the political/cultural forum by taking *critical* note of the issues taken up by artists with a cause – much as *Ars Americana, Ars Politica* attempts to do.

Notes

INTRODUCTION

1 For a critical definition and discussion of nobrow taste cultures, see Swirski, *From Lowbrow to Nobrow.*

2 *The Man* was reissued in 1999; *Parliament of Whores* in 2003; and *Stupid White Men* in 2004. Same paragraph, Auden in "The Poet and the City," 383.

3 Ambrose, 138; for background, see Greene online (2006).

4 Kennedy, "Sixth Annual Muggle Awards."

5 Orwell, 318; same paragraph, Furst, x.

6 See, for example, Speare, Milne, Howe, Aaron, Blotner, Wilding, Rideout, Horsley, Murphy, Whalen-Bridge, Foley, Wald, or Yerkes in the bibliography; for a good overview of the issue, see Denning, Kemme.

7 The canonical version is not the book published serially in 1904; see Sinclair, *The Jungle: The Uncensored Original Edition* (2003), and Swirski, "Upton Sinclair: *The Jungle* (1906); *Oil* (1927)."

8 Howe, 17; italics mine.

9 For a typically insightful account of the Clinton presidential campaigns and his two terms in the White House, see Halberstam.

10 Mailer's definition and an ironic coverage of this issue in Wolfe, 151. Wallace's sales figures from Folkart.

11 Swirski, *From Lowbrow to Nobrow.*

12 See Swirski, *From Lowbrow to Nobrow.*

13 My examples are perforce restricted to the United States; for a detailed and compelling study of political resonance in a more comparative context, see Hanne.

14 Clowers and Letendre, xi.

15 Moore in Headlam, 12; Condon, *And Then We Moved to Rossenarra*, 153; Wallace in Leverence, 199.

16 Not even Nobel Prize winners lie beyond the pale of such criticism; Alfred Kazin, for one, used to complain that Steinbeck's characters

are always on the verge of becoming human, but never do. As part of his revisionist theses from *The Cultural Front*, Michael Denning argues, however, that the formalistically maligned Marxist fiction of the 1930s would, in fact, "mount an opposition from within the commonplace forms of the culture," 61.

17 Not to be confused with Joan Didion's *Political Fictions* purveyed by the American press. Since my focus is on American criticism, I exclude studies like Horsley's *Political Fiction and the Historical Imagination* (1990) and others in the same category. I should also note the great number of South American political writers who fall, however, outside the scope of *Ars Americana*.

18 Quoted in McGrath, 14; same paragraph, Roth, 224.

19 Whalen-Bridge, 36. For a brief but serviceable review of "revision-ary scholarship," see the Introduction in Yerkes (2005); for recent examples of revisionist criticism, see Murphy, Foley, Denning, Wald.

20 Whitebrook, *Reading Political Stories*, 21

21 Reed, xiii.

22 Reed, Introduction, xvii.

23 Reed, xiv; see also Whitebrook. O'Rourke's 1987 collection is enti-tled *Republican Party Reptile*.

24 Properly speaking, as an acronym HAMAS should be capitalized; hereby I follow the common form of "Hamas."

25 See Hutcheon for a sketch of a politically engaged postmodernist scholarship. I would like to thank my research assistants Alice Tse and Hilton Hung for their help with the images for this book.

CHAPTER ONE

1 *Trevayne*, v; for discussion, see Swirski (1998).

2 In Leverence, 181.

3 Harwood, 3.

4 In Leverence, 135–8. David Shaw's 1986 review tips the compari-son between Wallace and Ludlum the other way.

5 In Leverence, 201.

6 See Wallechinsky.

7 See Lingeman, 45.

8 In Leverence, 206.

9 Shaw, 2. Wallace's first two books had been trimmed by 75,000 words before, presumably, he became too big to trim.

10 Lingeman, 45.

11 In Leverence, 215; next quote in Leverence, 217.

12 For background, see Leverence, especially 135, 138, 407–8.

13 Reed (44) provides a useful background to the timeline. For an insightful review of the film, including its political-yet-apolitical stance, see Canby; see also James Jones and pages 333–9 in Leverence.

14 In Leverence, 117.

15 In Leverence, 253; next quote below, in Leverence, 258.

16 See Brodie, chapter 10, "The First Law Case: Failure." For references to the case in Condon's *Death of a Politician*, see 33 and 65. On Victoria Woodhull, see Frisken.

17 Andersen, 45; following quotes by Tuchman (quoted in Shannon, 11) and Robertson, 310.

18 Similarly, although Roosevelt is sometimes taken as a patron of the muckrakers, his coinage was far from complimentary; his 1906 essay, "The Man with the Muck-Rake," called for discontinuing public exposés of corruption.

19 51.

20 Wintour and MacAskill, "1 in 3 Say Bush Is Biggest Threat"; Kessler and Allen, "Bush Faces Increasingly Poor Image Overseas"; see also TIME Europe poll, "Biggest Threat to Peace."

21 A good primer on the problem is Moore's *Downsize This!*; for background on the period, see Levy.

22 Levy, 12.

23 See Levine, 180; Levy, 6–14.

24 Jeffries, 64–5; Straub, 66; Thompson, 51.

25 Quoted in Stern, 62. "For Self-Defense" was later dropped from the party name.

26 Unger and Unger, 149; Carr, 186; for background see Abernathy, 118.

27 One of the defining moments for the party was the killing of Denzil Dowell by the Oakland Police Department, publicized in the very first communal newsletter; for a reproduction, see Foner, 9–12. For background, see Ogbar, 84; membership numbers from Boyd, 5.

28 Ogbar, 87. Other accounts can be found in Abernathy, 118; Foner, especially xi and xxi; Doss, 180. A more dramatic account of this "invasion" (as it was dubbed by the media) is provided by Reed, 40–1.

29 Clemens, 23–4. Thirty years later, Smith and Carlos, who eventually became high-school athletics coaches, were honoured for their part in furthering the civil rights movement in America.

30 Straub, 118.

31 Schultze, 75–6.

32 Paz. Levitt discusses at length the relation between the military and social wings of Hamas.

33 Leggett, A1. Byman quote, 270; following quote, Aufhauser online "Written Testimony."

34 Blackstock 7; also Marx, 434. For an exception to the official line on Hamas, see Beyer; Agha and Malley; for background, see Gunning.

35 Marx, 434–5; same paragraph, Chomsky online "Anarchy in the U.S.A.".

36 Charles E. Jones, 148. For the background to the rest of the paragraph, see Bloom and Breines, esp. 167; Brown, 266–7; Ward, 104–5. For Bunchy Carter, see Kelley 197.

37 See Ogbar, 88; Clemens, 36; Churchill, 92–3. Newton was eventually released but, scarred by prison, his later years were marked by heavy drug use, ended by a drug-related murder in 1989. Same paragraph, the FBI quote from Boyd, 5.

38 As Pearson reports (181), this led to at least several expulsions; same paragraph below, see O'Reilly, 298.

39 See Umoja, 417–42; Bukhari-Alston.

40 Finkle and Wallenstein, 26. For media portrayal of the party, see Chomsky, "Anarchy in the U.S.A"; Robinson, 1.

41 Ogbar, 121, 90.

42 Pearson, 237. For further material, see Jennings.

43 *The Black Panther* newsletter, 5 July 1969; reproduced in Foner, 171. Below, see Abron, 186.

44 Churchill, 87 and 89; the entire article details the FBI campaign.

45 Charles Jones, viii.

46 In Leverence, 266.

CHAPTER TWO

1 *And Then We Moved to Rossenarra*, 152. Parts of this chapter appeared previously in my "Literature as History: The Lives and Deaths of Richard Milhous Slurrie and Walter Bodmore Nixon."

2 Richler, 4; see also, Cochran, 188.

3 *Time*, "The Sustaining Stream." Same paragraph, subsequent quotes from Lingeman, 80; Braudy, BR5; Gold, 39.

4 Lehmann-Haupt, 31.

5 *Death*, 161; for background, see *Empires – The Medici: Godfathers of the Renaissance* (2004).

6 In Mitgang, C24. For closer analysis of some faults of the U.S. political system, see Swirski, *American Eutopia and Social Engineering*, chapter 2.

7 Edwards, "Terror in Freedonia," 34. For Braudy, see "*Winter Kills* by Richard Condon."

8 See Hofstadter, 4. Incidentally, Cochran errs when he declares on page 177 that Hofstadter defined paranoid style "as the exclusive property of 'the radical right.'" In fact, even in the introduction the historian states: "this is not the style of mind confined to the right wing. With modulations and differences, it exists today, as it has in the past, on the left," xi. On the very first page of the essay he refers to this "style of mind, not always right-wing in its affiliations," 3.

9 Hofstadter, 6.

10 For evidence of Nixon's paranoia, see Brodie, especially pages 17, 127, 189, 210, 310, 425, 446, 465, and 503–4. On Condon, see Cochran, 178.

11 Nixon's marital indifference and hints of homosexuality are a matter of record. His press secretary, James Bassett, for example, reported that Nixon suffered from and sought therapy for sexual impotence (Brodie, 331).

12 On McBain's documentary aesthetics, see Swirski, "A Is for American."

13 *The Truth*, 11.

14 There are well over a hundred instances of Condon using the names of his acquaintances as minor characters.

15 *The Whisper of the Axe*, 27.

16 For the dating of the Lansky connection, see Summers, 57; indeed, Summers appears to vindicate much of Condon's fiction with a detailed coverage of the underworld dimension in Nixon's career. Next paragraph, defence contract profits from Brandes, 275.

17 Summers, 180. Nixon was the strongest and most insistent proponent of CIA-led Cuban invasion and assassination of Castro. See Schifferes on corruption as a swing issue in the November 2006 congressional elections. For the missing billions in Iraq, see Gregory.

18 See Summers, especially 111–15, 127–8, and 243–5.

19 Facsimile reproduction of Hughes' notebook can be found in Summers, 279. On Hughes' "loan" to the Nixon family, see Brodie 436–7. Of course, not only Republican candidates are groomed and raced like so many depression-era Seabiscuits: Harry Truman, once a Missouri haberdasher, came out of the political stable of the Kansas boss Tom Pendergast.

20 See Kramer and Roberts's investigative biography of Rockefeller, *"I Never Wanted to Be Vice-president of Anything!"* (1973).

21 See Estulin.

22 Dewey's acknowledged connection with Lansky comes up in the context of wartime use of the mafia to secure military goals; see Richard Norton Smith, 570–3.

23 Reference to Slurrie's campaign manager in *Death of a Politician*, 16.
24 Sabato and Simpson, 149.
25 Keener, 114.
26 Lt. Jimmy Stewart, on a hiatus from Hollywood, who wondered
    how Nixon's "game became tops" in no time at all, was in fact
    duped by the man who had played and won for months before; see
    Aitken, 108.
27 Richard Norton Smith, 602; *Death of a Politician*, 227.
28 Genovese, 22. Data on Nixon's house improvements from Brodie,
    450; on Nixon's financial irregularities from Emery, 109. Informa-
    tion on Nixon's financial "irregularities" is abundant: beyond the
    biographies, the reader may start with Michael Johnston (1982);
    Welch (1997); and Genovese (1999).
29 Genovese, 23–5. For the Liddy Plan, see Chester Lewis, 135–6.
    See also *Watergate: A Third Burglary* (film time 24:46-26:15).
30 Quoted in Osborne, 7.
31 Miller, 178; below, Nixon quote in Furgurson, section 2:7. Widgery
    poll from Moore and Glynn, 206.
32 Books and Writers, online. Same paragraph, O'Neil quote in Welch,
    254.
33 James Wilson, 166.
34 Bauer, 117.
35 Benson, 179.
36 Bauer, 117. For Clinton, see Huffington, 97; for Bush Senior, see
    Parenti, *America Besieged*, 19; for Bush Junior, see Huffington, 149;
    for Lockheed-Martin, see Caldicott, 33–5.
37 In Harris, 335.

CHAPTER THREE

1 See Roger Cohen.
2 Stuttaford, 54; Brock, 57. Same paragraph, next quote, Grant, 69.
3 For an example of such attack, see Hardy and Clarke; a blistering
   and entertaining counterpoint is Franken's *Lies and the Lying Liars
   Who Tell Them*.
4 On gonzo and O'Rourke, see Sipchen; Goodrich.
5 Flynn online; next quote, Zinn, 5.
6 For background and self-assessment, see Reagan's inaugural
   and farewell speeches. For Friedman's role in shaping American
   economics as well as international programs of shock austerity,
   see Klein.
7 Wirls, 36.
8 Data from Philips, 82–3. In 1989 the Ford Foundation reported (6):

"nearly 25 percent of American's children under six now live in poverty. For minorities the percentage is 40 percent and both figures have been rising for more than ten years." Poverty-line data in the next line from Newman and de Zoysa, 88. For insider background, see Niskanen.

9   Reported in Hutton online. Same paragraph, data on political contributions from Collins and Yeskel, online, in the section "Why the Wealth Gap Matters." On America's wealthiest one percent, see also David Johnston.

10 Cox and Skidmore-Hess, 171. For a series of examples of how lax FDA enforcement affects consumers, see Schlosser, *Fast Food Nation*. For a good introduction to Reagan's economic policy, see Peretz; the Laffer Curve is also discussed in Cox and Skidmore-Hess, 168.

11 Harbutt, 296. For a hilarious but pointed discussion of similar "reversal of fortunes" involving Democrats and Republicans, see Franken, *Lies*, e.g. 103–9.

12 Hedrick Smith, 174.

13 Preceded by Black Thursday, 24 October, and followed by Black Tuesday, 29 October.

14 On page 15, Rodgers criticizes the official definition for these reasons.

15 In 1996 Rozin reported that, while people in Western countries spent about 21 percent of their income on food, this number rises to 50 percent in less wealthy countries such as India or China.

16 Pierson, 76; see also Jannson.

17 Imig, 17. On OASDI, see Martin, 50.

18 US Census Bureau, "Historical Poverty Tables."

19 Whites and blacks unemployment data from US Department of Labor: Bureau of Labor Statistics. Below, Lipscomb quote in Moore, *The Official Fahrenheit 9/11 Reader*, 91.

20 Powell, 270–1.

21 See Franklin's classic *War Stars* (revised and expanded in 2008) for a detailed analysis of America's love affair with super weapons.

22 Zinn, *The Twentieth Century*, 348.

23 US Census Bureau, "The 2008 Statistical Abstract" (item 522 under Government Transfer Payments, Social Assistance); see also Rivlin and Sawhill, 17.

24 O'Rourke, *Parliament of Whores*, 176.

25 Both quotes from Zinn, *The Twentieth Century*, 354.

26 See *Uncovered: The Whole Truth About the War in Iraq*.

27 See Froomkin.

28 Douglass, 452.

29 Bibby and Maisel, 31–4.

30 Winpisinger, 179.

31 For precisely this reason, Republican-voting Connecticut Democrat Joe Lieberman lost the 2006 Democratic primaries, after which he was, reportedly, approached by the Republican Party with offers of help in his campaign for re-election. (He is now serving in the Senate as an independent).

32 Keefe, 173, 182. For recent patterns of nonvoting, see Gant and Lyons.

33 Poll data from Johnson and Aldrich, 221. On 24 March 2001, at the Gridiron Club dinner in Washington, D.C., George W. Bush improved on Lincoln with: "You can fool some of the people all the time, and those are the ones you want to concentrate on."

34 For contemporary illustrations, see "Illinois Republican Party"; also Cigler and Loomis (1998).

35 BBC News online, "Profile: Nancy Pelosi."

36 Riley, 59. A more up-to-date popular primer on traditional conservative civics and constitutional politics can be found in former presidential candidate Ron Paul's exceedingly readable manifesto, *The Revolution*.

37 Another noteworthy study in Chomsky's political canon – not only for its readable style and format but also for having briefly become the focus of an American-Venezuelan political spat – is *Hegemony or Survival*.

38 Both quotes in this paragraph from Grant, 74.

39 See *WashingtonPost.com*.

CHAPTER FOUR

1 See Coyne for a recent survey of American political films.

2 McIntosh, 57.

3 As Moore and Glynn report in *Adventures in a TV Nation*, *Canadian Bacon* "was deemed 'too political' by most of the executives who read it" (2).

4 McIntosh, 65.

5 Leverence, 314.

6 All quotes in this paragraph from Turley online.

7 See Giles and Hamilton, 48.

8 Both quotes in this paragraph from Hirschberg, 24.

9 Quirk of fate or not, Capra's grandson was the movie's co-producer. To be exact, Beatty is *Bulworth*'s co-writer, with Jeremy Pikser.

10 See Massood, 287.

11 For the quotations, see in the order of appearance: Klawans, 32; Simon, 64; Dreher, 045; Kauffman, 25; Ansen, 71.

12 All quotes in this and the next paragraph from *Studio Briefing.*

13 Hirschberg, 11; next quote, Hirschberg, 12. For an insightful study of Socialism in American, see Lipset and Marks, *It Didn't Happen Here: Why Socialism Failed in the United States* (2000).

14 Blum et al., *The National Experience: A History of the United States*, 131 (emphasis added).

15 The notable exception – James Allen and Lawrence Goodheart's reflections on corporate capitalism and hip-hop politics – is a short academic paper published, of all places, in the *Journal of American Studies of Turkey.*

16 For background, see any number of standard histories, such as Tindall and Emory; Brinkley; or Rozwenc and Bender, for a documentary history of socialism in America from the revolutionary war until 1919, see Fried .

17 Hirschberg, 53.

18 *Outfoxed*, back cover, first paragraph.

19 Dennis and Merrill, 156. For Domke, see "The Press, Race Relations, and Social Change."

20 Chang and Diaz-Veizades, 60.

21 Cannon, 383; see also Mike Davis, online, "Burning Too Few Illusions."

22 Smith and Seltzer, 123; also Martindale and Dunlap, esp. 128. Ratings data from Chang and Diaz-Veizades, 60.

23 Page 53. For more on the authoritarian makeover, see Swirski, "Betrization Is the Worst Solution."

24 Hirshberg, 24. For an example of how life imitates art, see BBC News Online, "Rap Star Attacks Bush at Benefit."

25 According to Al Gore, the number can easily reach 80 percent; quoted in Young, (2006). An estimate from Joe Hansen, 2004 member of the Political Action Committee of the then Senate Minority Leader, Tom Daschle, is 90%. For an incisive analysis of contemporary marketing strategies, consumer culture, political advertising and communication, see Berger, *Ads, Fads, and Consumer Culture.*

26 Stevenson, 10.

27 US Department of State, 5; see Robert C. Allen for a classic collection of contemporary television analysis.

28 Patterson, 73–5.

29 US Department of State, 3. See Berger, *Media Analysis Techniques*, for an updated edition of his classic textbook on media analysis techniques.

30 Kerbel, 85. For a brief but incisive analysis, see also Hallin .

31 Dennis and Merrill, 85.

32 US Department of State, 5.

CHAPTER FIVE

1 Orwell, "Politics and the English Language," 170.

2 BBC News Online, "US Used White Phosphorus in Iraq."

3 See Swirski, *I Sing the Body Politic*.

4 Compiled and published by former magistrate David Crombie in *The World's Stupidest Laws*.

5 Berlau online.

6 In Allen-Mills, 8.

7 Moore, *Stupid White Men*, 2004 edition (henceforth *Stupid*), xvi.

8 Zeitchik, 15.

9 Moore and Glynn, *Adventures in a TV Nation*, x.

10 Moore, et al., online (on day five the book was in its ninth printing). Sales data from McEvoy, 31; Moore, *Stupid*, x. Data for Moore in Germany from Zeitchick, 15.

11 Allen-Mills, 8.

12 Allen-Mills, 8.

13 Clive Davis, 4.

14 Bruckner, 19. For other critical voices from France, see Douin, Graminiés.

15 Hitchens online; while Hitchens has made his name as a leftist, these days his views often coincide with those of the right. Friedman quote online.

16 Dobbs online.

17 Briley, 11. The same concerns abide in 2009; see Headlam. Below, Hardy and Clarke quote is the title of their chapter 2. Their labelling Moore as *the* voice of the left is as misleading and self-serving as comments by Larner; see Malanowski.

18 Hardy and Clarke, 40–1.

19 Data from T.C. Davis, et al, 96–7; and Cole, 16.

20 The "merit" of Hardy and Clarke's argument becomes apparent in their *non sequitur* to this assertion: "Moore loves the cap lock key more than anyone outside a jail cell," 41.

21 Moore, *Stupid*, 104. Buttressing his point, by 2005 a Congressman's salary was up by $17,000; average teacher's salary by less

than $5,500; data from Associated Press and CRS Report for Congress.

22 See American Federation of Teachers online.

23 Sanchez online; Kauffman, A19.

24 In Flesher, D6. Below, George Bush attack in Kasindorf and Keen, A.01.

25 All quotations in this paragraph from Blair online.

26 Hardy and Clarke, 11.

27 Hardy and Clarke, 39; same paragraph, Hitler quote, 37.

28 Hardy and Clarke, 13; the GM profits example also on 13.

29 Hardy and Clarke, 50; next quote, 50.

30 Both citations from Moore in this paragraph are from the original 2002 edition of *Stupid*. The revised 2004 edition corrects the first error by removing the reference to 2001 and changes "four" to "five" years (without correcting the error) in the second example.

31 Nolley, 15.

32 Larner, 6.

33 Larner substitutes "Union" for "Nation" as the final word of Moore's title on page 193; see also Malanowski's superb review of Larner's book.

34 Larner, 67.

35 Some of Kopel's points are, indeed, followed by what appear to be brief summaries of Moore's responses/rebuttals.

36 Ebert, 5.

37 Ebert, 5. Same paragraph, next sentence, Larner, 69. For a comprehensive analysis of the methodological and epistemological issues of representation and reduction, see Swirski, *Of Literature and Knowledge*.

38 Grierson, 13; following quotes: Ward 8; Bruzzi, 154; Nichols, 102. Less plausibly, Carl Plantinga goes as far as to maintain that there is "no necessary realism or resemblance between the nonfiction work and actuality," 18.

39 In Jacobson, 23.

40 Jacobson, 23.

41 Implicitly acknowledging the allegation, the 2004 edition of *Stupid White Men* (34) thanks Kirsten Selberg for the list of Bush's ruinous actions in office and directs readers to her original website; see also Hume.

42 Fox News, "Moore: 'Bush Didn't Tell the Truth.'"

43 Rich, 15.

44 Quoted in Macfarquhar, 134. Next quote in the same paragraph, Street-Porter, 22.

45 Hardy and Clarke, 112. Horton example in Larner, 136–7.
46 Moore, "My Oscar 'Backlash.'"
47 Blair.
48 Thoreau's work is better known as *Civil Disobedience.*
49 Kurtz, C01.
50 In Gavin Smith, 26.
51 McEvoy, 30–1.

CONCLUSION

1 On the American empire, see Paul Kennedy, Lefever, Burbach and
   Tarbell, Ferguson, Robin, Mann, Lieber, David and Grondin, Tony
   Smith, Swirski, "Literature as History."
2 Fiorina, 3.
3 Popkin, 35.
4 Larner, 185. Same paragraph, next quote in Young online.
5 In fact the only country to use chemical WMDs in Iraq is the United
   States; see BBC News Online, "US Used White Phosphorus in Iraq."
   The WMD saga can now be viewed on film: *Uncovered: The Whole
   Truth About the War in Iraq* (2004); Iraq WMD example in *Time
   Europe,* 12.
6 BBC News Online, "U.S. Senate Halts F-22 Jet Funding."
7 For more on Swiss democracy in the context of social engineering,
   see Swirski, *American Eutopia and Social Engineering*, chapter 2.
8 Mike Davis's Epilogue to *Prisoners of the American Dream* dis-
   turbingly anticipates the content of this paragraph.
9 In Chrisafis and Tilden. In this context, former criminal prosecutor
   Vincent Bugliosi's case-building study, *The Prosecution of George
   W. Bush for Murder*, is essential reading.

Works Cited

Aaron, Daniel. *Writers on the Left*. New York: Harcourt Brace and World, 1961.

Abernathy, Ralph. "Equal Protection Clause." *The Encyclopedia of Civil Rights in America. Vol 1*. Armonk, NY: Sharpe Reference, 1998.

Abron, JoNina M. "'Serving the People': The Survival Program of the Black Panther Party." In Jeffries, Judson L., et al. *The Black Panther Party [reconsidered]*. Baltimore: Black Classic Press, 1998. 177–92.

Abu-Jamal, Mumia. "A Life in the Party: An Historical and Retrospective Examination of the Projections and Legacies of the Black Panther Party." *Liberation, Imagination, and the Black Panther Party*. New York: Routledge, 2001.

Agha, Hussein, and Robert Malley. "The Road from Mecca." *Times Literary Supplement* 44, 8 (10 May 2007): 43–6.

A Huey P. Newton Story. Dir. Spike Lee. Black Starz! 2001.

Aitken, Jonathan. *Nixon, a Life*. Washington, DC: Regnery, 1993.

Allen, James, and Lawrence Goodheart. "*Bulworth*: The Hip-Hop Nation Confronts Corporate Capitalism." *Journal of American Studies of Turkey* 8 (1998): 73–80.

Allen, Robert C. *Channels of Discourse, Reassembled: Television and Contemporary Criticism*. London: Routledge, 1992.

Allen-Mills, Tony. "Capitalism Sucks, and I'm Going to Getya Dubya." *Sunday Times,* 14 April 2002, 8.

Alleva, Richard. "Beatty's Courage? 'Bulworth.'" *Commonweal,* 19 June 1998, 16–17.

Ambrose, Stephen E. *Nixon: The Education of a Politician, 1913–1962*. New York: Simon and Schuster, 1987.

American Civil Liberties Union. "ACLU of Massachusetts Condemns Censorship of 'Bowling for Columbine' at Local High School," 7 April 2003.
http://www.aclu.org/freespeech/censorship/11174prs20030407.html

American Federation of Teachers. "Funding." 2005.
http://www.aft.org/topics/nclb/funding.htm. 2 February 2007.

Andersen, Marie. "National History/Transnational Themes: Inaugural

Themes and American Mythology." In Duncan, Russell, and Clara
Juncker, eds. *Transnational America: Contours of National Modern
US Culture.* Copenhagen: Museum Tusculanum Press, 2004.

Ansen, David. "The Arts Shock to the System." *Newsweek,* 18 May
1998, 70–1.

Associated Press. "Teachers Paid an Average Salary of $46,752, Survey
Finds." *USA Today,* 25 June 2005. http://www.usatoday.com/news/
nation/2005-06-25-teacher-salary-raise_x.htm

Auden, W. H. "The Poet and the City." In Cook, Jon, ed. *Poetry in The-
ory: An Anthology 1900–2000,* 378–84. Oxford: Blackwell, 2004.

Aufhauser, David D. "Written Testimony of David D. Aufhauser, Gen-
eral Counsel, Before the House Financial Services Committee Subcom-
mittee on Oversight and Investigations September 24, 2003 – 10:00
AM, The United States House of Representatives." *Press Room: From
the Office of Public Affairs* 24 September 2003. http://www.ustreas.
gov/press/releases/js758.htm

Bauer, Monica. "Best Chance Since Watergate: Campaign Finance Re-
form in the 105th Congress." In Scheele, Paul E., ed. "*We Get What
We Vote For – or Do We?*": The Impact of Elections on Governing,
112–30. Westport, CN: Praeger, 1999.

BBC News Online. "Penn Says Movies Ignore Politics." 18 May 2004.
http://news.bbc.co.uk/2/hi/entertainment/3723925.stm Accessed 18
May 2004

– "Rap Star Attacks Bush at Benefit." 3 September 2005.
http://news.bbc.co.uk/2/hi/entertainment/4210808.stm Accessed 3
September 2005

– "US Used White Phosphorus in Iraq." 16 November 2005.
http://news.bbc.co.uk/2/hi/middle_east/4440664.stm Accessed 16
November 2005

– "Profile: Nancy Pelosi." 2 November 2006.
http://news.bbc.co.uk/2/hi/americas/6107062.stm Accessed 2
November 2006

– "US War Costs 'Could Hit $811bn.'" 28 April 2006.
http://news.bbc.co.uk/2/hi/business/4955418.stm. Accessed 28 April
2006

– "US Senate Halts F-22 Jet Funding." 22 July 2009.
http://news.bbc.co.uk/2/hi/americas/8162106.stm. Accessed 22 July
2009

Beard, Charles Austin. *An Economic Interpretation of the Constitution
of the United States.* New York, NY: Dover, 2004. (Orig. 1913).

Belknap, Micheal R. "The Mechanics of Repression: J. Edgar Hoover,
The Bureay of Investigations, and the Radicals 1917–1925." *Crime
and Social Justice* (Spring/Summer 1977).

Benson, George. *Political Corruption in America*. Lexington, MA: Heath, 1978.

Berger, Arthur Asa. *Ads, Fads, and Consumer Culture: Advertising's Impact on American Character and Society*. 3rd ed. New York: Rowman & Littlefield, 2007.

– *Media Analysis Techniques*. Thousand Oaks, CA: Sage, 2005.

Berges, Marshall. "Irving Wallace – A Good Ear for Words." *Los Angeles Times*, 27 Jan.1985, 1; 6.

Berlau, John. "Hog Wild: Stupid Ways States Waste Money." *Reader's Digest* (April 2004). http://www.rd.com/content/openContent. do?contentId=26729 Accessed 15 May 2004.

Beyer, Lisa. "Why the Middle East Crisis Isn't Really About Terrorism." *Time*, 7–14 August 2006, 14–18.

Bibby, John F., and L. Sandy Maisel. *Two Parties – or More? The American Party System*. Boulder, CO: Westview Press, 1998.

Blackstock, Nelson. *COINTELPRO: The FBI's Secret War on Political Freedom*. New York: Vintage, 1975.

Blair, Tim. "Sometimes Moore Is Less." *Fox News*, 22 March 2002. http://www.foxnews.com/story/0%2C2933%2C48562%2C00.html Accessed 30 July 2006

Blinder, Alan S. *The Quiet Revolution*. New Haven, CT: Yale University Press, 2004.

Bloom, Alexandra, and Breines, Wini, eds. *Takin' It to the Streets: A Sixties Reader*. New York: Oxford University Press, 1995.

Blotner, Joseph. *The Political Novel*. New York: Doubleday, 1956.

– *The Modern American Political Novel*. Austin: University of Texas Press, 1966.

Blum, John M., et al. *The National Experience: A History of the United States*. Forth Worth: Harcourt Brace Jovanovich, 1993.

Books and Writers. "Richard (Thomas) Condon (1915–1996)." (2002). http://www.kirjasto.sci.fi/condon.htm. Accessed 17 April 2008.

Boyd, Herb. "Focus Shifts to Black Panthers." *New Amsterdam News* 91, 17 (27 April 2000): 5.

Brandes, Stuart D. *Warhogs: A History of War Profits in America*. Lexington, KY: University Press of Kentucky, 1997.

Braudy, Leo. "*Winter Kills; By Richard Condon*." *New York Times Book Review*, 26 May 1974, BR5.

Briley, Ron. "*Fahrenheit 9/11*: Michael Moore Heats It Up." *Historians Film Committee: Special Report* 35, 2 (2005): 11–12.

Brinkley, Alan. *The Unfinished Nation: A Concise History of the American People*. Boston, MA: McGraw-Hill, 2000.

Brock, David. "Missing the Joke – *Parliament of Whores*." *Commentary* 92, 4 (1991): 57–8.

Brodie, Fawn M. *Richard Nixon: The Shaping of His Character*. Cambridge, MA: Harvard University Press, 1981.

Brown, Elaine. *A Taste of Power: A Black Woman's Story*. New York: Anchor, 1993.

Brownlow, Kevin. *Behind the Mask of Innocence*. London: Jonathan Cape, 1990.

Bruckner, Pascal. "Paris Dispatch: Tour de Farce." *New Republic* 231, 3 (19 July 2004): 19–20.

Bruzzi, Stella. *New Documentary: A Critical Introduction*. London: Routledge, 2000.

Bryson, Alex, and Stephen McKay, eds. *Is It Worth Working?* London: PSI Publishing, 1994.

Bugliosi, Vincent. *The Prosecution of George W. Bush for Murder*. Cambridge, MA: Vanguard, 2008.

Bukhari-Alston, Safiya. "We Too Are Veterans: Post-traumatic Stress Disorders and the Black Panther Party." *The Black Panther* (Feb 1991).

Bulworth. Dir. Warren Beatty. 20th Century Fox. 1998.

Burbach, Roger, and Jim Tarbell. *Imperial Overstretch: George W. Bush and the Hubris of Empire*. London, New York: Zed Books, 2004.

Byman, Daniel. *Deadly Connections: States that Sponsor Terrorism*. Cambridge: Cambridge University Press, 2005.

Caldicott, Helen. *The New Nuclear Danger: George W. Bush's Military-Industrial Complex*. New York: New Press, 2004.

Canby, Vincent. "Irving Wallace's 'The Man': Political Movie Stars James Earl Jones." *New York Times*, 20 July 1972, 26.

Cannon, Lou. *Official Negligence: How Rodney King and the Riot Changed Los Angeles and the LAPD*. New York: Times Books, 1997.

Carr, Robert. *Black Nationalism in the New World: Reading the African-American and West Indian Experience (Latin America Otherwise)*. Charleston, NC: Duke University Press, 2002.

Chandler, Raymond. "The Simple Art of Murder." *Later Novels and Other Writings*, 977–92. New York: Library of America, 1995.

Chang, Edward, and Jeanette Diaz-Veizades. *Ethnic Peace in the American City: Building Community in Los Angeles and Beyond*. New York: New York University Press, 1999.

Chomsky, Noam. *The Chomsky Quartet*. New York: Odonian Press, 2002.

– *Hegemony or Survival: America's Quest for Global Dominance*. New York: Henry Holt and Company, 2003.

– "Anarchy in the U.S.A." *The Noam Chomsky Website*. http://www.chomsky.info/interviews/19920528.htm Accessed 16 August 2006.

Chrisafis, Angelique, and Imogen Tilden. "Pinter Blasts 'Nazi America' and 'Deluded Idiot' Blair." *Guardian,* 11 June (2003). http://arts.guardian.co.uk/news/story/0,11711,975050,00.html Accessed 11 June 2003

Churchill, Ward. "To Disrupt, Discredit and Destroy: The FBI's Secret War against the Black Panther Party." In Cleaver, Kathleen, and George Katsiaficas, eds. *Liberation, Imagination, and the Black Panther Party,* 78–117. New York: Routledge, 2001.

Cigler, Allan J., and Burdett A. Loomis, eds. *Interest Group Politics.* Washington, DC: CQ Press, 1998.

Cleaver, Kathleen, and George Katsiaficas. *Liberation, Imagination and the Black Panther Party: A New Look at the Panthers and Their Legacy.* New York: Routledge, 2001.

Clemons, Michael L., and Charles E. Jones. "Global Solidarity: The Black Panther Party in the International Arena." In Cleaver, Kathleen, and George Katsiaficas, eds. *Liberation, Imagination, and the Black Panther Party* 20–39. New York: Routledge, 2001.

Clowers, Myles L., and Lorin Letendre. *Understanding American Politics Through Fiction.* New York: McGraw-Hill, 1973.

Cochran, David. *America Noir: Underground Writers and Filmmakers of the Postwar Era.* Washington, DC: Smithsonian, 2000.

Cohen, Nick. *What's Left? How Liberals Lost Their Way.* London: Fourth Estate, 2007.

Cohen, Roger. "The Media Business: The Atlantic Monthly Press Is Sold Out to One of Its Editors." *New York Times,* 30 Aug. 1991: Biography 1.

Cole, M.R. "The High Risk of Low Health Literacy." *Nursing Spectrum* 13 (15 May 2000): 16.

Collins, Chuck, and Felice Yeskel. *Economic Apartheid in America: A Primer on Economic Inequality and Insecurity.* New York: New Press, 2005.

Collins, Chuck, Chris Hartman, and Holly Sklar. "Divided Decade: Economic Disparity at the Century's Turn." *United for a Fair Economy,* 15 December 1999. http://www.faireconomy.org/press/archive/1999/Divided_Decade/divided_decade.html Accessed 12 June 2006

Condon, Richard. *And Then We Moved to Rossenarra.* New York: Dell, 1973.

– *Winter Kills.* New York: Dell, 1974.

– *The Whisper of the Axe.* New York: Dell, 1976.

– *Death of a Politician.* New York: Ballantine, 1978.

– *A Trembling Upon Rome.* New York: Pinnacle, 1983.

Cox, Ronald W., and Daniel Skidmore-Hess. *U.S. Politics and the*

Global Economy: Corporate Power, Conservative Shift. Boulder: Lynne Rienner, 1999.

Coyne, Michael. *Hollywood Goes to Washington: American Politics on Screen.* London: Reaktion Books, 2008.

Crombie, David. *The World's Stupidest Laws.* London: Michael O'Mara Books, 2000.

CRS Report for Congress. 18 April 2006. http://www.senate.gov/reference/resources/pdf/97-1011.pdf Accessed 1 September 2006

David, Charles-Philippe, and David Grondin. *Hegemony or Empire? The Redefinition of US Power under George W. Bush.* Aldershot, England: Ashgate, 2006.

Davis, Clive. "Not So Stupid White Men Fight Back." *The Times,* 18 June 2003, 4.

Davis, Mike. "Burning Too Few Illusions." *Left Turn Magazine.* http://www.leftturn.org/Articles/Viewer.aspx?id=366&type=M. Accessed 15 July 2006

– *City of Quartz: Excavating the Future in Los Angeles. New edition.* New York: Verso, 2006. (Orig. 1990).

– *Prisoners of the American Dream.* New York: Verso, 1986.

Davis, Richard, and Diana Owen. *New Media and American Politics.* New York: Oxford University Press, 1998.

Davis, T. C., et al. "Health Literacy, Part 1: How Poor Literacy Leads to Poor Health Care." *Patient Care* 30 (15 Oct. 1996): 96–7.

Dean, John W. *Worse than Watergate: The Secret Presidency of George W. Bush.* New York: Little, Brown, and Co., 2004.

Debs, Eugene V. "The American Movement." In Writing and Speeches of Eugene V. Debs. New York: Hermitage, 1948.

Deneen, Patrick J., and Joseph Romance, eds. *Reading America: On the Art of Reading Politically and Reading Political Art.* Lanham, MD: Rowman and Littlefield, 2005.

Denning, Michael. *The Cultural Front: The Laboring of American Culture in the Twentieth Century.* London: Verso, 1996.

Dennis, Everette E., and John C. Merrill. *Media Debates: Great Issues for the Digital Age.* Australia: Wadsworth Publishing, 2002.

Dickstein, Morris. *A Mirror in the Roadway: Literature and the Real World.* Princeton, NJ: Princeton University Press, 2005.

Dobbs, Lou. "Lou Dobbs Moneyline: Suicide Bomber Kills Six in Middle East; Venezuelan President Ousted." *Cnn.com* 12 April 2002. http://transcripts.cnn.com/TRANSCRIPTS/0204/12/mlld.oo.html Accessed 12 April 2002

Doctorow, Edgar Lawrence. "E.L. Doctorow, Novelist." In Flowers, Betty Sue. *A World of Ideas: Conversations with Thoughtful Men and*

Women about American Life Today and the Ideas Shaping Our Future, 83–95. New York: Doubleday, 1989.

Domke, David. "The Press, Race Relations, and Social Change." *Journal of Communication* (June 2001): 317–45.

Doss, Erika. "Revolutionary Art Is a Tool for Liberation: Emory Douglas and Protest Aesthetics at the *Black Panther*." In Cleaver, Kathleen, and George Katsiaficas, eds. *Liberation, Imagination, and the Black Panther Party*, 175–87. New York: Routledge, 2001.

Douglass, Frederick. *My Bondage and My Freedom*. New York: Auburn, Miller, Orton, & Co., 1857. Expanded as *Life and Times of Frederic Douglass; Written by Himself*. Hartford, CT: Park Pub. Co., 1881. Reprint: Secaucus, NJ: Citadel Press, 1983.

Douin, Jean-Luc. "La croisade anti-Bush d'un justicier cineaste." *Le Monde* 7 July 2004, 16.

Dowell, Pat, et al. "Warren Beatty's Bulworth: Will the Real Bulworth Please Stand Up?" *Cineaste* 24 (1998): 6–8.

Dreher, Rod. "A Load of 'Bulworth'; It's All a Lot of Bulworth." *New York Post*, 15 May 1998, 45.

Drew, Elizabeth. *Politics and Money*. New York: Macmillan, 1983.

Ebert, Roger. "The Cheapest Shots Attacks on 'Roger & Me' Completely Miss Point of Film." *Chicago Sun-Times*, 11 February 1990, 5.

Edwards, Thomas. "Terror in Freedonia." *New York Review of Books* 26, 4, 8 February (1979): 33–6.

Edwards, Thomas R. *Over Here: Criticizing America 1968–1989*. New Brunswick, NJ: Rutgers University Press, 1991.

Emery, Fred. *Watergate: The Corruption of American Politics and the Fall of Richard Nixon*. New York: Simon & Schuster, 1995.

Empires – The Medici: Godfathers of the Renaissance. DeVillier Donegan Enterprizes/Lion Television, (2004).

Estulin, Daniel. *The True Story of the Bilderberg Group*. Trine Day, 2009.

Fallow, James. "Rational Lampoon; Finally, P.J. O'Rourke Breaks from the Right-wing Bad Boys." *Washington Monthly* 23, 7–8 (1991): 54–7.

Ferguson, Niall. *Colossus: The Price of America's Empire*. New York: Penguin, 2004.

Finkle, Paul, and Peter Wallenstein. *The Encyclopedia of American Political History*. Washington: CCQ Press, 2001.

Fiorina, Morris P. *Retrospective Voting in American National Elections*. New Haven, CT: Yale University Press, 1981.

Fish, Stanley. *Professional Correctness: Literary Studies and Political Change*. New York: Oxford University Press, 1995.

Flescher, John. "Moore Turns Grim Grin on Terrorism." *The Gazette*, 30 Jan. 2004, D6.

Flynn, Dan. "Master of Deceit." *FrontPageMagazine.com*, 3 June 2003. http://www.frontpagemag.com/articles/Printable.asp?ID=8145 Accessed12 June 2006

Foley, Barbara. *Radical Representations: Politics and Form in U.S. Proletarian Fiction, 1929–1941*. Durham: Duke University Press, 1993.

Folkart, Burt A. "Irving Wallace Prolific Writer Reached Billion Readers." *Los Angeles Times*, 30 June 1990, A38-9.

Foner, Eric, ed. *The Black Panthers Speak*. New York: Da Capo, 1995.

Ford Foundation. *The Common Good: Social Welfare and the American Future*. San Diego: Ford Foundation, 1989.

Fox News. "Moore: 'Bush Didn't Tell the Truth.'" *FoxNews.com*. 29 July 2004. http://www.foxnews.com/story/0,2933,127236,00.html Accessed 29 July 2004

Franken, Al. *Rush Limbaugh Is a Big Fat Idiot and Other Observations*. New York: Dell, 1999.

– *Lies and the Lying Liars Who Tell Them: A Fair and Balanced Look at the Right*. London, New York: Plume, 2004.

– *The Truth (With Jokes)*. New York: Dutton, 2005.

Franklin, H. Bruce. *War Stars: The Superweapon and the American Imagination*. Amherst: University of Massachusetts Press, 2008.

Fried, Albert, ed. *Socialism in American from the Shakers to the Third International: A Documentary History*. New York: Columbia University Press, 1993.

Friedman, Roger. "Fahrenheit 9/11 Gets Standing Ovation." *FoxNews.15* June 2004. http://www.foxnews.com/story/0,2933, 122680,00.html Accessed 15 June 2004

Frisken, Amanda. *Victoria Woodhull's Sexual Revolution: Political Theater and the Popular Press in Nineteenth-century America*. Philadelphia: University of Pennsylvania Press, 2004.

Fritz, Ben. "One Moore Stupid White Man." *Salon.com*, 3 April 2002. http://dir.salon.com/story/politics/col/spinsanity/2002/04/03/moore/index.html?pn=1 Accessed 1 September 2006

Froomkin, Dan. "The Amazing Disappearing Trust Fund." *Washington-Post.com*, 11 February 2005. http://www.washintonpost.com/wp-dyn/articles/A16984-2005Feb11 Accessed 11 February 2005

Furgurson, Ernest B. "Nightmare of Nixon on TV Wasn't a Dream." *Los Angeles Times*, 4 December 1978. section 2:7.

Furst, Alan. "Introduction." In Greene, Graham. *The Ministry of Fear*. London: Penguin, 2005.

Gant, Michael M., and William Lyons. "Democratic Theory, Nonvoting, and Public Policy: The 1972–1988 Presidential Elections." *American Politics Quarterly* 21, 2 (1993): 185–204.

Garren, Samuel B. "'He Had Passion': William Attaway's Screenplay

Drafts of Irving Wallace's *The Man.*" *College Language Association Journal* 37 (March 1994, 245–60.

Geer, John G. *In Defense of Negativity: Attack Ads in Presidential Campaigns.* Chicago: Chicago University Press, 2006.

Genovese, Michael A. *The Watergate Crisis.* Westport, CT: Greenwood Press, 1999.

Ghosh, Nibir K. *Calculus of Power: Modern American Political Novel.* New Delhi: Creative Books, 1997.

Giles, Jeff, and Kendall Hamilton. "The Joys of Summer." *Newsweek,* 11 May 1998, 46–50.

Gold, Herbert. "Pop Goes the Novel." *New York Times Book Review,* 12 March 1978, 10, 39.

Goldberg, Bernard. *100 People Who Are Screwing Up America (And Al Franken is #37).* New York: HarperCollins, 2005.

Goldberg, Danny. "Hip Con – *Parliament of Whores: A Lone Humorist Attempts to Explain the Entire U.S. Government.*" *The Nation* 254, 24 (1992): 866–8.

Goldin, Claudia, and Gary D. Libecap, eds. *The Regulated Economy: A Historical Approach to Political Economy.* Chicago: Chicago University Press, 1994.

Goodrich, Chris. "P.W. Interviews: P.J. O'Rourke." *Publishers Weekly* 239 (1992): 60–1.

Graminiès, Clément. "Fahrenheit 9/11: The Totalitarianism of Michael Moore." Newropean Magazine, 21 July 2004. http://66.218.71.231/language/translation/translatedPage.php?tt=url& text=http%3a//newropeans-magazine.org/index.php%3foption=com_ content%26task=view%26id=1294%26Itemid=90&lp=fr_en&.intl=u s&fr=yfp-t-501 Accessed 15 July 2006

Grant, Thomas. "The 'Funny Republican:' P.J. O'Rourke and the Graying of Boomer Humor." In Sloane, David E.E., ed. *New Directions in American Humor.* Tuscaloosa: University of Alabama Press, 1998.

Greene, Richard Allen. "US Election Ads: Hitting Below the Belt." BBC News Online, 30 October 2006. http://news.bbc.co.uk/2/hi/ americas/6085922.stm Accessed 30 October 2006

Gregory, Mark. "The Baghdad Billions." BBC World Service, 9–10 November 2006. See also: http://news.bbc.co.uk/2/hi/middle_east/612 9612.stm and http://news.bbc.co.uk/2/hi/middle_east/6132688.stm Accessed 2 February 2009

Grierson, John. "First Principles of Documentary." In Hardy, Forsyth. *Grierson on Documentary.* Los Angeles: University of California Press, 1966.

Griffin, C.W. "Warren Beatty Is Trying to Say Something." *New York Times,* 31 May 1998. 14.

Gunning, Jeroen. *Hamas in Politics: Democracy, Religion, Violence.* New York: Columbia University Press, Hurst, 2008.

Gussow, Mel. "Richard Condon, Political Novelist, Dies at 81." *New York Times,* 10 April 1996, A16.

Halberstam, David. *War in a Time of Peace.* New York: Scribner, 2001.

Hallin, Daniel C. "Whose Campaign Is It, Anyway?" *Columbia Journalism Review* 29,5 (Jan/Feb 1991): 43–6.

Hanne, Michael. *The Power of the Story: Fiction and Political Change.* New York: Berghahn Books, 1994.

Hansen, Joe. Digital Video Conference on the US Presidential Election Campaign. United States Consulate General. 10 April 2004.

Harbutt, Fraser J. *The Cold War Era.* Malden, MA: Blackwell, 2002.

Hardt, Michael, and Antonio Negri. *Empire.* Cambridge, MA: Harvard University Press, 2000.

Hardy, David T., and Jason Clarke. *Michael Moore Is a Big Fat Stupid White Man.* New York: ReganBooks, 2004.

Harris, Leon. *Upton Sinclair: American Rebel.* New York: Crowell, 1975.

Harwood, Richard. "Hooked on the Lure of Ludlum." *Washington Post,* 23 March 1980, 3.

Headlam, Bruce. "Rabble-rousing as an Art Form." *International Herald Tribune,* 19–20 Sept. 2009, 11–12.

Hirschberg, Lynn. "Warren Beatty Is Trying to Say Something." *New York Times Magazine,* 10 May 1998, 20–5, 38–40, 53, 62–3.

Hitchens, Christopher. "Unfairenheit 9/11: The Lies of Michael Moore." *Slate.com.* 21 June 2004. http://www.slate.com/id/2102723/ Accessed 2 February 2007

Hofstadter, Richard. *The Paranoid Style in American Politics and Other Essays.* New York: Vintage, 1967.

Horsley, Lee. *Political Fiction and the Historical Imagination.* Basingstoke: Macmillan, 1990.

Howe, Irving. *Politics and the Novel.* Freeport, NY: Book for Libraries Press, 1970. (Orig. 1957).

Huffington, Arianna. *Pigs at the Trough: How Corporate Greed and Political Corruption are Undermining America.* New York: Crown, 2003.

Hume, Brit. "Special Report W/Brit Hume: Arafat's Power Still Strong." *Fox News.com,* 12 April 2002. http://www.foxnews.com/story/0%2C2933%2C50152%2C00.html Accessed 12 April 2002

Hutcheon, Linda. *The Politics of Postmodernism.* 2nd ed. London, New York: Routledge, 2002.

Hutton, Will. "Why America's Richest Love Taxes." *Observer,* 25 Feb 2001. http://observer.guardian.co.uk/comment/story/0,6903,442 671,00.html Accessed 17 October 2005

Illinois Republican Party. "Blagojevich Solicits Inaugural Donors." http://www.ilgop.org/demwatch/contentview.asp?c=3593 Accessed 30 December 2005

Imig, Douglas R. *Poverty and Power: The Political Representation of Poor Americans.* Lincoln: University of Nebraska Press, 1996.

Jacobson, Harlan. "Michael & Me." *Film Comment* 25, 6 (Nov 1989): 16–26.

Jannson, Bruce S. *The Reluctant Welfare State: American Social Welfare Policies: Past, Present and Future.* Belmont, CA: Thomson, 2005.

Jeffries, Judson L. "Black Radicalism and Political Repression in Baltimore: The Case of the Black Panther Party." *Ethnic and Racial Studies* 25, 1 (Jan. 2002): 64–98.

Jeffries, Judson L., et al. *The Black Panther Party [Reconsidered].* Black Classic Press, 1998.

Jennings, Billy X. "P.O.V. – A Panther in Africa. Black Panthers Today. Billy X. Jennings." *American Documentary,* 21 Sept. 2004. http://www.pbs.org/pov/pov2004/apantherinafrica/special_today_ jennings.html Accessed 18 July 2006.

Johnson, Paul E., and John H. Aldrich. *American Government.* US: Houghton Mifflin, 1990.

Johnston, David Cay. "Corporate Wealth Share Rises for Top-Income Americans." *New York Times,* 29 Jan. 2006, 1:22.

Johnston, Michael. *Political Corruption and Public Policy in America.* Monterey: Brooks/Cole Publishing, 1982.

Jones, Charles E. "'Talkin' the Talk and Walkin' the Walk': An Interview with Panther Jimmy Slater." In Jeffries, Judson L., et al. *The Black Panther Party [reconsidered].* Black Classic Press, 1998. 147–56.

Jones, James Earl. "Introduction." In Wallace, Irving. *The Man,* vii–xi. New York: ibooks, 1999.

Kasindorf, Martin, and Judy Keen. "'Fahrenheit 9/11': Will It Change Any Voter's Mind?" *USA Today,* 25 June 2004, A.01.

Katsiaficas, George. "The Case of the Black Panther Party and the Revolutionary People's Constitutional Convention of 1970." In Cleaver, Kathleen, and George Katsiaficas, eds. *Liberation, Imagination, and the Black Panther Party* 141–55. New York: Routledge, 2001.

Kaufman, Marc. "FY 2007 Budget Proposal: Agency-by-Agency Breakdown Domestic Programs Take the Hit: Budget Would Increase Security Spending but Cut or Curb 141 Programs." *Washington Post,* 7 February 2006, A19.

Kauffmann, Stanley. "Color Lines." *New Republic,* 8 June 1998, 24–5.

Keefe, William J. *Parties, Politics, and Public Policy in America.* Washington, DC: CQ Press, 1998.

Keener, John F. *Biography and the Postmodern Historical Novel.* Lewiston, NY: E. Mellen Press, 2001.

Kelley, Robin D. G. *Race Rebels: Culture, Politics, and the Black Working Class.* New York: Free Press, 1994.

Kemme, Thomas J. *Patterns of Power in American Political Fiction.* Lanham, MD: University Press of America, 2003.

Kennedy, Dan. "The Sixth Annual Muzzle Awards: Ten Who Undermined Freedom of Speech and Personal Liberties." *The Phoenix.com,* 4–10 July 2003. www.bostonphoenix.com/boston/news_features/top/features/documents/02990201.htm Accessed 29 April 2006

Kennedy, Paul. *The Rise and Fall of the Great Powers: Economic Change and Military Conflict from 1500–2000.* New York: Vintage, 1989.

Kerbel, Matthew Robert. "The Media: Viewing the Campaign Through a Strategic Haze." In Nelson, Michael. *The Elections of 1996,* 81–105. Washington, DC: CQ Press, 1997.

Kessler, Glenn, and Mike Allen. "Bush Faces Increasingly Poor Image Overseas." *Washington Post,* 24 February 2003, A01.

Klawans, Stuart. "Bulworth *Life of Jesus* The Last Days of Disco." *Nation,* 15–22 June 1998, 32–5.

Klein, Naomi. *The Shock Doctrine.* London: Penguin, 2007.

Koch, Edward I. "Koch: Moore's Propaganda Film Cheapens Debate, Polarizes Nation." *World Tribune,* 29 June 2004. www.worldtribune.com/worldtribune/WTARC/2004/guest_koch_6_28.html Accessed 29 June 2004

Kopel, David. "Fifty-nine Deceits in Fahrenheit 9/11." 12 November 2004. http://www.davekopel.com/Terror/Fiftysix-Deceits-in-Fahrenheit-911.htm Accessed 12 June 2006

Kramer, Michael, and Sam Roberts. *"I Never Wanted to Be Vice-president of Anything!" An Investigative Biography of Nelson Rockefeller.* New York: Basic, 1973.

Kurtz, Howard. "Moore's Spin Spotlights Revolving Doors." *Washington Post.* 6 Sept. 6 2004, C01.

Larner, Jesse. *Forgive Us Our Spins: Michael Moore and the Future of the Left.* Hoboken, NJ: John Wiley & Sons, 2006.

Lasky, Victor. *It Didn't Start with Watergate.* New York: Dutton, 1977.

Layman, Richard, ed. *American Decades 1960–1969.* Detroit: Gale, 1994.

Lefever, Ernest W. *America's Imperial Burden: Is the Past Prologue?* Boulder: Westview Press, 1999.

Leggett, Karby. "One Man's Zeal Typifies How Hamas Is Evolving into Gaza Political Force; Activist Once Imprisoned for Violence Remains on the Case Through Aid Job; Filling a Void Left by Arafat." *Asian Wall Street Journal,* 22 April 2004, A1.

Lehmann-Haupt, Christopher. "Behind the Assassination." *New York Times,* 24 May 1974, 31.

Leverence, John. *Irving Wallace: A Writer's Profile.* With an Introduction by Jerome Weidman, and interview by Sam L. Grogg, Jr., and an afterword by Ray B. Browne. Bowling Green, OH: Popular Press, 1974.

Levine, Michael L. *African Americans and Civil Rights, From 1619 to Present.* Phoenix, AZ: Oryx, 1996.

Levitt, Matthew. "Moderately Deadly: Yassin's Long History of Terror." *National Review Online,* 26 March 2004. http://www.nationalreview.com/comment/levitt200403261126.aspz Accessed 6 July 2006.

Levy, Peter B. *The Civil Rights Movement.* Westport, CN: Greenwood, 1998.

Lewis, Chester, et al. *Watergate: The Full Inside Story.* New York: Ballantine, 1973.

Lewis, Justin, Sut Jhally, and Michael Morgan. "The Gulf War: A Study of the Media, Public Opinion and Public Knowledge." The Center for the Study of Communication, University of Massachusetts, Amherst. 1 April 2004. http://www.umass.edu/communication/resources/special_reports/gulf_war/index.shtml Accessed 12 June 2006

Lieber, Robert J. *The American Era: Power and Strategy for the 21st Century.* Cambridge: Cambridge University Press, 2005.

Lingeman, Richard R. "Happy Irving Wallace Day." *New York Times,* 15 March 1972, 45.

Lingeman, Richard. "A Thriller of the Condon Class." *New York Times,* 21 May 1976, 80.

Lipset, Seymour Martin, and Gary Marks. *It Didn't Happen Here: Why Socialism Failed in the United States.* New York: Norton, 2000.

Lowenkopf, Shelley. "CONDON, Richard (Thomas)." In Henderson, Lesley, ed. *Twentieth-century Crime and Mystery Writers.* 3 rd ed. Chicago, London: St James Press, 1991.

Ludlum, Robert. *Trevayne.* New York: Dell, 1989. (Orig. 1973).

Lynn, Jonathan. In *A Short History of Yes, Minister. Yes, Minister.* BBC Video DVD (2002).

Macaulay, Sean. "Sean Macaulay's TV Film of the Week." *Times Online,* 23 March 2006. http://entertainment.timesonline.co.uk/article/0,14931-2098345,00.html Accessed 23 march 2006

Macfarquhar, Larissa. "The Populist; Profiles." *The New Yorker,* 80, 1 (16 Feb. 2004): 132–45.

Malanowski, Jamie. "The Loud Mouth: What Aristotle Would Like about Michael Moore." *The Washington Monthly* 38, 11 (Nov. 2006): 41–2.

Mann, Michael. *Incoherent Empire*. London and New York: Verso, 2005.

Martin, George T., Jr. *Social Policy in the Welfare State*. Englewood Cliffs, NJ: Prentice Hall, 1990.

Martindale, Carolyn, and L. R. Dunlap. "The African Americans." In Keever, Beverly Ann Deepe, and Carolyn Martindale, and Mary Ann Weston, eds. *US News Coverage of Racial Minorities: A Sourcebook, 1934–1996*, 122–30. Westport, CN: Greenwood Press, 1997.

Marx, Gary T. *Racial Conflict*. Boston: Little & Brown, 1971.

– "Thoughts on a Neglected Category of Social Movement Participant: The Agent Provocateur and the Informant." *American Journal of Sociology* 80 (1974): 402–42.

Massood, Paula J. "Ghetto Supastar: Warren Beatty's Bulworth and the Politics of Race and Space." *Film Literature Quarterly* 30, 4 (2002): 287–93.

McChesney, Robert W. *The Problem of the Media: U. S. Communications Politics in the Twenty-First Century*. New York: Monthly Review Press, 2004.

McEvoy, Dermot. "Michael Moore Bareknuckle Liberal." *Publishers Weekly* 250, 42 (20 Oct 2003): 30–1.

McGrath, Patrick J. "True Unbeliever: Arthur Koestler and the 'Political Libido.'" *Times Literary Supplement*, 6 June 2008, 14–15.

McIntosh, William, et al. "Are the Liberals Good in Hollywood? Characteristics of Political Figures in Popular Films from 1945 to 1998." *Communication Reports* 16, 1 (2003): 57–68.

McKibbin, Tony. "The Thickening Centre: *Fahrenheit 9/11*." *Senses of Cinema: An Online Film Journal* 33 (Oct–Dec 2004). http://www.sensesofcinema.com/contents/04/33/fahrenheit_9_11.html Accessed 12 June 2006

Mencken, Henry L. *In Defense of Women*. Garden City, NY: Knopf, 1922. (Orig. 1918).

Miller, Merle. *Plain Speaking: An Oral Biography of Harry S. Truman*. New York: Putnam, 1974.

Mills, Bart, and David Wallechinsky. "Relative Values. Wearing the Right Hat: Authors Irving Wallace and His Son David Wallechinsky Talk to Bart Mills." *Sunday Times Magazine*, 18 September (1983): 9.

Milne, Gordon. *The American Political Novel*. Norman, OK: University of Oklahoma Press, 1966.

Mitgang, Herbert. "Condon's Prizzis Turn into a Series." *New York Times*, 29 October 1986, C24.

Moore, Michael. *Downsize This!* New York: HarperPerennial, 1997. (Orig. 1996).

– "My Oscar 'Backlash': 'Stupid White Men' Back At #1, 'Bowling' Breaks New Records." 7 April, 2003. http://www.michaelmoore.com/ words/message/index.php?messageDate=2003-04-08 Accessed 8 April 2003

– "My Wild First Week with *Fahrenheit 9/11*." 4 July 2004. Personal email.

– *The Official Fahrenheit 9/11 Reader.* New York: Simon & Schuster, 2004.

– *Stupid White Men... and Other Sorry Excuses for the State of the Nation.* New York: Regan Books, 2004. (Orig. 2002).

– *Mike's Election Guide 2008.* New York: Grand Central Publishing, 2008.

Moore Michael, and Kathleen Glynn. *Adventures in a TV Nation.* New York: HarperPerennial, 1998.

Moore, Michael, et al. "Welcome to ... MICHAELMOORE.COM." http://www.michaelmoore.com/books-films/index.php Accessed 16 Jan. 2007

Morgan, Michael, Justin Lewis, and Sut Jhally. "The Media and the War: Public Conceptions and Misconceptions. In Gerbner, G., et al, eds. *Global Deception: The Media's War in the Persian Gulf – An International Perspective*, 216–33. Boulder, CO: Westview, 1992.

Morrow, Frederick E. *Black Man in the White House: A Diary of the Eisenhower Years by the Administrative Officer for Special Projects, the White House, 1955–1961.* New York: Coward-McCann, 1963.

Murphy, James F. *The Proletarian Moment: The Controversy over Leftism in Literature.* Urbana, Chicago: University of Illinois Press, 1991.

Newman, Otto, and Richard de Zoysa. *The American Dream in the Information Age.* New York: St. Martin's, 1999.

Nichols, Bill. *Blurred Boundaries.* Bloomington and Indianapolis: Indiana University Press, 1994.

Niskanen, William A. *Reaganomics: An Insider's Account of the Policies and the People.* New York: Oxford University Press, 1988.

Nocera, Joseph. "How Hunter Thompson Killed New Journalism." *Washington Monthly* 13, 2 (1981): 44–50.

Nolley, Ken. "*Fahrenheit 9/11*: Documentary, Truth-telling, and Politics." *Historians Film Committee: Special Report* 35, 2 (2005): 12–16.

Ogbar, Jeffrey O.G. *Black Power: Radical Politics and African American Identity.* Baltimore, MD: Johns Hopkins University Press, 2004.

O'Reilly, Kenneth. *Racial Matters: The FBI's Secret File on Black America 1960–1972.* New York: Free Press, 1989.

O'Rourke, Patrick J. *Parliament of Whores: A Lone Humorist Attempts to Explain the Entire U.S. Government.* New York: Vintage, 1991.

– *All the Trouble in the World: The Lighter Side of Overpopulation,*

Famine, Ecological Disaster, Ethnic Hatred, Plague, and Poverty. New York: Atlantic Monthly Press, 1994.

– *Republican Party Reptile.* New York: Atlantic Monthly Press, 1987.

Orwell, George. "Politics and the English Language." In Orwell, Sonia, and Ian Angus, eds. *The Collected Essays, Journalism and Letters of George Orwell, Vol. 4: In Front of Your Nose 1945–1950.* London: Penguin, 1970.

– "Why I Write." In Davison, Peter, ed. *The Complete Works of George Orwell, vol. 18. Smothered Under Journalism 1946,* 316–21. London: Secker and Warburg, 1998.

Osborne, John. "White House Watch: The China Caper." *New Republic,* 20 March 1976, 7.

Outfoxed: Rupert Murdoch's War on Journalism. Dir. Robert Greenwald. Carolina Productions; MoveOn.Org, 2004.

Panther. Dir. Mario van Peebles. Gramercy Pictures, 1995.

Parenti, Michael. *Make-believe Media: Politics of Entertainment.* New York: St. Martin's, 1992.

– *America Besieged.* San Francisco: City Lights Books, 1998.

Patterson, Thomas E. *Out of Order: An Incisive and Boldly Original Critique of the News Media's Domination of America's Political Process.* New York: Vintage, 1994.

Paul, Ron. *The Revolution.* New York, Boston: Grand Central Publishing, 2008.

Paz, Reuven. "Islamic Palestine or Liberated Palestine?" The Institute for Counter-Terrorism, 20 July 2001. http://www.ict.org.il/articles/articledet.cfm?articleid=377 Accessed 25 July 2006.

Pearson, Hugh. *The Shadow of the Panther: Huey Newton and the Price of Black Power in America.* New York: Addison-Wesley, 1994.

Pearson, Richard. "Charles "Bebe" Rebozo, 85, Dies." *Washington Post,* 10 May 1998, B08.

Peretz, Paul. *The Politics of American Economic Policy Making.* Armonk, NY: M.E. Sharpe, 1996.

Peterson, Karen S. "IRVING WALLACE; The Storyteller Works Late into the Night, Dreaming Up Critic-proof Best Sellers." *USA TODAY,* 5 May 1987, 04.D.

Philips, Kevin. *The Politics of Rich and Poor: Wealth and the American Electorate in the Reagan Aftermath.* New York: Random, 1990.

Pierson, Paul. *Dismantling the Welfare State?: Reagan, Thatcher, and the Politics of Retrenchment.* Cambridge: Cambridge University Press, 1994.

Plantinga, Carl. *Rhetoric and Representation in Nonfiction Film.* Cambridge: Cambridge University Press, 1997.

Powell, John A. "Race, Poverty, and Social Security." In Hartman,

Chester, ed. *Challenges to Equality: Poverty and Race in America.*
   Armonk, New York: M.E. Sharpe, 2001.
Primeau, Françoise. *American Dissident: The Political Art of Michael
   Moore.* Lulu.com, 2007.
Reagan, Ronald. "Farewell Address to the Nation," 11 Jan. 1989.
   www.reagan.utexas.edu/archives/speeches/1989/011189i.htm
   Accessed 2 February 2007
– "Inaugural Address," 20 January 1981. www.reagan.utexas.edu
   archives/speeches/1981/12081a.htm Accessed 2 February 2007
Reed, Thomas Vernon. *The Art of Protest: Culture and Activism from
   the Civil Right Movement to the Streets of Seattle.* Minneapolis:
   University of Minnesota Press, 2005.
Rich, B. Ruby. "Mission Improbable." *Sight & Sound* (July 2004): 14–16.
Richler, Mordecai. "A Captivating but Distorted Image." *Book Week
   (Sunday Herald Tribune),* 13 September 1964, 4, 19.
Rideout, Walter. *The Radical Novel in the United States, 1900–1954:
   Some Interrelations of Literature and Society.* New York: Columbia
   University Press, 1992. (Orig. 1956).
Riley, Michael. "No Deficit of Laughs." *Time* 138 (8 July, 1991): 59.
Rivlin, Alice M., and Isabel Sawhill, eds. *Restoring Fiscal Sanity: How
   to Balance the Budget.* Washington, DC: Brookings Institution Press,
   2004.
Robertson, James Oliver. *American Myth, American Reality.* New York:
   Hill & Wang, 1980.
Robin, Corey. *Remembrance of Empires Past: 9/11 and the End of the
   Cold War.* New York: New Press, 2004.
Robinson, John. "Black Panthers; Revolution and Social Change." *News
   America,* 6 Sept. 1970.
Rodgers, R. Harell, Jr. *American Poverty in a New Era of Reform.* Armonk,
   NY: M.E. Sharpe, 2000.
Roosevelt, Theodore. "The Man with the Muck-Rake." *New York
   Tribune,* 15 April 1906, 1, 4.
Roth Philip. *Our Gang (Starring Tricky and His Friends).* New York:
   Random House, 1971.
– *I Married a Communist.* London: Jonathan Cape, 1998.
Rozin, Paul. "Towards a Psychology of Food and Eating: From
   Motivation to Module to Model to Marker, Morality, Meaning and
   Metaphor." *Current Directions in Psychological Science* 5 (1996):
   970–86.
Rozwenc, Edwin Charles, and Thomas Bender. *The Making of American
   Society. Volume II since 1865.* New York: Knopf, 1978.
Sabato, Larry J., and Glenn R. Simpson. *Dirty Little Secrets: The Persist-
   ence of Corruption in American Politics.* New York: Times Books, 1996.

Samway, Patrick H. "An Interview with Walker Percy." In Lawson, Lewis A., and Victor A. Kramer, eds. *More Conversations with Walker Percy,* 127–33. Jackson, MS: University Press of Mississippi, 1993.

Sanchez, Claudio. "An Inside Look: President Bush's 2007 Budget: Education Spending Declines." *National Public Radio,* 7 Jan 2007. http://www.npr.org/templates/story/story.php?storyId=5192631 Accessed 2 February 2007

Schifferes, Steve. "Domestic Issues Swing It for Democrats." *BBC News Online,* 8 November 2006. http://news.bbc.co.uk/2/hi/americas/ 6126176.stm Accessed 8 November 2006

Schlosser, Eric. *Fast Food Nation: The Dark Side of the All American Meal.* New York: Perennial, 2002.

– *Reefer Madness: Sex, Drugs, and Cheap Labor in the American Black Market.* Boston, New York: Mariner, 2004.

Schulze, Kirsten E. *The Arab-Israeli Conflict.* London: Longman, 1999.

Shannon, William Vincent. *They Could Not Trust the King.* New York: Collier, 1974.

Shaw, David. "*The Seventh Secret,* by Irving Wallace." *Los Angeles Times,* 2 March 1986, 2.

Siebers, Tobin. *Cold War Criticism and the Politics of Skepticism.* New York: Oxford University Press, 1993.

Simon, John. "Rappers and Whisperers." *National Review,* 22 June 1998, 63–4.

Sinclair, Upton. *The Jungle: The Uncensored Original Edition.* Tucson: See Sharp Press, 2003.

– *Boston. A Documentary Novel of the Sacco-Vanzetti Case.* Cambridge, MA: Robert Bentley, 1978.

Sipchen, Bob. "Button-Down Gonzo Journalist P.J. O'Rourke Would Rather Be Fun Than Right: Is He Either?" *Los Angeles Times,* 16 Nov. 1988, 1.

Smith, Gavin. "The End Is Up to You." *Film Comment* (Jul/Aug 2004): 26.

Smith, Hedrick. "The Power Game: How Washington Works." In Breidlid, Anders, et al. *American Culture: An Anthology of Civilization Texts,* 172–4. London: Routledge, 1996.

Smith, Richard Norton. *Thomas E. Dewey and His Times.* New York: Touchstone, 1982.

Smith, Robert C., and Richard Seltzer. *Contemporary Controversies and the American Racial Divide.* Lanham, MD: Rowman and Littlefield, 2000.

Smith, Tony. *A Pact with the Devil: Washington's Bid for World Supremacy and the Betrayal of the American Promise.* New York: Routledge, 2007.

Speare, Morris Edmund. *The Political Novel: Its Development in England and America*. Oxford: Oxford University Press, 1924.

Stein, Jean. "The Art of Fiction XII: William Faulkner." *The Paris Review* 12 (Spring 1956): 29–52.

Stern, Sol. "The Call of the Black Panthers." *New York Times Magazine*, 6 August 1967, 62.

Stevenson, Adlai. "Texts of Governor Stevenson's Speeches During His Invasion of Ohio." *New York Times*, 4 October 1952, 10.

Straub, Deborah Gillan, ed. *African American Voices*. Vol 1. Detroit, MI: U.X.L., 1996.

Street-Porter, Janet. "Subtle, He Ain't. Fat, He May Be. But Stupid?" *The Independent on Sunday*, 4 July 2004, 22.

Studio Briefing. "Beatty's Political Ploy at 20th." *The Internet Movie Database*. 11 May 1998. http://www.imdb.com/news/sb/1998-05-11#film2 Accessed 19 September 2003

Stuttaford, Genevieve. "Non-fiction – *Parliament of Whores: A Lone Humorist Attempts to Explain the Entire U.S. Government*, by P.J. O'Rourke." *Publishers Weekly* 238, 18 (1991): 54.

Summers, Anthony, with Robbyn Swan. *The Arrogance of Power: The Secret World of Richard Nixon*. New York: Viking, 2000.

Swirski, Peter. "Robert Ludlum: *The Cry of the Halidon*." In Beetz, Kirk, ed. *Beacham's Encyclopedia of Popular Fiction*, 9: 5343–54. Osprey, FL: Beacham Publishing, 1998.

– *From Lowbrow to Nobrow*. Montreal, London: McGill-Queen's University Press, 2005.

– "Betrization Is the Worst Solution... with the Exception of All Others." In Swirski, Peter, ed. *The Art and Science of Stanislaw Lem*. Montreal, London: McGill-Queen's University Press, 2006.

– *Of Literature and Knowledge: Explorations in Narrative Thought Experiments, Evolution, and Game Theory*. London, New York: Routledge: 2006.

– "Upton Sinclair: *The Jungle* (1906); *Oil* (1927)." In Irons-Georges, Tracy, ed., *Magill Survey of American Literature; Revised Edition*, 2335–41. Pasadena, CA: Salem Press, 2006.

– "A Is for American, B Is for Bad, C Is for City: Ed McBain and the ABC of Urban Procedurals." In Swirski, Peter, ed. *All Roads Lead to the American City*. Hong Kong, London: Hong Kong University Press, 2007.

– "The Historature of the American Empire: Joseph Heller's *Picture This*." *I Sing the Body Politic: History as Prophecy in Contemporary American Literature*. Montreal, London: McGill-Queen's University Press, 2009. 47–81.

– "Literature as History: The Lives and Deaths of Richard Milhous

Slurrie and Walter Bodmor Nixon." *Journal of American Studies* 43, 3 (2009): 1–18.

– *American Eutopia and Social Engineering: American Literature, History, and Experience 1948–2008.* Forthcoming, 2011.

The Pew Charitable Trusts. "Improving Elections. Related Grantee Reports." http://www.pewtrusts.com/ideas/index.cfm?page= 8&name=Grantee%20Reports&issue=9 See also http://www.pewtrusts.org/resource_library_search. aspx?keyword=related%20grantee%20reports

The Player. Dir. Robert Altman. Avenue Productions; Guild; Spelling Entertainment (1992).

The Sentencing Project and Human Rights Watch. "Losing the Vote: The Impact of Felony Disenfranchisement Laws in the United States." *The Sentencing Project* (1998). http://www.hrw.org/reports98/vote/

Thompson, Peter. *Cassell's Dictionary of Modern American History.* London: Cassell & Co., 2000.

Time. "Numbers." 7–14 August 2006, 12.

– "The Sustaining Stream." 1 February 1963, 82–4. See also http://www.time.com/time/magazine/article/0,9171,829810-7,00.html Accessed 3 February 2008

TIME Europe. "The Biggest Threat to Peace." http://www.time.com/ time/europe/gdml/peace2003.html Accessed 2 February 2007

Tindall, George Brown, and David Emory Shi. *America: A Narrative History.* New York: Norton, 2003.

Turley, Jonathan. "Hollywood Isn't Holding Its Lines Against the Pentagon." *Los Angeles Times,* 19 August 2003. http://www.common dreams.org/views03/0819-05.htm Accessed 19 August 2003

Umoja, Akinyle Omowale. "Set Our Warriors Free: The Legacy of the Black Panther Party and Political Prisoners." In Jeffries, Judson L., et al. *The Black Panther Party [reconsidered],* 417–42. Black Classic Press, 1998.

Uncovered: The Whole Truth About the War in Iraq. Dir. Robert Greenwald. The Disinformation Company DVD (2004).

Unger, Irwin, and Debi Unger. *The Times Were A-changin' – The Sixties Reader.* New York: Three Rivers Press, 1998.

U.S. Census Bureau. "The 2007 Statistical Abstract." 22 December 2006. http://www.census.gov/compendia/statab/past_years.html Accessed 17 April 2008

– "Historical Poverty Tables." Updated 14 Dec 2005. http://www.census.gov/hhes/www/poverty/histpov/hstpov2.html Accessed 17 April 2008

U.S. Department of Labor: Bureau of Labor Statistics. "Employment and Unemployment." www.bls.gov Accessed 7 May 2006

U.S. Department of State. *Election Focus 2004.* 1, 11. 21 May 2004.

Vonnegut, Kurt. *Slaughterhouse-five, or, The Children's Crusade.* New York: Delacorte, 1994. (Orig. 1969).

Wald, Alan M. *Exiles from a Future Time... the Forging of the Mid-Twentieth-Century Literary Left.* Chapel Hill: University of North Carolina Press, 2002.

Wallace, Irving. *The Man.* Introduction by James Earl Jones. Afterword by David Wallechinsky. New York: ibooks, 1999. (Orig. 1964).

– *The R Document.* New York: Forge, 2006. (Orig. 1976).

Wallechinsky, David. "Afterword." In Wallace, Irving. *The Man.* New York: ibooks, 1999.

Wal-Mart: The High Cost of Low Price. Dir. Robert Greenwald. Brave New Films DVD, 2005.

Ward, Brian, ed. "Jazz and Soul, Race and Class, Cultural Nationalism and Black Panthers: A Black Power Debate Revisited." *Media, Culture, and the Modern African American Freedom Struggle,* 161–96. Orlando: University Press of Florida, 2001.

Ward, Paul. *Documentary: The Margins of Reality.* London and New York: Wallflower, 2005.

WashingtonPost.com. "P.J. O'Rourke: Writer and Humorist." 10 September 2001. http://discuss.washingtonpost.com/wp-srv/zforum/01/author_orourke091001.htm Accessed 12 May 2006

Watergate: A Third Burglary. Gold, Mike, dir. Discovery Enterprise Group, 1994.

Welch, Susan, et al. *Understanding American Government.* 4th ed. Belmont, CA: West/Wadsworth, 1997.

West, Cornel. *Race Matters.* Boston: Beacon Press, 1993.

Whalen-Bridge, John. *Political Fiction and the American Self.* Urbana, Chicago, IL: University of Illinois Press, 1998.

Whitebrook, Maureen, ed. *Reading Political Stories: Representations of Politics in Novels and Pictures.* Lanham, MD: Rowman and Littlefield, 1992.

Wilding, Michael. *Political Fictions.* London: Routledge and Kegan Paul, 1980.

Wilson, James Q. *American Government.* 6th ed. Boston: Houghton Mifflin, 2003.

Wilson, Michael, dir. *Michael Moore Hates America.* HCW Films, 2004.

Winpisinger, William W. "The Democratic Party Does Not Effectively Represent Americans." In Tipp, Stacey L., and Carol Wekesser, eds. *Politics in America: Opposing Viewpoints,* 177–81. San Diego, CA: Greenhaven Press, 1992.

Wintour, Patrick and Ewen MacAskill. "1 in 3 Say Bush Is Biggest Threat." *Guardian,* 14 November 2002, 17. See also:

http://www.guardian.co.uk/usa/story/0,12271,839417,00.html
Accessed 15 July 2006

Wirls, Daniel. *Buildup:The Politics of Defense in the Reagan Era*.
Ithaca: Cornell University Press, 1992.

Wisconsin Advertising Project. Goldstein, Ken, and Joel Rivlin. "Volume and Targeting of Election Advertising." *Political Advertising in the 2002 Elections*. 2004. http://www.polisci.wisc.edu/tvadvertising/Political%20Advertising%20in%20the%202002%20Elections.htm

Wolfe, Tom. *Hooking Up*. New York: Farrar, Straus and Giroux, 2000.

Yerkes, Andrew C. *"Twentieth-Century Americanism:" Identity and Ideology in Depression-Era Leftist Fiction*. New York, London: Routledge, 2005.

Young, Kevin. "US Politics 'Obsessed' with Ads." *BBC News Online*, 27 August 2006. http://news.bbc.co.uk/2/hi/entertainment/5291298.stm Accessed 27 August 2006

Zeitchik, Steven. "Michael Moore: The New JFK?" *Publishers Weekly* 250, 43 (27 Oct. 2003): 15.

Zinn, Howard. *Declarations of Independence: Cross-Examining American Ideology*. New York: HarperCollins, 1990.

– *The Twentieth Century: A People's History*. New York: Perennial, 2003.

Index